THE NEW YORK TIMES ENCYCLOPEDIA OF SPORTS **Volume 14**

INDEX AND BIBLIOGRAPHY

THE NEW YORK TIMES ENCYCLOPEDIA OF SPORTS

Vol. 1   FOOTBALL
Vol. 2   BASEBALL
Vol. 3   BASKETBALL
Vol. 4   TRACK AND FIELD
Vol. 5   GOLF
Vol. 6   TENNIS
Vol. 7   BOXING
Vol. 8   SOCCER/PROFESSIONAL HOCKEY
Vol. 9   WINTER SPORTS
Vol. 10   OUTDOOR SPORTS
Vol. 11   INDOOR SPORTS
Vol. 12   WATER SPORTS
Vol. 13   HORSE RACING/AUTO RACING
Vol. 14   INDEX AND BIBLIOGRAPHY

THE NEW YORK TIMES
ENCYCLOPEDIA OF SPORTS

VOLUME 14

INDEX AND BIBLIOGRAPHY

EDITED BY
GENE BROWN
INTRODUCTION BY
FRANK LITSKY

ARNO PRESS
A NEW YORK TIMES COMPANY
NEW YORK 1979

GROLIER EDUCATIONAL CORPORATION
SHERMAN TURNPIKE, DANBURY, CT. 06816

ISBN 0-405-12626-3

Manufactured in the United States of America

The editors express special thanks to The Associated Press, United Press
International, and Reuters for permission to include a number of dispatches
originally distributed by those news services.

The New York Times Encyclopedia of Sports

Founding Editors: Herbert J. Cohen and Richard W. Lawall
Project Editors: Arleen Keylin and Suri Boiangiu
Editorial Assistant: Jonathan Cohen

CONTENTS

BASEBALL

Allen, Ethan N., *Baseball Play and Strategy,* 2d ed. (Ronald 1969).
Allen, Lee, *The American League Story* (Hill & Wang 1962).
Allen, Lee, *The National League Story* (Hill & Wang 1961).
Anderson, Clary, *The Young Sportsman's Guide to Baseball* (Nelson 1963).
Baseball Register (Spink, C.C. annually).
Crossetti, Frank, *Secrets of Baserunning and Infield Play* (Putnam 1966).
Danzig, Allison, and Reichler, Joe, *The History of Baseball, Its Great Players, Teams and Managers* (Prentice-Hall 1959).
Hollander, Zander, *The Complete Handbook of Baseball* (NAL 1977)
Koppett, Leonard, *All About Baseball,* rev ed. (Quadrangle 1974).
Lieb, Frederick G., *Baseball As I Have Known It* (Coward 1977).
Macmillan, *The Baseball Encyclopedia* (Macmillan 1976).
Official Baseball (Spink, C.C. annually).
Olan, Ben, *Big-time Baseball* (Hart 1965)
Reichler, Joe, ed., *Ronald Encyclopedia of Baseball,* 2d ed. (Ronald 1964).
Rickey, Branch, and Riger, Robert, *The American Diamond* (Simon & Schuster (1965).
Turkin, Hy, and Thompson, S.C., *Official Encyclopedia of Baseball, 9th ed. (Barnes, A.S. 1977).*
Wolfe, Harold H., The Complete Book of Baseball Strategy (Cornerstone 1977).

FOOTBALL

American Football League, *Official Guide* (St. Louis, current ed.).
Andres, Bruce, *Australian Football Handbook* (Adelaide, current ed.).
Canadian Football League, *Official Record* (Toronto, current ed.).
Daley, Arthur, *Pro Football's Hall of Fame* (New York 1968).
Higdon, Hal, *Pro Football USA* (New York 1968).
Kramer, Jerry, *Instant Replay* (New York 1968).
Maule, Tex, *The Game,* rev. ed. (New York 1967).

National Collegiate Athletic Association, *Official Football Guide* (Phoenix, current ed.)

National Federation of State High School Athletic Associations, *Football Handbook——Six Man Football and Touch Football* (Chicago, current ed.)

Sporting News, *Football Register* (St. Louis, current ed.).

Treat, Roger, *The Official Encyclopedia of Football,* 6th rev. ed. (New York 1968).

BASKETBALL

Auerbach, Arnold, (Basketball (New York 1961).

Bee, Clair F., and Norton, Ken, *Basketball Fundamentals and Techniques* (New York 1959).

Bell, Mary M., *Women's Basketball* (Dubuque, Iowa 1964).

Bunn, John W., *Basketball Techniques and Team Play* (Englewood Cliffs, NJ 1964.

Naismith, James, *Basketball, Its Origin and Development* (New York 1962).

Newell, Pete, and Bennington, John, *Basketball Methods* (New York 1962).

Wooden, John R., *Practical Modern Basketball* (New York 1966).

TRACK AND FIELD

Amateur Athletic Union, *The Official AAU Track and Field Handbook and Rules* (New York annually).

American Association for Health, Physical Education, and Recreation, *Track and Field Guide* (Washington biennially).

Bresnahan, George T., and others, *Track and Field Athletics,* 7th ed. (St. Louis, 1969).

International Amateur Athletic Federation, *Official Handbook* (London annually).

Jordan, Payton and Spencer, Bud, *Champions in the Making,* Englewood Cliffs, NJ 1969).

National Collegiate Athletic Association, *The NCAA Official Track and Field Guide* (Phoenix annually).

Parker, Virginia, and Kennedy, Robert, *Track and Field Activities for Girls and Women* (Philadephia 1969).

GOLF

Gibson, Nevin H., *A Pictorial History of Golf, rev. ed. (Barnes A.S. 1974).*

Graffis, Herb B., *The PGA* (Crowell 1975).

Jones, Robert T., *Bobby Jones on Golf* (Doubleday 1966).

Nicklaus, Jack, *Golf My Way* (Pocket Books 1977).

Palmer, Arnold, *My Game and Yours* (Simon & Schuster 1965).

Price, Charles, *The World of Golf* (Random House 1962).

Steel, Donald, and others, *Encyclopedia of Golf* (Viking 1975).

U.S. Golf Association, *Golf Rules in Pictures* (Grosset 1977).

TENNIS

Barnaby, John M., *Racket Work: The Key to Tennis* (Rockleigh, NJ 1969).
Brady, Maurice, *Lawn Tennis Encyclopedia* (New York 1969).
Davidson, Owen, and Jones, C.J., *The Great Ones* (London 1970).
Gensemer, Robert E., *Tennis* (Philadelphia 1969).
United States Lawn Tennis Association, *The Official Yearbook and Tennis Guide*
New York current edition).

BOXING

Amateur Athletic Union, *Official AAU Boxing Guide* (New York annually)
Fleischer, Nat, *50 Years at Ringside* (New York 1958).
Fleischer, Nat, *The Heavyweight Champion* (New York 1949).
Fleischer, Nat, and Andre, Sam. *A Pictorial History of Boxing* (New York 1959).
Grombach, John V., *The Saga of Sock* (New York 1949).
Heinz, W.C., ed., *The Fireside Book of Boxing* (New York 1961).
Liebling, A.J., *The Sweet Science* (New York 1956).

SOCCER

Arnold, Peter, and Davis, Christopher, *Hamlyn Book of World Soccer,* (Hamlyn
(1976).
Bradley, Gordon, and Toye, Clive, *Playing Soccer the Professional Way
(Harper 1973).*
Glanville, Brian, *Soccer: A History of the Game* (Crown 1968).
Toye, Clive, *Soccer* (Watts 1968).
Universal Guide For Referees (Federation of International Football Associations
annually).

HOCKEY

Beddoes, Richard, and others, *Hockey: The Story of the World's Fastest Sport,* 3d
rev. ed. (Macmillan, NY 1973).
Eskenazi, Gerald, *Hockey,* (Follett 1971).
Sullivan, George, *Face-Off: A Guide to Modern Hockey* (Van Nostrand Reinhold
1968).

WINTER SPORTS

Skating

Amateur Skating Union of the United States, *Official Handbook,* (Amateur Skating
Union).
Brown, Nigel, *Ice Skating, A History* (Barnes, A.S. 1959)

Lussi, Gustave, and Richards, Maurice, *Championship Figure Skating* (Barnes, A.S. 1951).
Ogilvie, Robert S., *Basic Ice Skating Skills* (Lippincott 1968).
Owen, Maribel Vinson, *The Fun of Figure Skating* (Harper 1960).
Richardson, T.D., *The Art of Figure Skating* (Barnes, A.S. 1962).
U.S. Figure Skating Association, *The Rulebook* (USFSA Biannually).
U.S. Figure Skating Association, *Evaluation of School Figure Errors,* 7th ed., (USFSA 1970).

Skiing

Bradley, David et al, *Expert Skiing* (Grosset 1963).
Caldwell, John, *New Cross-Country Ski Book* (Greene 1971).
Jerome, John, and others, *Sports Illustrated Book of Skiing,* rev. ed., (Lippincott).
Lederer, William J., and Wilson, Joe P., *Complete Cross-Country Skiing and Touring* (Norton 1970).
Scharff, Robert, and others, eds., *Ski Magazine's Encyclopedia of Skiing* (Harper 1970).

OUTDOOR SPORTS

Shooting

Consult Chapel, Charles E., *Feld, Skeet, and Trap Shooting* (New York 1949).
Amateur Trapshooting Association, *Official Trapshooting Rules,* rev. (Vandalia, Ohio 1962).

Soaring

Bowers, Peter M., *Soaring Guide* (Sports Car 1966).
Ellison, Norman, *British Gliders and Sailplanes, 1922-1970 (Barnes & Noble 1971).*
Lincoln, Joseph C., *Soaring for Diamonds,* 2d ed. (Northland, 1967).
Piggott, Derek, *Gliding: A Handbook on Soaring Flight,* 2d ed. (Barnes & Noble 1967).

Rugby

Greenwood, Jim, *Total Rugby* (Lepus Books 1978).
Rea, Chris, *Rugby: A History of Rugby Union Football* (Hamlyn 1977).
Reyburn, W., *All About Rugby Football* (Allen, W.H. 1976).
Rugby Football Union, *A Guide for Players* (1978).
Thomas, J.B.G., *Rugby: Men, Matches and Moments* (Pelham Books 1970).
Wallace, J.M., *The Rugby Game* (Kaye & Ward 1976).

Polo

Disston, Harry, *Beginning Polo* (Barnes, A.S. 1973).
Mountbatten of Burma, *An Introduction to Polo,* rev. ed. (British Book. Centre 1973).

Mountain Climbing

Bonington, Chris, *Everest the Hard Way* (Random House 1976).
Engel, Claire E., *They Came to the Hills* (Allen G. 1952).
Herzog, Maurice, *Annapurna* (Dutton 1953)
Hunt, Sir John, *The Conquest of Everest* (Dutton 1954).
Jones, Chris, *Climbing in North America* (Univ. of Calif. Press 1976).
Ullman, James Ramsey, *The Age of Mountaineering* (Lippincott 1954).
Ward, Michael, ed. *The Mountaineer's Companion* (Eyre 1966).
Whymper, Edward, *Scrambles Amongst the Alps* (John Murray 1871).
Williams, Cicely, *Women on the Rope* (Allen, G. 1973).

Hunting

Boone and Crockett Club, *Records of North American Big Game,* rev. ed. (New York 1964).
Duggey, David Michael, *Bird Hunting Know How* (Princeton 1968).
Hibben, Frank C., *Hunting in Africa* (New York 1962).
MacKenty, John G., *Duck Hunting,* rev. ed. (New York 1964).
Morris, Desmond, *The Mammals* (New York 1965).
Moyer, J.W. *Trophy Heads* (New York 1962).
Ormond, Clyde, *The Complete Book of Hunting* (New York 1962).
Ruark, Robert, *Use Enough Gun* (New York 1966).
Rue, Leonard Lee, *Sportsman's Guide to Game Animals* (New York 1968).

Fishing

Bates, Joseph D., Jr., *Streamer Fly Tying and Fishing* (Harrisburg, Pa., 1966).
Bauer, Erwin A., *The Salt Water Fisherman's Bible* (New York, 1962).
Brooks, Joseph W., *Complete Book of Fly Fishing,* rev. ed. (New York 1968).
Evanoff, Vlad. *The Fresh-Water Fisherman's Bible* (New York 1964).
Evanoff, Vlad. *1001 Fishing Tips and Tricks* (New York 1966)
McClane, A.J., *McClane's Standard Fishing Encyclopedia* (New York 1963).

Bicycling

Athletic Institute, *How to Improve Your Cycling* (Chicago, no date.).
Baranet, Nancy N., *The Turned Down Bar* (New York 1964).
Bicycle Institute of America, *The Bicycle Story* (New York 1965).
Bicycle Institute of America, *Bike Racing on the Campus* (New York 1966).
English, Ronald, *Cycling for You* (London 1964).
Huffman Manufacturing Company, *A Handbook on Bicycle Tracks and Cycle Racing* (Dayton, Ohio, no date).

Bullfighting

Arruza, Carlos, *My Life as a Matador* (Boston 1956).
Conrad, Barnaby, *The Encyclopedia of Bullfighting* (Boston 1961).
Daley, Robert, *The Swords of Spain* (New York 1967).
McCormick, John, and Mascarenas, Mario Sevilla, *The Complete Aficionado* (Cleveland 1967).
Tynan, Kenneth, *Bull Fever,* rev. ed. (New York 1966).

INDOOR SPORTS

Squash

Khan, Hashim, and Randall, Richard E., *Squash Racquets: The Kahn Game* (Wayne State Univ. Press 1967).

Molloy, Albert, Jr., with Lardner, Rex, *Sports Illustrated Book on Squash* (Lippincott 1963).

U.S. Squash Racquets Association *Year Book* (U.S.S.R.A. annually).

Judo

Kano, Jigoro, *Judo* (Tokyo 1937).

Stone, Henry A., *Wrestling* (New York 1939)

Hikoyama, Kozo, *Sumo* (South Pasadena, CA 1940).

Takagaki, Shinzo and Sharp, Harold E., *The Techniques of Judo* (Rutland VT, 1957).

Brown, Robert L, and Ober, D.K., *Complete Book of High School Wrestling* (Englewood Cliffs, N.J. 1962).

Jiu-jitsu

Hancock, H.I., and Higasm, K., *The Complete Kano Jiu-jitsu* (1905; reprint, Dover, 1961).

Nakae, Kiyose, and Yeager, Charles, *Jiu Jitsu Complete* (Citadel 1974).

Tegner, Bruce, *Bruce Tegner's Complete Book of Jukado Self-Defense: Jiu Jitsu Modernized* (Thor 1968).

Karate

Nishiyama, Hidetaka, and Brown Richard C., *Karate: The Art of "Empty Hand" Fighting* (Tuttle 1959).

Parker, Edmund K., *Secrets of Chinese Karate* (Prentice-Hall 1963).

Son, Duk Sung, and Clark, Robert, *Korean Karate: The Art of Tae Kwon Do* (Prentice-Hall 1968).

Tegner, Bruce, *Bruce Tegner's Complete Book of Karate,* 2d rev. ed., (Thor 1970).

Tegner, Bruce, *Karate: Self Defense & Tradition Sport Froms* (Thor 1973).

Equestrian

Blake, Neil F., *World of Show Jumping* (New York 1967).

Self, Margaret Cabell, *The American Horse Show* (New York 1958).

Self, Margaret Cabell, *At the Horse Show* (New York 1966).

Steinkraus, William, *Riding and Jumping* (New York 1961).

Williams, Jennifer and Dorian, *Show Pony* (New York 1965).

Gymnastics

Baley, James A., *Gymnastics in the Schools* (Boston 1965).

Carter, Ernestine, *Gymnastics for Girls and Women* (Englewood Cliffs NJ 1968).

Hughes, Eric, *Gymnastics for Girls* (New York 1963).

Hughes, Eric, *Gymnastics for Men* (New York 1966).

Musker, Frank F., Casady, Donald R., and Irwin, Leslie W., *A Guide to Gymnastics* (New York 1968).

United States Gymnastic Federation, Federation of International Gymnastics, *Code of Points* (Tucson, AZ current ed.).

Fencing

Amateur Fencers League of America, *Fencing Rules* (West New York, NJ 1968).
American Association for Health, Physical Education, and Recreation, *Fencing Guide* (Washington, biennially).
Castello, Hugo, and Castello, James, *Fencing* (New York 1962).
Garret, Maxwell R., *How to Improve Your Fencing* (Chicago, no date).

Bowling

American Association for Health, Physical Education, and Recreation (Division for Girls and Women's Sports), *Bowling—Fencing—Golf Guide* (biennually).
American Bowling Congress, *Constitution Specifications and Rules* (Milwaukee, Wis. annually).
McDonough, Patrick J., *Official Bowling Guide* (Largo FL, 1966).
National Duckpin Bowling Congress, *Rules and Regulations,* (Washington annually).
Woman's International Bowling Congress, *Constitution and Rules* (Columbus, Ohio, annually).

Billiards

Billiard Congress of America, *Official Rules Books for All Pocket Carom Billiard Games,* rev. ed. (Chicago 1966).
Cottingham, Clive, Jr., *The Games of Billiards (Philadelphia 1964).*
Crane, Irving and Sullivan, George, The Young Sports man's Guide to Pocket Billiards (New York 1964).
Lassiter, Luther, and Sullivan, George, *Billiards for Everyone* (New York 1965).
Mosconi, Willie, *Winning Pocket Billiards* (New York 1965).

Badminton

American Association for Health, Physical Education, and Recreation, Tennis—Badminton Guide (Washington, current ed.).
American Badminton Association, *Official Handbook* (Waban, MA, current ed.).
Davis, Patrick Ronald, *Badminton Complete* (New York 1967).
The Athletic Institute, *How to Improve Your Badminton* (Chicago, no date).

WATER SPORTS

Water Skiing

Hardman, Thomas C., and Clifford, William D., *Let's Go Water Skiing* (Hawthorn 1969).

Swimming and Diving

Billingsley, Robert H. and H. Sherwood, *Swimming and Diving* 5th ed. (St. Louis, Mo. 1968).
Billingsley, Hobie, *Diving Illustrated* (New York 1965).
Fairbanks, Anne Ross, *Teaching Springboard Diving* (Englewood Cliffs, NJ 1963).
Moriarty, Phil, *Springboard Diving* (New York 1959).

Boating

Chapman, Charles F., *Piloting, Seamanship and Small Boat Handling* (Hearst 1976).
Fox, Uffa, *Seamanlike Sense in Powercraft* (Davies 1968).
Lord, Lindsay, *Naval Architecture of Planning Hulls* (Cornell Martime 1963).
Teal, John, *High-Speed Motor Boats* (Nautical Pub. Co.1969).

Surfing

Dixon, Peter, *Complete Book on Surfing* (New York 1965).
Dixon, Peter, *Where the Surfers Are* (New York 1968).
Houston, James D., and Finney, B.R. *Surfing: The Sport of Hawaiian Kings* (Rutland, VT 1968).
Olney, R.R. and Graham, R.., *Kings of the Surf* (New York 1970).
Severson, John Hugh, ed., *Great Surfing* (New York 1967).
Wagenvoord, James, and Bailey, Lynn, *How to Surf* (New York 1968).

Yachting

Aymar, Gordon C., *Yacht Racing Rules and Tactics* (New York, current ed.)
Barrault, Jean M., *Great Moments of Yachting* (New York 1967).
Bavier, Robert N., Jr., *New Yacht Racing Rules,* rev. ed. (New York 1969).
Carric, Robert W., and Rosenfeld, Stanley Z., *Defending the America's Cup* (New York 1969).
Heaton, P., *The Yachtsman's Vade Mecum,* 2d ed. (London, 1969).
Hewitt, R.L., *Foreign Cruising* (London 1969).
Lauer-Leonardi, Boris and Heffeshoff, Lewis Francis, *Yachts* (New York 1967).
Lloyds Register of American Yachts (London and New York, current ed.).
Murrant, Jim, ed., *Yachting Down Under* (Boston 1966).
Robinson, Bill, *The World of Yachting* (New York 1966).

HORSE RACING

Ainslie, Tom, *Complete Guide to Thoroughbred Racing* (New York 1968).
Ainslie, Tom, *The Jockey Book: The Relationship of Jockeys to the Winning and Losing of Horse Races* (New York 1967).
Alexander, David C., *Sound of Horses* (Indianapolis 1966).
Bomze, Henry, comp., *A Treausry of American Turf* (New York 1968).
Cooper, John E., *Steeplechasing in America* (New York 1968).
Malloy, Michael T., *Racing Today: A New Look at the Whirling World of Thoroughbreds* (Silver Spring, MD, 1968).
Robertson, William H.P., *History of Thoroughbred Racing in America* (Englewood Cliffs, NJ 1964).
Welsh, Peter C., *Track and Road: The American Trotting Horse* (New York 1968).

AUTO RACING

Bloemaker, Al, *500 Miles to Go,* rev. ed. (New York 1966).

Clifton, Paul, *The Fastest Men on Earth* (New York 1966).

Frere, Paul, *Sports Car and Competition Driving* (Cambridge, MA 1963).

Hough, Richard, and Frostick, Michael, *A History of the World's Racing Cars* (New York 1965).

Moss, Stirling, and Purdy, Ken W., *All but My Life* (New York 1963).

Parks, Wally, *Drag Racing Yesterday and Today* (New York 1966).

Rudeen, Kenneth, *The Swiftest* (New York 1966).

Shaw, Wilbur, *Gentlemen, Start Your Engines* (New York, 1955).

Stone, William S., *Guide to American Sports Car Racing,* rev. ed. (Garden City, NY 1963).

Aaron, Hank, **2**:120, 122, 171-72, 191
Aaron, Tommy, **5**:145-46
Aarons, Ruth Hughes, **11**:38
ABC-TV, **7**:193-94, 198-99
Aberdare, Lord, **11**:13
Abertondo, Antonio, **12**:67
Abrahams, Harold, **4**:34-37
Acthon Major, **8**:54-55
Adams, Arthur, **1**:47
Adams, Frank, **8**:62-63
Adcock, Joe, **2**:106, 123
Adderley, Herb, **1**:137
Adios, Butler, **8**:107-10
Adios, Harry, **8**:103, 105
Adios, Vic, **8**:114
Affirmed, **8**:85-91
Aga Khan, **8**:21-22
Agostini, Giacomo, **10**:90
airplanes and hunting, **10**:154
Aitkenhead, Andy, **8**:121-22
Akii-Bua, John, **4**:176-77
Alabama University basketball team, **3**:49
Alabama University football team, **1**:26-27, 50-51, 82-83
Alaskan bear hunting, **10**:175
Albert, King of Belgium, **4**:28
Albright College, **1**:178
Albright, Tenley, **9**:73-75, 82-83, 87-88
Alcindor, Ferdinand Lewis. *See* Jabbar, Kareem Abdul-
Alcott, Amy, **5**:193-194
Alekseyev, Vasily, **11**:112, 113, 117
Alexander, A.V., **8**:27
Alexander, Grover Cleveland, **2**:22, 41, 138-40
Ali, Muhammad
    Army induction refusal, **7**:171-72, 178
    vs Frazier 1971, **7**:176-78; 1974, **7**:183-84
    heavyweight champion 1964, **7**: 155-59; 1965, **7**:161-65; 1966, **7**:168; 1967, **7**:169; 1974, **7**:185-86; 1975, **7**:186-88; 1976, **7**:188-90, 192-93
    at 1960 Olympics, **7**:139
    vs Norton 1973, **7**:182-83
    portrait of, **7**:154-55, 165-66

purse of, **7**:160, 61
    vs Quarry 1970, **7**:175-76
    relicensing of, **7**:174-75
    and Ring Magazine, **7**:168-69
    shuffle of, **7**:168
    vs Spinks 1978, **7**:195-96
Allais, Emile, **9**:42
All-American Football Conference, **1**:99-100, 103
Allan, Liz, **12**:110-11
All Comers' Tournament 1915, **6**:8
Allen, Forrest C., **3**:22
Allen, George, **1**:153-54, 183
Allen, Greg, **1**:180
Allen, Scott, **9**:115-16, 120-121
All England tennis title. *See* Wimbledon matches champions
Allison, Donnie, **8**:190-91
Allison, Wilmer, **6**:49-50, 53
Alliss, Percy, **5**:54
All-New York, **8**:4-5
All Star games. *See* individual sports
Almer, Jack, **11**:67
Alps, **10**:116-17
Alston, Walter E. (Smokey), **2**:111-13
Altoona 200-mile auto race, **8**:132-33
Altwegg, Jeanette, **9**:61-62, 69
Alvarez, Elia de, **6**:38-39
Alvarez, Lili de, **6**:53
Alworth, Lance, **1**:148, 151
Alydar, **8**:85-91
Amateur Athletic Union and basketball, **3**:3-4, 8
Amateur Athletic Union and handball. *See* handball champions (AAU)
Amateur Athletic Union and swimming
    Age Group, **12**:71-73
    championships 1915, **7**:5; 1919, **12**:8; 1923, **12**:11; 1925, **12**:15; 1929, **12**:22; 1931, **12**:22; 1934, **12**:31; 1942, **12**:42-43
    penalties, **12**:103-04
Amateur Athletic Union and track and field
    barring of Didrikson from Oylmpics, **4**:72-73
    Duffey confession, **4**:8-9

marathon race rules, **4**:25
-NCAA dispute, **4**:150, 161
Santee suspension, **4**:116
Thorpe disqualification, **4**:24
track and field meet 1918, **4**:26-27; 1922, **4**:33; 1961, **4**:146-47; 1963, **4**:152; 1967, **4**:163, 1971, **4**:174
and women athletes, **4**:33, 185
Amateur Hockey Association, **9**:48, 50, 57-59
Ambers, Lou, **7**:66-67, 69-70
Ameche, Alan, **1**:49, 113-15
Ameche, Don, **1**:97
American Association of Baseball Clubs, **2**:3, 158
American Automobile Assocation, **8**:158
American Basketball Association,
    Barry signed for, **3**:159
    championship 1973, **3**:178-79; 1975, **3**:184-85; 1976, **3**:188-89
    Mikan as commissioner of, **3**:157
    and NBA, **3**:160, 170, 191-92
    and Porter, **3**:82-83
    star subsidies from, **3**:187-88
American Basketball League, **3**:143-44
American Bowling Congress, **11**:69
American Boxing Association of the United States, **7**:13
American Football League, **1**:88, 92, 117, 128-29
American Humane Association, **10**:132-33
American Kennel Club, **11**:171
American League. See baseball, American League
American Motorcycle Association, **10**:90-93
American Powerboat Association race 1920, **7**:118-20
American Professional Basketball League, **3**:112-13
American Professional Golfers, **5**:156
American Soccer League, **8**:8-9, 15-16, 18
America's Cup Yachting competition
    history of, **12**:129-31
    winners: Columbia 1958, **12**:160-61; Constellation 1964, **12**:166-68; Courageous 1974, **12**:179-80, 1977, **12**:185; Enterprise 1930, **12**:131-33; Intrepid 1967, **12**:172-73, 1940, **12**:174-75; Rainbow 1934, **12**:139; Ranger 1937, **12**:144-46; Weatherly 1962, **12**:163-64, 1963, **12**:164-66
Amour, Drake, **13**:53
amphetamines. See drugs
Anakin, Doug, **9**:117
Anapurna Peak, **10**:111
Ancestor, **13**:62-63
Andersen, Greta, **12**:44-45, 47
Andersen, Hjalmar, **9**:65-67
Anderson, Bob, **1**:52-53, 60-62
Anderson, Dick, **1**:164
Anderson, Donnie, **1**:135-36
Anderson, Gary, **10**:51-52
Anderson, Heartley, **1**:23-24
Anderson, James O., **6**:22, 25-26
Anderson, Jimmy, **8**:195
Anderson, John, **4**:64-65
Anderson, John G., **5**:9
Anderson, Malcolm, **6**:117-18, 120-21
Anderson, Miller, **12**:45, 50-51

Anderson, Paul, **11**:108
Anderson, Sparky, **2**:179-83
Anderson, Stephen, **4**:55
Andersson, Arne, **4**:89
Andras, Chris, **10**:179-80
Andretti, Mario, **13**:178-79, 185
Andrianov, Nikolai, **9**:132, 134, 136
animal welfare, **10**:132-33
Anke, Hannelore, **7**:97-98
Anoufriev, Aleksandr, **4**:102, 104
Anquetil, Jacques, **10**:104
Ansterberg, Ernie, **13**:133
antelope hunt, **10**:175
Anthony, Earl, **11**:75
anthropology and football, **1**:185-86
anti-trust laws and
    baseball, **2**:19, 157, 167-68
    basketball, **3**:170
    boxing, **7**:128-29
    football, **1**:112-13
apartheid, and
    golf, **5**:134, 179
    tennis, **6**:135, 185, 201
    see also blacks
Apps, Sylvanus, **7**:127, 133
Arantes, Edison. See Pele
Arcaro, Eddie, **13**:38-40, 51-52, 56-61
    criticism of Seattle Slew, **13**:83
    4th victory at Kentucky Derby 1948, **13**:49-51
    in Kentucky Derby 1957, **13**:63-64
    record 1952, **13**:56
    retirement of, **13**:68-69
archery, **10**:2-6
Archibald, Nate, **3**:178
Arfons, Art, **13**:176
Argentina polo team, **10**:20, 24-25, 28
Argentina, soccer and, **8**:19-20, 64, 74
Argentina soccer team
    vs France 1930, **8**:19
    vs United States 1930, **8**:19
    vs Uruguay 1930, **8**:19
    World Cup victory 1978, **8**:96-97
Ariuza, Carlos, **10**:140
Arizin, Paul, **3**:34, 127
Arkansas University football team, **1**:68
Armour, Tommy, **5**:34-35, 54
Armstrong, Henry
    vs Ambers 1939, **7**:69-70
    featherweight champion 1937, **7**:63
    Hall of Fame, **7**:118-19
    lightweight champion 1938, **7**:66-67
    welterweight champion 1938, **7**:64-65
    vs Zivic 1940, **7**:70
Armstrong, Michael, **7**:194
Armstrong, Murray, **8**:137
Armstrong, Wally, **5**:192-93
Army
    vs Columbia University 1947, **1**:39-41

lonesome end play of, **1**:58-59
losses to Notre Dame, **1**:15
vs Michigan 1949, **1**:41-42
vs Navy 1946, **1**:36-39; 1950, **1**:44-45; 1959, **1**:60-62
vs Notre Dame games disbanded, **1**:178-79
vs Notre Dame 1913, **1**:7-8; 1929, **1**:20-22; 1946, **1**:35-36; 1957, **1**:52-53
vs. Yale 1929, **1**:18-20
Army, United States, **7**:171-72; **10**:51
Arnold, Billy, **13**:136-38
Arnold, Claude, **1**:43
Arnold, Steve, **1**:155
Aronson, Jim, **10**:126
Arsenal Gunners
English Football Association Cup 1930, **8**:18; 1936, **8**:25; 1950, **8**:31-32; 1971, **8**:72-73
vs. Newcastle United 1952, **8**:33
artificial snow, **9**:13, 101-02
artificial turf, **2**:145
Artoe, Lee, **1**:96
Arvidsson, Par, **12**:104-5
Arzhanov, Yevgeny, **4**:176-77
Aschenbach, Georg, **9**:156-57
Ashe, Arthur, **6**:160-62, 177, 187-88
Ashenfelter, Horace, **4**:106-07
Ashford, Emmett L., **2**:143
Ashworth, Jeanne, **9**:105, 127-28
Assault, **13**:45-49
Associated Press
football poll, **1**:78-79
swimming poll, **12**:49
Association of Independent Tennis Professionals, **4**:167
Aston Villa, **8**:38-39
Atkins, Geoffrey, **9**:19-21
Atkinson, Sidney J., **4**:49
Atlanta Braves, **2**:171-72
Atlanta Chiefs, **8**:57-58, 64
Atlanta Hawks, **3**:162, 173
Atlas, Charles, **11**:113
Attell, Abe, **7**:11
Attles, Al, **3**:185
Atuegbu, Andy, **7**:85
Auerbach, Arnold (Red), **3**:154, 183
Augusta National Golf Club Course, **5**:52-53, 65
Auguste, Arsene, **8**:85
Austin, H.W. (Bunny), **6**:57, 63, 72-73
Austin, Tracy, **6**:199
Australia, boating in, **12**:185
Australia, cricket in, **10**:53-56, 62
Australia, rugby team of, **10**:79
Australia, swim team of, **12**:55-56
Australia, tennis in, **6**:90-151
Davis Cup 1939, **6**:75-76; 1950, **6**:90-92; 1955, **6**:108-10; 1956, **6**:114
matches: Connolly 1953, **6**:97; Court 1960, **6**:125; Laver 1960, **6**:125, 1962, **6**:128; Perry 1934, **6**:63
Austria, soccer in, **8**:16
Austria, soccer team of

expulsion from Italy, **8**:26-27
vs Italy 1934, **8**:21; 1936, **8**:26; 1937, **8**:26
Austria, toboggan team of, **9**:113
auto and hunting, **10**:151
auto industry, **8**:158, 170
auto polo, **10**:15-16
auto racing, **13**:120-98
and American Auto Association, **13**:158
and balloon tire, **13**:158
blacks in, **13**:196
buffs of, **13**:192
cars, **13**:136, 170, 172-73, 176-77, 184; *see also* individual cars
Daytona Beach, **13**:123, 137, 150, 160
Daytona 500-mile stock car race winners: Andretti 1967, **13**:178-79; Beauchamp 1959, **13**:162; Johnson 1960, **13**:164-65; Pearson 1976, **13**:193-94; Petty (Lee) 1959, **13**:162; Petty (Richard) 1974, **13**:190-91; Roberts 1962, **13**:168-69; Yarborough 1977, **13**:194-95
Daytona Grand National, **13**:154, 159
Daytona, 24 Hours of, **13**:192-93
deaths. *See* deaths, auto-racing
Delage car, **13**:127-29
dirt mile tracks, **13**:125-26
as experimentation, **13**:158
Grand Prix auto, **13**:170
Grand Prix of Belgium, **13**:165
Grand Prix of Endurance, **13**:159
Grand Prix of France, **13**:126, 163-64
Grand Prix of Germany, **13**:175-76
Grand Prix of Italy, **13**:152, 158-59, 165, 167-68, 171
Grand Prix of United States, **13**:150, 153
history of, **13**:122-23
hot rod races, **13**:159, 183-84
Indianapolis 500, accidents at, **13**:187-88
Indianapolis 500, deaths at, **13**:130, 136-37, 154-56; *see also* deaths, auto-racing
Indianapolis 500-mile auto race winners: Andretti 1969, **13**:185; Arnold 1930, **13**:136-37; Chevrolet 1920, **13**:131; Clark 1965, **13**:175; Corum 1924, **13**:133; de Palma 1915, **13**:129-30; de Paolo 1925, **13**:134; Donohue 1972, **13**:188-89; Foyt 1961, **13**:166, 1964, **13**:173-74, 1977, **13**:195-96; Frame 1932, **13**:138; Harroun 1911, **13**:125; Hill 1966, **13**:177; Jones 1963, **13**:171-72; Meyer, 1928, **13**:134, 1936, **13**:141; Milton 1923, **8**:132; Murphy 1922, **13**:131-32; Rose 1941, **13**:147, 1947, **13**:147-48, 1948, **13**:148-50; Shaw 1937, **13**:142-43, 1939, **13**:144-45, 1940, **13**:146; Swikert 1955, **13**:154-55; Unser 1971, **13**:187-88, 1978, **13**:197-98; Vukovich 1954, **13**:153; Wallard 1951, **13**:150-51; Ward 1962, **13**:169-70
Indianapolis Speedway safety, **13**:139, 189-90
Le Mans auto race, **13**:151-52, 157, 179
Mille Miglia race, **13**:160-61
Motor Racing Drivers' Association of American, **13**:125-26
National Association for Stock Car Auto Racing, **13**:170, 182-83, 187

National Circuit auto-racing, **13**:124-25
national convertible championship, **13**:160
night, **13**:137
Pan American Road Races 1953, **13**:152
perils of, **13**:123, 125-26
pit gang, **13**:156-57
popularity of, **13**:137
Professional Drivers' Association, **13**:187
Purolator 500-mile stock car race 1975, **13**:193
radio broadcast of, **13**:136
and rear view mirror, **13**:158
records. *See* records, auto racing
Riverside 500-mile stock car race 1966, **13**:177
safety measures, **13**:125-26, 189-90
Sebring race. *See* Grand Prix of Endurance
Sports Car Club of America, **13**:181-82
stock cars, **13**:170, 84
U.S. Automobile Club, **13**:183
in U.S., **13**:134, 180-84
Vanderbilt Cup race, **13**:122, 127, 129, 143-44
and women, **13**:127
autos, U.S., **13**:134
Avant, Bob, **4**:146-47
Averina, Tatyana, **9**:154, 158
Avilov, Nikolai, **4**:181-82, 194-95
Ayres, **13**:114
Azam Khan, **11**:20
Azzaro, Joe, **1**:65-66

Baas-Kaiser, Stien, **9**:149
Babando, Pete, **8**:144-45
Babashoff, Jack, **12**:97, 99
Babashoff, Shirley
  in 1972 Olympics, **12**:86
  in 1976 Olympics, **12**:92-93, 95, 97, 99
  training of, **12**:101
Babcock, Carolyn, **6**:55-56, 58-59
Babka, Richard, **4**:141
Baby Gar IV, **12**:123-24
Bacallao, Pedro, **11**:24
Badger, Sherwin C., **9**:7, 15
badminton, **11**:34-37
Baer, Buddy, **7**:71-72
Baer, Max
  vs Braddock 1935, **7**:51-53
  heavyweight champion 1934, **7**:48
  vs Louis 1935, **7**:54-56
Baeza, Braulio, **13**:78-79
Bagby, Jim, Jr., **2**:71
Bahr starting gate, **13**:19
Baier, Ernst, **9**:35, 37
Bailey, Ace, **8**:122, 124
Bailey, H.M., **10**:44

Bajukov, Nikolai, **9**:157-58
Baker, David, **1**:58
Baker, Steve, **10**:94
Baker, Thane, **4**:117-18, 120-21
Baker Field, **1**:12
Balassi, Gerry, **8**:46, 50
bald eagle, **10**:162
Baldini, Ercole, **10**:101
Baldwin, Howard, **1**:155; **8**:204
Baldwin-Wallace College basketball team, **3**:47
balkline billiards. *See* billiards
Ball, Catie, **12**:79-80
Ballengrud, Ivar, **9**:10-11, 17, 19-20, 33-34, 36-37
Ball, Frank, **5**:26-27
Ballesteros, Severiano, **5**:187-88
Baltimore baseball team, **2**:4
Baltimore Bays, **8**:63
Baltimore Bullets, **3**:117, 123-24, 152, 172-73
Baltimore Colts, **1**:113-15, 127, 139-41, 150-51
Baltimore Orioles, **2**:101-02, 133, 156-57
Baltimore Zephyrs, **3**:146
Baltusrol Golf Club, **5**:87
Balukas, Jean, **9**:64-66
Banfrica, **8**:63
Bang Away, **9**:174, 176
Bangu, **8**:45-46
Banks, Ernie, **2**:111
Bannister, Roger, **4**:112-15
bantamweight championship 1922, **7**:21-22
Banuet, Alfred, **11**:15
Barabas, Al, **1**:25-26
Barbuti, Ray, **4**:51-52
Baric, Rudy, **3**:18-19
Barilko, Bill, **8**:145
Barkman, Jane, **12**:78
Barna, Victor, **11**:38
Barnes, Erich, **1**:20
Barnes, Jim, **5**:18, 21-22
Barnett, Dick, **3**:143, 169
Barnstable, Dale, **3**:42-45
Barnum, Len, **1**:94
barrel-jumping, **9**:74
Barrett, Bill, **1**:44
Barrett, H.R., **6**:2
Baron, H.E., **4**:28-29
Barrow, Joseph Louis. *See* Louis, Joe
Barrow soccer team, **8**:12
Barry, Marty, **8**:128
Barry, Rick, **3**:153, 159, 185-88
Barthel, Joseph, **4**:107
Bartholomew, Ken, **9**:48-49
Bartsch, James R., **5**:143
baseball, amateur, **2**:2
baseball, professional
  All Stars game 1933, **2**:46, 48-49; 1934, **2**:49-51; 1941, **2**:68-69; 1955, **2**:109-11; 1967, **2**:145-46
  American League, **2**:4, 128-29, 147-48, 158, 169, 185-86; *See also* baseball, pennant, American League

anti-trust suit, **2**:19, 157, 167-68
balls used, **2**:24, 31, 35
batting records. *See* records, baseball, batting
batting rules, **2**:154
as big business, **2**:123-24
and blacks, **2**:75, 80, 143, 161-65, 175
championship, **2**:2, 6-8
closing of, **2**:22
consecutive play record, **2**:64-66
disagreement, **2**:19, 30
fans, **2**:31
fielding, **2**:49, 74-75
fixing, **2**:25-28, 32
free agents, **2**:141-42, 184-85, 187-89
gambling in, **2**:79
Hall of Fame, **2**:57, 161-65
hitters, designated, **2**:169, 179
hitting records. *See* records, baseball, batting
home run records. *See* records, baseball, home run
longest games, **2**:135-36, 173-74
Major League Baseball Players Association, **2**:105, 167-68, 184-85, 187-89
Major League Umpires Association, **2**:159-60
minor leagues, **2**:4
national agreement, **2**:4
National Association of Professional Baseball Players, **2**:157
National League, **2**:127-28, 141, 148-49, 170; *see also* baseball, pennant race, National League
National League of Professional Baseball clubs, **2**:4, 157-58
new clubs, **2**:128-29, 185-86
night games, **2**:56, 62-63
numbers, **2**:20
pennant, American League 1934, **2**:53-54; 1945, **2**:76-77; 1948, **2**:85-86; 1949, **2**:87-88; 1951, **2**:92-93; 1967, **2**:146-47; 1976, **2**:189-90
pennant, National League 1908, **2**:11-12; 1934, **2**:53-54; 1942, **2**:74; 1946, **2**:77-78; 1949, **2**:87-88; 1950, **2**:88-89; 1959, **2**:124-25; 1964, **2**:140-41; 1972, **2**:168-69
pension plan, **2**:78-79, 105
pitchers, **2**:21, 139-40, 169
pitches, **2**:22, 151-52
pitching records. *See* records, baseball, pitching
pitching rules, **2**:154
players, **2**:12, 23, 157-58, 167-68. 188-89
radio broadcasts, **2**:35, 67
reserve system, **2**:157-58, 167-68, 188-89
riots, **2**:54-56
rules. *See* rules, baseball
salaries, **2**:17, 188
stolen bases. *See* records, baseball, stolen bases
strike of players, **2**:13, 166-67
strike of umpires, **2**:159-60
stud spikes, **2**:154
Supreme Court ruling on, **2**:167-68
on television, **2**:67
trading, **2**:171
training, **2**:75, 188-89

umpires, **2**:143, 159-60
union, **2**:157-58
World Series 1912, **2**:14-16; 1919, **2**:25-28, 32; 1920, **2**:28-29; 1926, **2**:36-38; 1929, **2**:41-42; 1932, **2**:45-46; 1934, **2**:54-56; 1941, **2**:72-73; 1947, **2**:81-85; 1953, **2**:102-04; 1954, **2**:107-08; 1955, **2**:111-13; 1956, **2**:116-19; 1957, **2**:121-23; 1960, **2**:125-26; 1961, **2**:132-33; 1965, **2**:143-44; 1968, **2**:152-54; 1969, **2**:156-57; 1974, **2**:176-78; 1975, **2**:179-83; 1977, **2**:192-95
See also softball
Baseball Writers' Association, **2**:113-14
Basilio, Carmen
vs Gavilan 1953, **7**:114
middleweight champion 1957, **7**:129-30
vs Robinson 1958, **7**:130-31
welterweight champion 1955, **7**:119-20; 1956, **7**:124-25
basketball, amateur, **3**:82-83
Basketball Association of America, **3**:113, 116-18
basketball, college. *See* college basketball
basketball, professional, **3**:112-203
All Star game 1964, **3**:147; 1970, **3**:165-66
American Basketball Association. *See* American Basketball Association
American Professional Basketball League, **3**:112-13
American Basketball League, **3**:143-44
antitrust violations, **3**:170
Basketball Association of America, **3**:113, 116-18
blacks in, **3**:135, 154-55, 174, 186
computers in, **3**:197-99
fans, **3**:124-26, 189-90, 197-99
free agents, **3**:144
gambling in, **3**:122-23
Hall of Fame, **3**:183
league mergers, **3**:113, 118, 170, 191-92
at Madison Square Garden, **3**:172
National Basketball Association. *See* National Basketball Association; National Basketball Association champions
National Basketball League, **3**:116-17
pension plan, **3**:148
plays, **3**:124-25
Professional Basketball League of America, **3**:116
records. *See* records, basketball
recruiting of players, **3**:96-97, 159-60, 170-71, 173, 180-81
referees, **3**:197-99
rules. *See* rules, professional basketball
salaries. *See* salaries, basketball
swearing ban, **3**:112
on television, **3**:192
violence in, **3**:196-97
Bass Clef, **13**:67-68
Bass, Mike, **1**:153
Bassett, John, Jr., **1**:155, 158
Bassey, Hogan, **7**:131
Bathgate, Andy, **8**:159
Bauer, Bobby, **8**:134, 138
Bauer, Hank, **2**:103, 112-13
Bauer, Sybil, **12**:10, 13

Baugh, Sam, **1**:29-30, 93, 95-99, 102, 121-23
Baum, Abe, **10**:171
Bauman, Charlie, **1**:80-81
Baumholtz, Frank, **3**:17-18
Bausch, Jim, **4**:69-70
Bavaria, **13**:62-63
Bavier, Robert N., Jr., **12**:167
Baylor, Elgin, **3**:135-37, 141, 144-45, 162
Baysinger, Reaves, **1**:38-39
Beamon, Bob, **4**:169-70
Beard, Butch, **3**:185
Beard, Ralph, **3**:26, 29, 42-45
bear hunting, **10**:175
Beathard, Pete, **1**:62
Beatty, Jim, **4**:149
Beauchamp, Johnny, **13**:162
Beban, Gary, **1**:63-64
Beccali, Luigi, **4**:66-67
Beckenbauer, Franz, **8**:87-89
Becker, Wayland, **1**:91
Beck, Hans, **9**:23
Behra, Jean **13**:163-64
Behr, Johnny, **7**:80
Beirne, Jim, **1**:66
Beiser, Trude, **9**:53
Belgium soccer team, **8**:19
Beliveau, Jean, **8**:160
Bell, Bert, **1**:16, 96, 100-05, 108, 112-13
Bell, Greg, **4**:130
Bell, James (Cool Papa), **2**:162-64
Bellamy, Walt, **3**:62, 143
Bellino, Joe, **1**:60-62
Belmonte, Jan, **10**:137-38
Belmont Park, **13**:2-5, 16-17
Belmont Stakes winners
    Affirmed 1978, **13**:90-91
    Assault 1946, **13**:47-48
    Citation 1948, **13**:52
    Colin 1908, **13**:5-6
    Count Fleet 1943, **13**:43-45
    Gallant Fox 1930, **13**:22-23
    Man o' War 1920, **13**:10
    Needless 1956, **13**:61-62
    Omaha 1935, **13**:28-29
    Seattle Slew 1977, **13**:83-85
    Secretariat 1973, **13**:76-77
    Sir Barton 1919, **13**:8-9
    Twenty Grand 1931, **13**:24
    War Admiral 1937, **13**:33-34
    Whirlaway 1941, **13**:40
Belote, Melissa, **12**:89-90
Belousova, Ludmila, **9**:104, 121, 131-32, 138
Beloussov, Vladimir, **9**:136-37
Beman, Deane, **5**:144-45
Bench, Johnny, **2**:180-81
Bender, Charles Albert, **10**:42
Bender, Jules, **10**:3
Benedict, Sleepy, **8**:106-07

Benfica, **8**:50
Benham, Stan, **9**:70
Benitez, Manuel, **10**:144-45
Benner, Huelett, **10**:48-50
Benvenuti, Nino, **7**:170, 176
Bergmann, Arnfinn, **9**:71-72
Berg, Patty, **5**:58, 63, 74, 81, 106
Berkeley ski jump contest 1934, **9**:27
Bermudez, Marian, **11**:102
Berra, Yogi, **2**:92-93, 113-14, 125-26
Berruti, Livio, **4**:137-38
Berry, Raymond, **1**:113-15, 121-23, 127
Bertelsen, Jim, **1**:68, 71-72
Berthod, Madeleine, **9**:82
Berwanger, Jay, **1**:28, 75, **10**:74
Best, Clyde, **8**:85
Bethea, Tom, **7**:196
Bethlehem Steel Company soccer team, **8**:8
Bettenhausen, Tony, **13**:154-55
betting
    in golf, **5**:138
    in soccer, **8**:21-25, 38, 44-45
    See also gambling
Betz, Pauline, **6**:77-79, 81-82
Bevens, Floyd (Bill), **2**:81-82
Beyaert, J., **10**:100
Bibeault, Paul, **8**:139
Bicknell, C., **8**:27
bicycle racing, **10**:95-108
bicycling, women's, **5**:5-6
Biddles, George, **7**:131
Biebl, Heidi, **9**:90-91
Bigos, Al, **3**:38
Bikila, Abebe, **4**:144-45, 160, 171-72
Biletnikoff, Fred, **1**:167-68
billiards, **11**:47-66
    business boom, **11**:63
    halls, **11**:54-55
    number of players, **11**:54
    table, **11**:62
    techniques, **11**:50-53
Billick, George, **11**:69
Billows, Ray, **5**:61-63
Bingham, William, **1**:177
birds, preservation of, **10**:152
Birmingham City soccer team, **8**:19, 37-38
Bissbi, **12**:135-36
Bixler, E.G., **1**:178
Bjurstedt, Molla. *See* Mallory, Molla
Black, E.D., **6**:2
Black, James, **5**:155-56
Black, John, **5**:22-23
Blackburn Rovers, **8**:27
Black Muslims, **7**:158-59, 165-66, 168
Blackpool soccer team, **8**:33-34, 42
blacks and auto racing, **13**:196
blacks and baseball
    banned from stadium, **2**:75

in Hall of Fame, **2**:161-65
  Robinson as manager, **2**:175
  Robinson purchase, **2**:80
  umpire, **2**:143
blacks and basketball, **3**:54, 78, 98, 135, 154-55, 174, 186
blacks and bowling, **11**:69, 74-75
blacks and boxing
  Dempsey against, **7**:17
  deterioration of, **7**:12
  Johnson, **7**:8-11
  mixed bouts banned, **7**:9-11
blacks and fencing, **11**:124, 127
blacks and football, **1**:179-80, 182
blacks and golf
  apartheid, **5**:134, 179
  Elder in Masters, **5**:181-82
  PGA, **5**:71, 85, 113
blacks and golf
  Powell, **5**:189-90
  race-baiting, **5**:157-58
  Siffords victory, **5**:156-57
  United Golfers' Association Tournament, **5**:155-56
blacks and hockey, **8**:145
blacks and lacrosse, **10**:82
blacks and rugby, **10**:78-79
blacks and tennis
  apartheid, **6**:135, 185, 201
  banning of, **6**:47
  Gibson, **6**:87
  players, **6**:159
  and West Side Tennis Club, **6**:124-25
blacks, and track and field, **4**:76, 87, 166-69
blacks and wrestling, **11**:86, 100-02
Blackstock, Marshall, **11**:85
Blackwell, Ewell, **2**:109
Blaik, Earl, **1**:35-36, 53, 138
Blake, Hector (Toe), **8**:137, 170, 174
Blancard, Theresa Weld. *See* Weld, Theresa
Blancas, Homero, **5**:121
Blanchard, Felix (Doc), **1**:35-36, 38-40, 75, 179
Blanda, George, **1**:103-04, 123
Blankers-Koen, Fanny, **4**:95, 97-98, 105-07
Blaze Hanover, **13**:109
Bleibtrey, Ethelda, **12**:8-9
Bleier, Rocky, **1**:170
Blenheim, **13**:21-22
Blouin, Jimmy, **11**:67
Blubaugh, Doug, **11**:95
Bluebird, **12**:171-72
Bluebird II, **12**:149
Bluebird VII, **12**:158-59
Blue Dan, **11**:167-68
Blue Prince, **13**:25
Blue Ridge College, **1**:178
Blue Swords, **13**:41-42
Blue, Vida, **2**:187-88
Bluth, Ray, **11**:72
boating, **12**:114-86

popularity of, **12**:181-84
Jacoby on racing, **12**:148
see also individual races
Bobet, Louison, **10**:100
Bob Hope Desert Classic 1975, **5**:180-81
Bobick, Duane, **7**:179-81
bobsled race
  Garmisch 1953, **9**:72-73
  world contest 1961, **9**:100
  see also Olympic bobsled race winners
Bodnar, Gus, **8**:147
body building, **11**:113-16
Boeckl, Willi, **9**:13
Boe, Roy, **3**:192-94
Bogdanov, Anatole, **10**:49
Bogdanovskii, Fedor, **11**:108
Boglioli, Wendy, **12**:96-97, 99-100
Bogner, Willy, **9**:94-95
Bohemian Actress, **11**:140
Boillot, **13**:126
Boiteux, Jean, **12**:53-54
Boit, Mike, **4**:176-77
Bold Minstrel, **11**:158-59
Bold Ruler, **13**:63-64
Bold Venture, **13**:29-30
Bolero, **13**:55-56
Bologna-Genoa soccer game 1925, **8**:13
Bolshov, Viktor, **4**:135, 150
Bolton Wanderers
  vs Blackpool 1953, **8**:34
  English Soccer Cup winners 1929, **8**:18; 1958, **8**:39
  vs Manchester City 1926, **8**:15
Bonallack, Michael, **5**:162-63
Bond, Julian, **7**:168
Bonhag, George V., **4**:12
Bonlieu, François, **9**:110-11
Bonomi, John B., **7**:133-34, 139
Bonsack, Klaus, **9**:136
Bonthron, Bill, **4**:73-75
Boomer, Aubrey, **5**:33-36
Booth, A., **1**:18-20
Boozer, Bob, **3**:56
Borah, Charles, **4**:47-48
Borah, William, **13**:30
Borg, Arne, **12**:13-14, 20
Borg, Bjorn, **6**:190-93, 197-98
Boros, Julius, **5**:122-24
Borotra, Jean, **6**:36, 38, 53
Borzov, Valery, **4**:175-76, 178-79, 182, 187-89
Boston Americans
  vs Cleveland team 1909, **2**:12
  vs New York Yankees 1908, **2**:8
  vs Pittsburgh Nationals 1903, **2**:6
Boston Braves
  vs Brooklyn Robins 1920, **2**:23-24
  move to Milwaukee, **2**:100
  vs New York Giants 1916, **2**:20-21
Boston Bruins

vs Chicago Black Hawks 1933, **8**:120
vs Detroit Red Wings 1943, **8**:135
vs Los Angeles Kings 1971, **8**:13-84
vs Montreal Canadiens 1930, **8**:113-14; 1931, **8**:115; 1946, **8**:137-38; 1953, **8**:149; 1957, **8**:156-57; 1958, **8**:158; 1977, **8**:203-04; 1978, **8**:205-06
vs New York Rangers 1926, **8**:107-08; 1939, **8**:130-32
  Orr on, **8**:175-79
vs Ottawa Senators 1927, **8**:109
vs Philadelphia Flyers 1974, **8**:193
vs Philadelphia Quakers, 1930, **8**:114
vs St. Louis Blues 1969, **8**:180-82
Stanley Cup victors 1929, **8**:112-13, 1939, **8**:133; 1941, **8**:134; 1970, **8**:182-83; 1972, **8**:187-88
vs Toronto Maple Leafs 1933, **8**:121-22
Boston Celtics
  Auerbach as coach, **3**:154
  vs Cincinnati Royals 1965, **3**:150
  vs Los Angeles Lakers 1963, **3**:145-46
  vs Minneapolis Lakers 1959, **3**:135
  NBA champions 1957, **3**:130-31; 1959, **3**:135-36; 1960, **3**:140-41; 1962, **3**:144; 1964, **3**:149; 1965, **3**:151-52; 1966, **3**:155; 1968, **3**:162; 1969, **3**:162-63; 1974, **3**:181-82; 1976, **3**:190-91
  NBA Eastern title 1968, **3**:160
  vs New York Knicks 1958, **3**:132-33; 1960, **3**:139
  vs Philadelphia 76ers 1965, **3**:151
  vs Philadelphia Warriors 1960, **3**:141
  vs Phoenix Suns 1976, **3**:189-90
  record 1962, **3**:143
  Russell as coach, **3**:154-55
  vs Saint Louis Hawks 1958, **3**:133-35
Boston Marathon, **4**:44, 162
Boston, Ralph, **4**:132, 140, 169
Boston Redskins, **1**:92
Boston Red Sox
  vs Cincinnati Reds 1975, **2**:179-83
  vs Cleveland Indians 1948, **2**:85-86
  Lynn as Most Valuable Player, **2**:183-84
  vs Minnesota Twins 1967, **2**:146-47
  vs New York Giants 1912, **2**:14-16
  vs New York Yankees 1949, **2**:87-88; 1951, **2**:92-93; 1956, **2**:116; 1961, **2**:129-30
  vs Philadelphia Athletics 1941, **2**:72
  voided player purchase of, **2**:187-88
  vs Washington Senators 1917, **2**:21
  and Yawkey, **2**:56
Bothner, George, **11**:78
Bottom, Joe, **12**:95, 102-03
Bottomley, James, **2**:33
Bott, R.E.A., **9**:49
Boucher, Frank, **8**:109-12, 119-20, 136
Boucher, George, **8**:109
Boudreau, Lou, **2**:85-86, 109
Boudreaux, Johnny, **7**:193
Bourland, Dave, **1**:52-53
Bovard, **13**:51-52
Bovee, Roy E., **10**:12

bow and arrow hunting, **10**:163-64, 177-78
Bower, Johnny, **8**:167
Bowers, Anderson (Dick), **12**:140
bowling, **11**:67-75
  alleys, **11**:69-70, 72
  popularity of, **11**:67, 69-70, 73
  business of, **11**:73
Bowling Green State University basketball team, **3**:24-25
bowls, football, **1**:12-13, 68-70; *see also* specific Bowls
Bowman Challenge Cup, **11**:151-52
Bowman, Chester, **4**:34-35
boxing, **7**:1-199
  American Boxing Association of the U.S., **7**:13
  antitrust laws, **7**:128-29
  ban, **7**:12, 148-49
  blacks in, **7**:8-12, 17
  blows, **7**:122-23
  boxers' names, **7**:13
  brain damage from, **7**:138, 142-44
  champions. *See* individual titles
  court ruling on, **7**:128-29
  deaths. *See* deaths, boxing
  exhibition fights, **7**:74
  and fencing, **7**:122-23
  films, **7**:9-11
  fixing, **7**:81-82, 134-35
  gloves, **7**:83, 122-23, 149-50
  Hall of Fame, **7**:118-19
  International Boxing Club, **7**:119, 128-29, 139-41
  Jewish managers in, **7**:50
  knockouts, **7**:138
  monopoly in, **7**:128-29
  National Boxing Association. *See* National Boxing Association
  Olympic. *See* Olympic boxing
  promoters, **7**:13-15, 128-29, 138
  punch drunk boxers, **7**:138
  purses, **7**:14, 160-61
  and racketeers, **7**:133-35, 139-41
  rankings, **7**:119
  records. *See* records, boxing
  referees, **7**:20, 143-44
  ringside stretchers, **7**:39
  riots, **7**:24-26
  rules. *See* rules, boxing
  safety measures, **7**:83, 149-50
  scoring, **7**:189-90
  social acceptability of, **7**:27-28
  style, **7**:6-7, 82, 87
  Supreme Court ruling on, **7**:139, 178
  on television, **7**:63, 100, 114-17, 119, 128, 193-94
  titles, **7**:47-48, 74; *see also* individual titles
  trial, **7**:133-34
  United States Boxing Championship, **1**:93-94
  weight divisions, **7**:13
  women, **7**:179
  World Boxing Championship Commission, **7**:119
  World Boxing Council, **7**:167-68, 184, 196

Boyarskikh, Claudia, **9**:113-14
Boyd, Jim, **7**:126
Boykoff, Harry, **3**:27-28
Bozon, Charles, **9**:95, **10**:116-17
Braddock, James
  heavyweight champion 1935, **7**:51-53
  vs Louis 1937, **7**:60-62
  suspension of, **7**:59-60
Bradley, Bill, **3**:70, 169, 180-81
Bradley University basketball team, **3**:35-37, 42, 54-55, 57-60
Bradshaw, Terry, **1**:162, 166, 169-71
Brady, Bob, **11**:21
Bragg, Don, **4**:131, 141-42
Braid, James, **5**:7
brain damage, **7**:138, 142-44
Brabham, Jack, **13**:165
Bramlett, Leon, **1**:38-39
Branca, Ralph, **2**:94-95
Brand, Ester, **4**:109
Brant, Joseph, **10**:167-68, 172-74
Brasher, Chris, **4**:124-27
Bratton, Johnny, **7**:102
Braun, Joe, **3**:118
Brazil soccer team
  vs England 1970, **8**:68
  vs Hungary 1954, **8**:36; 1966, **8**:54-55
  and Pélé, **8**:73, 77-78
  vs Uruguay 1950, **8**:32
    World Soccer Cup victors 1958, **8**:40-41; 1962, **8**:50; 1966, **8**:53-54; 1970, **8**:69-70
Brazil water polo team, **12**:23
Breadon, Sam, **2**:80
Breedlove, Craig, **13**:172-73, 176-77
Breen, George, **12**:59, 61, 67
Bregman, Jim, **11**:97
Brenden, Hallgeir, **9**:66-67, 78-79
Brennan, Terry, **10**:35-36
Bresnahan, Roger, **2**:6-7, 19
Bret Hanover, **13**:114-16
Brett, George, **2**:189
Brewer, Gay, **5**:134-35
Brickley, Charles, **1**:86
Bridgeport University soccer team, **8**:43
Bridle n' Bit, **13**:73
Briggs, Peter, **11**:26
Brimsek, Frankie, **8**:130, 135, 138-39
Briscoe, Bennie, **7**:184-85
Britain, *See also* British; England; English
Britain, cricket in, **10**:53-56, 62
Britain, croquet in, **10**:12-14
Britain, equestrian team of, **11**:155
Britain, fishing in, **10**:192-93
Britain, golf in, **5**:33-34, 40-41, 54, 61-63, 162-63; *see also* British Open Golf Tournament
Britain, lacrosse team of, **10**:81
Britain, mountain climbing and, **10**:111-14
Britain, Olympic bobsled team of, **9**:107-08

Britain, Olympic yachting team of, **12**:141
Britain, polo team of, **10**:16-20, 26-27, 32
Britain, rugby in, **10**:79
Britain, tennis and
  Davis Cup 1933, **6**:57; 1934, **6**:63
  Lawn Tennis match, **6**:2
  open Wimbledon, **6**:154; *see also* Wimbledon tennis matches winners
  tennis method of, **6**:6-7
  Wightman Cup 1958, **6**:118-19
Britain, soccer in, **8**:23-25, 91-92; *see also* England soccer team; English football Association Cup; English Soccer Cup
See also England
British Football Association Cup. *See* English Football Association Cup
British Open Golf Tournament winners
  Hagen 1922, **5**:21-22; 1928, **5**:38-39; 1939, **5**:39-40
  Hogan 1953, **5**:92-93
  Hutchison 1921, **5**:19
  Jones 1926, **5**:29-30; 1927, **5**:25-26; 1930, **5**:41-42
  Locke 1950, **5**:81
  Miller 1976, **5**:187-88
  Nicklaus 1966, **5**:142-43; 1970, **5**:160-61
  Palmer 1961, **5**:113-14; 1962, **5**:119-20
  Player 1959, **5**:106; 1968, **5**:154-55; 1974, **5**:180
  Sarazen 1932, **5**:50-51
  Taylor 1913, **5**:9
  Thomson 1956, **5**:99; 1966, **5**:132-34
  Trevino 1971, **5**:164-65; 1972, **5**:172-73
  Vardon 1898, **5**:2-3
  Watson 1977, **5**:190-91
Britton, Jack
  vs Walker 1922, **7**:23-24
  welterweight champion 1919, **7**:15; 1922, **7**:20-21
See long jump; records, track and field, broad jump
Brock, Lou, **2**:152-53, 172-74
Brodsky, Abraham, **7**:133-34
Brokaw, Irving, **9**:2, 6
Bromwich, John, **6**:75-76, 90-92
bronco riding, **10**:130, 132-35
Brookes, Norman, **6**:75-76
Brooker, Tom, **1**:123
Brooklyn Arcadians, **3**:112
Brooklyn College basketball team, **3**:10-11
Brooklyn Country Club, **5**:8
Brooklyn Dodgers
  vs Cincinnati Reds 1938, **2**:62-63
  vs Milwaukee Braves 1954, **2**:106
  move to Los Angeles, **2**:120-21
  vs New York Giants 1934, **2**:53-54; 1951, **2**:94-95
  vs New York Yankees 1941, **2**:72-73; 1947, **2**:81-85; 1953, **2**:102-04; 1955, **2**:111-13; 1956, **2**:116-19
  vs Philadelphia Phillies, 1949, **2**:87-88; 1950, **2**:88-89; 1951, **2**:93
  vs Pittsburgh Pirates 1956, **2**:115
  purchase of Robinson, **2**:80
  vs St. Louis Cardinals 1934, **2**:52-53; 1946, **2**:77-78

suspension of Durocher, **2**:79
Brooklyn Robins
  vs Boston Braves 1920, **2**:23-24
  vs Cleveland Indians 1920, **2**:28-29
  vs St. Louis Cardinals 1924, **2**:33
Brooks, Joe, **11**:18
Brooks, Steve, **13**:55-56
Brooks, Tony, **13**:163-64
Broomstick, **13**:7
Brotherhood War, **2**:157-58
Brough, Louise
  in U.S. matches 1942, **6**:77-78; 1948, **6**:83-84, 1957,
    6:117-18
  in Wimbledon matches 1952, **6**:95-96; 1954, **6**:105;
    1956, **6**:112
  Wimbledon winner 1948, **6**:83; 1950, **6**:87; 1955, **6**:108
Broughton, John, **7**:122-23
Browden, Jefferson, **7**:138
Brown, Drew, **7**:175-76
Brown, Hubie, **3**:184
Brown, Ivan, **9**:36-38
Brown, Jim, **1**:57, 113, 126
Brown, Joe, **7**:124, 145
Brown, Pat, **8**:185
Brown, Pete, **5**:157
Brown, "Three-Fingered", **2**:11-12
Brown, Tom, **6**:81-82
Brown, Vivian, **4**:149-50
Browne, Mary K., **6**;19, 34
Browning, Dave, **12**:50-51
Browning, Jim, **11**:85
Brown University football team, **1**:8-9, 178
Bruce-Brown, David, **13**:126
Bruen, Jimmy, **5**:61-63
Brugnon, Jacques, **6**:39
Brumbaugh, Carl, **1**:89-92
Brumel, Valeri, **4**:135, 149-50, 159
Brundage, Avery
  and boxing, **7**:173
  and Holm, **12**:32
  and track and field, **4**:26, 58, 73
  at Winter Olympics, **9**:30-32, 51, 86-87, 141-42
Bruner, Mike, **12**:91-92
Brunet, Mme. Pierre, **9**:15
Brunet, Pierre, **9**:15
Brunner, Melitta, **9**:15-16
Bruno, Al, **1**:46
Bryan, Bucky, **1**:27-28
Bryan, Jimmy, **13**:153
Bryant, Nelson, **10**:186-90
Bryant, Paul, **1**:27, 82-83
Buchanan, Ken, **7**:179
Bucher, Carl, **11**:84
Bucknell University football team, **1**:177
Buckner, Bill, **2**:176-78
Budd, Frank, **4**:134-35, 142, 146-47
Budge, Don
  in Davis Cup matches 1937, **6**:71-72

record 1938, **6**:73
  in U.S. matches 1936, **6**:66-69
  U.S. matches winner 1938, **6**:73-74
  Wimbledon winner 1961, **6**:69-70; 1938, **6**:72-73
Budin, David, **3**:65
Bueno, Maria
  in U.S. matches 1960, **6**:126-27
  U.S. matches winner 1966, **6**:144
  in Wimbledon matches 1965, **6**:142; 1966, **6**:143
  Wimbledon winner 1959, **6**:124; 1964, **6**:137
Buff, Johnny, **7**:21-22
Buffalo Bills, **1**:156-57
Buffalo Sabres, **8**:199-200
Buhan, Jean, **11**:124
Buivid, Ray, **1**:30
Bukich, Rudy, **1**:49
Bulgaria soccer team, **8**:53-54
Bulger, Jim, **1**:71-72
Bulla, Johnny, **5**:71-72
bullfighting, **8**:13, **10**:137-47
Bullock, Fred, **5**:106
bulls, rodeo, **10**:134-35
Bunce, Don, **1**:73-74
Bunche, Ralph, **6**:124-25
Bunche, Ralph, Jr., **6**:124-25
Bungert, Wilhelm, **6**:146
Bunning, Jim, **2**:136-37
Burdette, Lew, **2**:121-23
Burgess, Charles, **8**:6
Burgess, William, **12**:4
Burghley, David, **4**:45-46
Burglund, Wilfred, **6**:124-25
Burka, Petra, **9**:121
Burka, Sylvia, **9**:147
Burke, Billy, **5**:49-50, 55-56
Burke, Jack, Jr., **5**:85-86, 98-99
Burke, Lynn, **12**:66-67
Burke, Michael, **2**:154-55
Burke, T.W., **4**:4
Burkemo, Walter, **5**:84
Burman, George, **1**:183
Burns, Tommy, **7**:7-8
Burnside, Dave, **8**:62-63
Burr, Janette, **9**:60-61
Burse, Ray, **10**:78-79
Burton, Mike, **12**:82, 89-90
Burton, Nelson, Jr., **11**:73
Bush, Lesley, **12**:70
Bushnell, Asa, **1**:48
Bushuev, Viktor, **11**:110
business
  baseball as, **2**:123-24
  billiards as, **11**:63
  bowling as, **11**:73
  of college basketball, **3**:39
  golf as, **5**:136-39
Butler, Bernie, **10**:164
Butler, Sol, **4**:28

Button, Richard
 "Ice Capades" contract, **9**:72
 in national figure skating contest 1945, **9**:44; 1960, **9**;61
 in Olympic figure skating contest 1948, **9**:50-51, 54-55; 1952, **9**:67-69
 in world figure skating contest 1947, **9**:45; 1948, **9**:50-51, 59-60
Buz On, **13**:72
Byrne, Tommy, **2**:111-13
Byrnes, John A., **3**:37-38

Cable, **13**:47-48
Cabrera, Delfo, **4**:98, 100
caddies, **5**:108-09
Cagle, Chris (Red), **1**:20-21
Cahill, Thomas W., **8**:9-10, 17-18
Cain, Bobby, **2**:95-97
Cain, Jim, **1**:41-42, 45
Calcuttas, golf, **5**:138
Calder, Frank, **8**:109, 126-27, 129, 134-35; *see also* National Hockey League
Caldwell, Joe, **1**:60-62
Calhoun, Lee, **4**:123-24, 131, 138-39
California Angels, **2**:174
California basketball team, **3**:27, 58-59, 61
California, boxing banned in, **7**:12
California, University of. *See* University of California, University of California (Los Angeles); University of Southern California
Calmat, Alain, **9**:115-16
Calnan, George, **11**:122
Calumet Butler, **13**:98
Cambridge University crew team, **12**:136
Cambridge University rugby team, **10**:77, 79
Cameron, Bob, **1**:45
Camp, Walter, **1**:5, 10-12, 174
Campanella, Roy, **2**:111-14
Campaneris, Bert, **2**:188
Campbell, Bill, **5**:162-63
Campbell, Clarence, **8**:142, 150-51, 155, 182, 186, 192, 195; *see also* National Hockey League
Campbell, Donald, **12**:158-59, 171-72
Campbell, Sir Malcolm, **12**:149, **13**:139-41
Campbell, Milton, **4**:107-08, 125, 128
Campbell, Thomas, **4**:28
Campi, Louis, **11**:70-72
Canada, curling team of, **9**:6, 18, 27
Canada, equestrian team of, **11**:160
Canada, hockey team of
 1920, **9**:7
 1932, **9**:23-24
 1936, **9**:39
 1952, **9**:69
 1956, **9**:84-86
 1960, **9**:95-96
 1964, **9**:119
 1968, **9**:135
 1973, **8**:189-90
Canada, hunting and fishing in, **10**:158-60
Canada, lacrosse team of, **10**:81
Canada, Olympic bobsled team of, **9**:116-17
Canada, ladies golf championship in 1913, **5**:11
Canario, Arthur, **11**:99
Cane Futurity 1959, **13**:107-08
Canfield, Robert W., **10**:47-48
canoe race, Olympic. *See* Olympic canoe race
Cantello, Al, **4**:130
Cantlon, William (Shorty), **13**:147-48
Cantreall, Bill, **12**:157-58
Canzoneri, Tony
 lightweight champion 1930, **7**:42; 1931, **7**:42-43
 vs Ross 1933, **7**:45
Capadrutt, Reto, **9**:20-22
Capilla, Joaquin, **12**:53, 60-61
Carbo, Bernie, **2**:179
Carbo, Frankie, **7**:81-82, 133-34, 139-41, 148
Cardiff City soccer team, **8**:13, 15
Cardigan Bay, **13**:115
Career Boy, **13**:61-62
Carleton, Tex, **2**:46-48
Carlisle Indian School, **1**:7, **4**:24
Carlton, Steve, **2**:155-56
Carmen, Clarence, **10**:89
Carnegie Fund Study, **1**:174-78
Carnera, Primo
 vs Baer 1934, **7**:48
 heavyweight champion 1933, **7**:45-46
 vs Louis 1935, **7**:53-54
 and wrestling, **9**:94-95
Carney, Les, **4**:137
Carpenter, Bill, **1**:60-62
Carpenter, Ken, **4**:80-81
Carpenter, Lew, **1**:113
Carpentier, Georges, **7**:17-20
Carr, Bill, **4**:67-69
Carr, Henry, **4**:157-58
Carr, Joe, **1**:86, 89
Carr, Roddy, **5**:162-63
Carr, Savin, **4**:43, 48-49
Carroll, Dan, **9**:143-44
Carruthers, Louis, **6**:53
Carry Back, **13**:67-68
Carry Message, **13**:57
Carson, Bill, **8**:112
Carter, Don, **11**:69, 71-73
Caruccio, Consetta, **11**:128
Carveth, Jack, **8**:135
Casa, Victoria, **8**:67
Casals, Rosie, **6**:158, 169-72, 194-95
Casey, Hugh, **2**:72-73, 81-82, 84-85
Caslavska, Vera, **11**:131
Casper, Billy, **5**:140-42, 144-45, 154-55, 157

Cassidy, George, **13**:22
Cassidy, Thomas, **13**:19
Castellotti, Eugenio, **13**:159
Catalina swim 1927, **12**:18-20
Catt, Dierdre, **6**:134
cattle-grazing, **5**:65
Cattrano, Jimmy (the Cat), **11**:64
Cauthen, Steve, **13**:79-80, 85-87, 90-91
Cavanaugh, John, **1**:178-79
Cavender, Regis, **1**:64-66
Cawley, Evonne Goolagong. *See* Goolagong, Evonne
Cawley, Rex, **4**:156
CBS-TV, **4**:201, **10**:185-90
Cecil, Richard, **8**:57-58
Cecotto, Johnny, **10**:93
Celtic soccer team, **8**:20
Cepeda, Orlando, **2**:136
Cerbonney, Jules, **4**:48
Cerdan, Marcel, **7**:90-91, 93, 134
Cevert, Françoise, **13**:190
Chabot, Lorne, **8**:121-22
Chadwick, Florence, **12**:49-50
Challedon, **13**:35-36
Chamberlain, Wilt
    in NBA championship game 1967, **3**:158; 1969, **3**:162-63; 1973, **3**:178
    vs New York Knicks 1970, **3**:168
    on Philadelphia 76ers, **3**:150
    record 1960, **3**:137; 1961, **3**:142, 1962, **3**:142-43; 1963, **3**:146; 1966, **3**:153; 1972, **3**:74
    vs Seattle Supersonics 1972, **3**:176
    superstar on Kansas University team, **3**:53-54
    traded to Los Angeles Lakers, **3**:162
Chambliss, Chris, **2**:189-90, 194
Chammartin, Henri, **11**:158
Champi, Frank, **1**:67
Chance, Britton, **12**:156
Chance, Dean, **2**:145-47
Chandler, Albert (Happy), **2**:76, 78-79, 86-87
Chandler, Don, **1**:115, 137
Chandler, Jenni, **12**:94
Chaney, Darrel, **2**:168
Chapman, Colin, **13**:170
Chapman, Ray, **2**:25
Charles, Bob, **5**:126-28, 154-55, 160-61
Charles, Ezzard
    heavyweight 1949, **7**:94-95; 1950, **7**:99-100
    vs Marciano 1954, **7**:117-18
    vs Walcott 1951, **7**:103-04
Chataway, Christopher, **4**:105-06, 112, 115
Cheny, Tom, **2**:133
Cheng, Chi, **4**:173
Chepulis, Ionas, **7**:173
Cherry, Don, **8**:205-06
Chevallier, B.M., **11**:152
Chevrolet, Gaston, **13**:131
Chevy Chase Club, **6**:159
Chewning, Lynn, **1**:38-39

Chicago Bears
    vs All Stars 1934, **1**:91
    Grange on, **1**:87-88
    vs New York Giants 1925, **1**:87-88; 1933, **1**:89-91; 1934, **1**:91-92
    vs Portsmouth Spartans 1932, **1**:89
    vs St. Louis Cardinals 1949, **1**:103-04
    vs San Francisco 49ers 1965, **1**:128
    vs Washington Redskins 1937, **1**:93-94; 1940, **1**:95-96; 1943, **1**:97-99
Chicago Black Hawks
    vs Boston Bruins 1933, **8**:120
    vs Detroit Red Wings 1934, **8**:124-25
    vs Montreal Canadiens 1931, **8**:115-18; 1944, **8**:137; 1952, **8**:147-48; 1960, **8**:160; 1965, **8**:169-70; 1971, **8**:184-85; 1973, **8**:190-91
    vs New York Rangers 1952, **8**:147; 1962, **8**:161-62
    Stanley Cup victors 1934, **8**:125; 1938, **8**:129-30; 1961, **8**: 161
Chicago Bricklayers, **8**:16-17
Chicago Bulls, **3**:152, 171
Chicago Cardinals, **1**:119
Chicago Cubs
    vs Cincinnati Reds 1917, **2**:21
    vs Cleveland 1908, **2**:10
    vs Los Angeles Dodgers 1965, **2**:142-43
    vs Milwaukee Braves 1957, **2**:120
    vs New York Giants 1908, **2**:9-12; 1912, **2**:13-14
    vs New York Mets 1973, **2**:170
    vs New York Yankees 1932, **2**:45-46
    vs Philadelphia Athletics 1929, **2**:41-42
    vs Philadelphia Phillies 1976, **2**:186-87
    vs Pittsburgh Pirates 1938, **2**:63-64; 1975, **2**:178
    vs St. Louis Cardinals 1942, **2**:74; 1955, **2**:111
    and Santo trade, **2**:171
Chicago Hornets, **1**:103
Chicago Packers, **3**:136, 142
Chicago Stags, **3**:114, 116
Chicago University football team, **1**:11, 32
Chicago White Sox
    vs Cincinnati Reds 1920, **2**:25-28
    vs Cleveland Indians 1940, **2**:68
    vs Detroit Tigers 1922, **2**:32
    World Series fixing 1919, **2**:25-28, 32
Chik T'Sun, **11**:176
Chile soccer team, **8**:32
Chinaglia, Giorgio, **8**:89-90
Chinese angler, **10**:167
Chinese Communist table tennis team, **11**:40-41, 43
Chmielewski, Bill, **3**:66-67
Chocolate, Kid, **7**:42-45
Christenberry, Robert, **7**:107, 119, 167-68
Chrystal, William, **3**:65
Church, George, **6**:7
Churchill, Tom, **4**:52-53
Churchill, Winston, **8**:33
Cicotte, Eddie, **2**:25-28, 32
Cincinnati Reds

vs Boston Red Sox 1975, **2**:179-83
vs Brooklyn Dodgers 1938, **2**:62-63
vs Chicago Cubs 1917, **2**:21
vs Chicago White Sox 1920, **2**:25-28
vs New York Giants 1937, **2**:61
vs New York Yankees 1961, **2**:132-33
vs Philadelphia Phillies 1935, **2**:56
vs Pittsburgh Pirates 1972, **2**:168-69
vs St. Louis Cardinals 1920, **2**:24; 1934, **2**:53-54
Cincinnati Royals, **3**:150, 164-65
Cincinnati University basketball team
vs Louisville 1959, **3**:59
NCAA champions 1961, **3**:63-64; 1962, **3**:67-68
vs New York University 1960, **3**:61
vs St. John's 1964, **3**:70-71
vs Wichita 1960, **3**:59
City College of New York basketball team
vs Bradley 1950, **3**:35-37
coaches of, **3**:5
game-fixing, **3**:38-39, 47
and Holman, **3**:49-50
NCAA champions 1950, **3**:36-37
vs New York University 1934, **3**:9; 1947, **3**:27-28
Clancy, Charles, **4**:24
Clancy, King, **8**:118-19
Clark, Bob, **4**:83-85
Clark, Clarence, **5**:59-60
Clark, Ellery, **4**:4
Clark, Jimmy, **13**:167-68, 170-72, 175-77
Clarke, Ron, **4**:153, 160
Clay, Cassius. *See* Ali, Muhammed
Clements, Jack, **11**:18
Cleveland Barons, **8**:206
Cleveland baseball team
vs Boston 1909, **2**:12
vs Chicago Cubs 1908, **2**:10
vs St. Louis 1910, **2**:12
Cleveland Browns, **1**:93, 101, 105-09, 113
Cleveland Indians
vs Boston Red Sox 1948, **2**:85-86
vs Brooklyn Robins 1920, **2**:28-29
vs Chicago White Sox 1940, **2**:68
vs Detroit Tigers 1915, **2**:19; 1927, **2**:40; 1938, **2**:64; 1951, **2**:90-91; 1954, **2**:107
vs New York Giants 1954, **2**:107-08
vs New York Yankees 1941, **2**:71
numbers on uniforms, **2**:20
vs Philadelphia Athletics 1925, **2**:34
Robinson as manager of, **2**:175
vs St. Louis Browns 1936, **2**:60; 1952, **2**:95-97
season victory record 1954, **2**:107
Cleveland Pipers, **3**:143
Cleveland Rams, **1**:100
Cleveland Rosenblums, **3**:112-13
Clifton, Nat (Sweetwater), **3**:119
Clothier, William, **6**:4
Clotworthy, Robert, **12**:50-51, 56
coaching, football. *See* football, college coaching; football,

professional, coaching
Coaltown, **13**:49-51
Coan, Andy, **12**:104-05
Coates, Jim, **2**:132-33
Cobb, John Rhodes, **12**:156-57
Cobb, Ty
and baseball strike, **2**:13
in Hall of Fame, **2**:57
vs Johnson, **2**:17
records, **2**:12-13, 34
salary of, **2**:17
Cobb, W. Montague, **4**:76
Cochet, Henri
in Davis Cup matches 1927, **6**:40-42; 1932, **6**:53; 1933, **6**:57
French hard court tournament winner 1930, **6**:48
in U.S. matches 1932, **6**:56-57
U.S. matches winner 1926, **6**:35-37
in Wimbledon matches 1927, **6**:38
Cochran, Barbara, **9**:148-49, 166
Cochran, Roy, **4**:89, 91-92
Cochran, Welker, **11**:59-60, 62
Cochrane, George, **11**:85
Cody, William, **10**:151
Coe, Charley, **5**:106-07, 111-13
Coffin, Roy, **9**:15
Colavito, Rocky, **2**:151
Cole, Tom, **13**:151-52
Colella, Tom, **1**:101
Coleman, Georgia, **12**:22, 26, 29
Coles, Neil, **5**:175-76
Colgate University football team, **1**:57
Colin, **13**:5-6
college basketball, **3**:2-109
and Amateur Athletic Association, **3**:3-4, 8
basket height, **3**:11
blacks in, 7:54, 78, 98
as business, **3**:39
coaches of, **3**:96-97
control of, **3**:3
fans, **3**:7
in Far East, **3**:5
fixing, **3**:22, 37-39, 41-46, 63-66
gambling, **3**:22, 38
Intercollegiate Basketball League, **3**:5
at Madison Square Garden, **3**:9-10, 40-42
National Collegiate Association. *See* National Collegiate Athletic Association; and basketball; National Collegiate Athletic Association, basketball champion
officials, **3**:7
Olympic. *See* Olympic basketball
popularity of, **3**:14
records. *See* records, college basketball
recruiting of players by professional teams, **3**:96-97, 159-60, 170-71, 173, 180-81
rules. *See* rules, college basketball
U.S. World Basketball Tournament team, **3**:56-57
women's, **3**:2, 5, 98-101, 105-06

writers about, **3**:13

zone defense, **3**:14-15

college crew races. *See* crew races, intercollegiate

college fencing, **11**:125-26

college football, **1**:2-83, 174-78

  All Star football club, **1**:91

  Associated Press poll, **1**:78-79

  bowls, **1**:12-13, 68-70; *see also* college football, individual bowls

  cleats, **1**:17

  coaching, **1**:8-10, 75-77

  dead ball, **1**:25

  death, **1**:5

  defense, **1**:2-3, 23-25, 53-54

  elbow pads, **1**:16

  equipment, **1**:17, 25

  fans, **1**:28

  films, **1**:10-11

  formations, **1**:34, 51, 53, 59

  Four Horsemen, **1**:15-16

  goal posts, **1**:16-17, 60

  huddle, **1**:16

  Intercollegiate Football Rules Committee, **1**:5, 7

  Ivy League, **1**:47-48

  Joint Rules Committee, **1**:8

  kick, **1**:5, 7, 17, 25

  Lewisohn Stadium, **1**:12

  Los Angeles Coliseum, **1**:12

  NCAA, **1**:15, 47, 68-70, 184-85

  night game, **1**:17

  numbers, **1**:7

  offense, **1**:5, 16-17, 23, 33-34, 53-54

  pass, **1**:5, 7, 16

  penalties, **1**:16

  periods, **1**:7

  plays, **1**:53, 58-60

  poll, **1**:78-79, 151

  Quantico Stadium, **1**:13

  radio broadcast of, **1**:18

  ratings, **1**:16

  records, **1**:57, 62, 63

  reform of, **1**:2

  revenue, **1**:10

  Rice Memorial Stadium, **1**:12

  riots, **1**:28

  Rose Bowl 1928, **1**:18; 1933, **1**:25-26; 1934, **1**:26-27; 1939, **1**:30-31; 1940, **1**:33, 1953, **1**:49; 1956, **1**:55; 1963, **1**:62; 1966, **1**:63-64; 1967, **1**:66; 1972, **1**:73-74; 1975, **1**:74; 1977, **1**:77-78

  rules. *See* rules, college football

  scoreboard, **1**:16

  signal-calling, **1**:75-77

  slush funds for, **1**:174-78

  vs soccer, **8**:5, 7-8

  Southeastern Conference, **1**:70

  substitutions, **1**:25, 33-34, 49-50, 63

  Sugar Bowl: 1935, **1**:27-28; 1950, **1**:46; 1956, **1**:54-55, 179-80;1968, **1**:137; 1979, **1**:82-83

  tackle, **1**:7

  on television **1**:31-32, 47, 70, 77-78

  two-point conversion, **1**:58

  United Press International poll, **1**:78-79

  Yankee Stadium, **1**:12-13

  see also football and society; football, professional

college gymnastics, **11**:128-29

college lacrosse, **10**:80-83

College of the Holy Cross. *See* Holy Cross basketball team

college polo, **10**:23-24, 32

college riflery, **10**:45

college rodeo, **10**:134

college rugby, **10**:75-76

college soccer, **8**:5-8, 74-75; *see also* National Collegiate Athletic Association soccer champions; soccer champions,intercollegiate

college tennis, **6**:172

college wrestling, **11**:86-87, 97, 104

college track and field

  cross country running, **4**:16, 26

  Dillard records, **4**:89

  ICAAA meet 1928, **4**:43-44

  Pacific 8 Conference 1978, **4**:201

  Princeton meet 1934, **4**:73-74

  recruiting of foreign athletes for **4**:199-200

  relay races, **4**:25

  UCLA-Southern California Pacific Coast Conference 1954, **4**:112-13 *see also* National Collegiate Athletic Association

Collett, Glenna, **5**:40, 46-47, 58

Collett, Wayne, **4**:179-82

Colledge, Cecelia, **9**:28-29, 34, 38-39

Colliard, Renee, **9**:78-79

Collier, James, **3**:182-83

Collier, Jeanne, **12**:67

Collier, Sam, **13**:150

Collings, Earl, **5**:191-92

Collins, Ted, **1**:97, 103

Colorado University basketball team, **3**:13-14, 16-17

Colo, Zeno, **9**:60, 64

Columbia, **12**:160-61

Columbia University athletic meet 1906, **4**:9

Columbia University football team, **1**:12, 25-26, 39-41, 177

Columbia University soccer team, **8**:8

Colville, Mac, **8**:130

Colville, Neil, **8**:133

Comaneci, Nadia, **11**:132-36

Combs, Clarence (Buddy), **10**:28

Comiskey, Charles, **2**:25-28, 32

Complex II, **12**:156

Compston, Archie, **5**:33-34, 38-39

computers in sports, **1**:132-33, **3**:197-99

Conacher, Charlie, **8**:118-20

Conacher, Lionel, **8**:118-19

Conacher, Roy, **8**:133

Cone, Carin, **12**:59

Conerly, Charles, **1**:113-15, 122-23

Conger, Ray, **4**:49-50

Conn, Billy, **7**:72-77, 167-68
Conn, Mark, **7**:172
Connecticut University basketball team, **3**:40-41
Connie Hawkins Story, The (Wolf), **3**:175-76
Connell, Alex, **8**:126
Connolly, Hal, **4**:117-18, 120, 130-31, 136-38
Connolly, Maureen (Mo)
   Australian matches winner 1953, **6**:97
   French matches winner 1953, **6**:97-98
   grand slam winner 1953, **6**:102-03
   portrait of, **6**:100-01
   U.S. matches winner 1951, **6**:93-94; 1952, **6**:96-97
   Wimbledon winner 1952, **6**:95-96; 1953, **6**:100: 1954,
6:105
Connors, Jimmy
   doubles with Evert, **6**:190
   vs Laver 1975, **6**:185
   vs Nastese 1977, **6**:195
   NCAA winner 1971, **6**:172
   in U.S. Open 1975, **6**:189-90; 1977, **6**:200-01
   U.S. Open winner 1974, **6**:184-85; 1976, **6**:193
   in Wimbledon matches 1975, **6**:187-88; 1977 **6**:197;
     1978, **6**:202
   Wimbledon winner 1974, **6**:183-84
Consolini, Adolfo, **4**:93
conservation of wildlife, **10**:153-54, 157-58, 162, 191-92
Constantine, Prince, **4**:2, 4, **12**:163
Constellation, **12**:166-68
Conti, Roger, **11**:56-57
Continental League, **2**:123-24
Cook, Arthur, Edwin, **10**:48
Cook, Bill, **8**:121-22
Cooke, Sarah Palfrey. *See* Palfrey, Sarah
Coolidge, Thornton, **9**:14
Cooper, Ashley, **6**:117-22
Cooper, Brad, **12**:91
Cooper, Earl, **13**:133
Cooper, Harry, **5**:34-35, 56-57, 59-60
Cooper, Joe, **8**:128
Cooper, Joyce, **12**:22
Copeland, Lillian, **4**:62-63
Coppi, Fausto, **10**:100, 102-03
Corbally, John, **1**:180
Corbett, George, **1**:91
Corbett, James, **7**:2-4, 12
Corcoran, Tom, **9**:91
Corey, Albert, **4**:7
Cornaggia-Medici, G., **11**:123
Cornell College wrestling team, **11**:87
Cornell University football team, **1**:7
Cornell University lacrosse team, **10**:84, 86
Corrock, Susan, **9**:142
Corum, L.L., **13**:133
Cosell, Howard, **7**:143
Cotelli, Mario, **9**:152
Cotton Bowl 1937, **1**:29-30; 1954, **1**:50-51; 1971, **1**:70-71
Coulter, Art, **8**:13
Counsilman, Jim, **12**:84-86

Count Fleet, **13**:41-45
Courageous, **12**:179-80, 185
Court, Margaret Smith
   Australian matches winner 1960, **6**:125
   grand slam winner, **6**:171-72
   vs Riggs 1972, **6**:179
   U.S. matches winner 1962, **6**:130; 1970, **6**:171-72; 1973,
     6:182
   in Wimbledon matches 1962, **6**:128; 1964, **6**:137; 1971,
     6:172-73
   Wimbledon winner 1963, **6**:133; 1965, **6**:142; 1970,
     6:167-69
Courtney, Tom, **4**:121-23
Cousy, Bob, **3**:120, 133-34, 135-36, 140-41, 145, 164-65
Covell, B.C., **6**:24-25
Coward, Thomas R., **11**:6-7, 9-10
Cowens, Dave, **3**:181-82, 190-91
Cowhig, Gerry, **1**:35-36
Cox, Johnny, **3**:56
Cox, Mark, **6**:165
Cox, Wiffy, **5**:56-57
Cox, William, **8**:43, 53
Coy, Robert, **10**:126
Crabbe, Clarence (Buster), **12**:22, 26
Crack Brigade **13**:19-20
Craig, Ralph, **4**:17-18
Crampton, Bruce
   earnings of, **5**:176
   Masters Golf Tournament 1972, second place, **5**:165-66
   Professional Golfers' Association Tournament 1963,
     third place, **5**:124; 1973, second place, **5**:176; 1975,
     second place, **5**:184-85
   United States Open Golf Tournament 1972, second
place, **5**:166-67
Crane, Irving, **11**:62-63
Cranz, Christel, **9**:29-20
Craven race 1930, **13**:20
Crawford, Hasely, **4**:187-89
Crawford, Jack, **6**:61-63
Crawley, Leonard, **5**:61-63
crawl, swimming, **12**:2-5
Crescent Athletic-Hamilton Club 1936, **3**:10-11
Cresceus, **13**:94
crew. *See* Olympic rowing; records, rowing
crew race, intercollegiate
   Cambridge vs Oxford 1933, **12**:136
   Harvard victory 1914, **12**:115-16; 1927, **12**:125-27;
     1937, **12**:143-44; 1938, **12**:146, 1948, **12**:151-52
   Navy victory 1925, **12**:124-25
   Washington victory 1923, **12**:121-22; 1937, **12**:142-43
   Yale victory 1921, **12**:120-21; 1949, **12**:154-55
cricket, **8**:9, **10**:53-56, 62
Crisler, H.O., **1**:49-51, 77
Crockett, Ivory, **4**:185-86
Cronin, Joe, **2**:128-29, 144, 166
Crook, Eddie, **7**:139
croquet, **10**:11-14, 53-62
Cross, George, **1**:48

cross-country skiing, 9:43, *see also* Olympic ski race champions, cross country
Crozier, 13:67-68
Cruguet, Jean, 13:80-85
Cruickshank, Robert, 5:24-25, 51-52, 56-57
Crump, Diane, 13:72-73
Crusader, 12:156-57
Crutchfield, Jimmie, 2:162-65
Cruyff, Johan, 8:97
Csermak, Jozsef, 4:105
Csik, Ferenc, 12:33-35
Csonka, Larry, 1:151-54, 157-59, 162, 164-65
Cuff, Ward, 1:94
Cullinan, Craig F., Jr., 2:127
Cummings, Dorothy Smith, 10:4
Cunningham, Briggs, 12:160-61
Cunningham, Glenn, 4:73-75, 82
Cuozzo, Gary, 1:127
Cupit, Jack, 5:123-24
Curd, Ed, 3:44-45
curling, 9:5-6, 18, 62; *see also* Gordon International Medal
Curry, Bill, 1:143-46
Curry, John, 9:159, 161
Curtice, Jack, 1:63
Curtis, Ann, 4:94, 98, 12:43-48
Cutbill, Harold, 4:33
Cuthbert, Betty, 4:122-24, 128
Cutter, Kiki, 9:127, 129, 139
cycling, Olympic, 12:62
Czechoslovakia, canoe team of, 12:154
Czechoslovakia, gymnastics of, 11:129
Czechoslovakia, Olympic hockey team of, 9:98-99, 164, 167
Czechoslovakia, soccer team of, 8:21, 50, 52

Dahlgren, Ellsworth (Babe), 2:64
Dahlstrom, Cully, 8:129
Daland, Peter, 12:72-73, 91
D'Alesandro, Thomas, 2:101-02
Dallas Cowboys
    vs Baltimore Colts 1971, 1:150-51
    vs Denver Broncos 1978, 1:168-69
    vs Green Bay Packers 1968, 1:135-36
    vs Houston Oilers 1962, 1:123
    vs Miami Dolphins 1972, 1:151-53
    vs Pittsburgh Steelers 1976, 1:165-66; 1979, 1:169-71
Dallas Rangers, 1:118
Daller, Jiri, 10:104
Dalton, Mel, 4:49
Daly, Maurice, 11:47-48
Dambrot, Irwin, 3:35-37
Dame Pattie, 12:172-73

Dancer's Image, 13:70-72
Dancer, Stanley, 13:104
Danek, Ludvik, 4:154-56
Daniels, C.M., 12:2
Danielsen, Egil, 4:122
Danneberg, Jochen, 9:156-57
Danowski, Ed, 1:91-92, 94
Dan Patch, 13:94
Dark, Alvin, 2:176
Dark Star, 13:56-57
Dartmouth University football team, 1:178
Daugherty, Duffy, 1:63-64
Davenport, Ira, 4:18-19
Davenport, Willie, 4:167-68, 192-93
Davidson, Gary, 1:155
Davidson, Gary, 8:185
Davies, John, 12:55
Davies, W.H., 5:54
Davis, Anthony, 1:74-75
Davis, Dwight, 6:2
Davis, Floyd, 13:147
Davis, Glenn, 1:35-36, 38-40, 75 105-06, 179
Davis, Glenn, 4:117-18, 120, 130, 135-36
Davis, Howard, 7:191-92
Davis, Jack, 4:105-06
Davis, Jim, 10:89
Davis, John, 11:107
Davis, Otis, 4:139-42
Davis, Suzanne, 9:15
Davis, Walter, 4:102
Davis, Willie, 1:138
Davis Cup (matches)
    to Australia 1907, 6:3; 1939, 6:75-76; 1950, 6:90-92; 1955, 6:108-10; 1956, 6:114
    to Britain 1933, 6:57; 1934, 6:63
    to France 1927, 6:40-42; 1932, 6:53
    Nastase in 1969, 6:165
    South Africa banned from, 6:201
    to South Africa 1974, 6:185
    organization on challenge basis, 6:113-14
    to Sweden 1975, 6:190-91
    U.S. in challenge 1937, 6:71-72
    to U.S. 1923, 6:25-26; 1954, 6:106-07; 1958, 6:121-22; 1963, 6:131
    withdrawals from, 6:196
Dawkins, Peter, 10:76-77
Dawson, Joe, 13:127
Dawson, Len, 1:128, 130, 148
Daytona Beach, auto racing at. *See* auto racing, Daytona
Daytona 200-mile national motorcycle championship 1951, 10:89; 1969, 10:91; 1976, 10:93; 1977, 10:94
Dayton University basketball team, 3:48, 50-51, 66-67
Dean, Dan, 4:62
Dean, Jerome (Dizzy), 2:52-56
Dean, Paul, 2:52-53
Dean, Ted, 1:119-20
deaths, auto racing
    Ansterberg, 13:133

Bruce-Brown, **13**:127
Cantlon, **13**:147-48
Chevrolet, **13**:131
Cole, **13**:151-52
Collier, **13**:150
at Indianapolis 500, **13**:130, 136-39, 156, 189-90
Italians, **12**:136
Lecocq, **13**:130
at Le Mans auto race, **13**:157
MacDonald, **13**:173-74
in 1924, **13**:133
Revson, **13**:191-92
Roberts, **13**:144-45
Sachs, **13**:173-74
Thurman, **13**:130
of top racers, **13**:191
von Trips, **13**:167-68
Wilcox, **13**:132-33
deaths, bicycling, **10**:102-3, 106
deaths, boating
Campbell, **12**:171-72
Cobb, **12**:156-57
in President's Cup race 1965, **12**:169-70
deaths, bobsledding, **9**:72-73
deaths, boxing
Doyle, **7**:78
McCarty, **7**:11-12
Moore, **7**:148-49
Pacheco, **7**:138
Paret, **7**:144
deaths, fencing, **11**:125
deaths, football, **1**:5
deaths, hang-gliding, **10**:127
deaths, hunting, **10**:150
deaths, Israeli at 1972 Olympics, **4**:180
deaths, motorcycling, **10**:88
deaths, mountain-climbing, **10**:116-17
deaths, skiing, **9**:103-04
deaths, sky-diving, **10**:125-26
deaths, U.S. skaters', **9**:100-01
Debaets, Gerard, **10**:99
Debernard, Danielle, **9**:164, 167
De Busschere, Dave, **3**:168-69
deCapriles, Jose R., **11**:122, 124
deCapriles, Miguel, **11**:123-24
decathlon records. *See* records, track and field decathlon
decathlon winners, Olympic
Avilov 1972, **4**:181-82
Bausch 1932, **4**:69-70
Campbell 1956, **4**:128
Holdorf 1964, **4**:158
Jenner 1976, **4**:194-95
Johnson 1960, **4**:139-40
Mathias 1948, **4**:97-98; 1952, **4**:107-08
Morris 1936, **4**:84-85
Osborne 1924, **4**:40
recount 1920, **4**:30-31
Thorpe 1912, **4**:22-24
Toomey 1968, **4**:170-71
Yrjola 1928, **4**:52-53
Decker, Fred, **8**:79
deer hunting, **10**:154
DeForest, Jimmy, **7**:45
Degener, Richard, **12**:31, 34-36
DeGroot, Edward, Jr., **11**:45-46
DeJesus, Estebu, **7**:194
Delage car, **13**:127-29
de la Hunty, Shirley Strickland, **4**:105-07, 126
Delaney, Loral I., **10**:51
deLeeuw, Dianne, **9**:164, 168
Delfino, Guiseppe, **11**:125-26
DeLisle, Coquelin, **10**:44
Delvecchio, Alex, **13**:152
DeMar, Clarence, **4**:41, 44
DeMarco, Tony, **7**:119-20
Demaret, Jimmy, **5**:77-78, 101
Dementieva, Elisaventa, **12**:159
DeMerode, Alexandre, **12**:90
DeMont, Rick, **12**:89-91
Dempsey, Jack
and black challengers, **7**:17
greatest fighter, **7**:96-97
in Hall of Fame, **7**:118-19
heavyweight champion 1919, **7**:16-17; 1921, **7**:17-20; 1923, **7**:24-26; 1927, **7**:34-36
vs Tunney, 1926, **7**:29-32; 1927, **7**:36-39
Dempsey, Tom, **1**:149-50
Denmark soccer team, **8**:46-70
Denneny, Cy, **8**:109
Denney, Jim, **9**:156-57
Dennis, Clare, **12**:24-25
Denver Broncos, **1**:168-69
Denver Nuggets, **3**:188-89, 200-01
Denver Rockets, **3**:164
DeOro, Alfredo, **9**:48, 50
dePalma, Ralph, **13**:123, 126, 129-31
dePaolo, Peter, **13**:134
DePaul University basketball team, **3**:20, 24-26
dePietro, J.N., **11**:106
dePortago, Alfonso (Marquis), **13**:160-61
Depthios, Charlie, **11**:112
Derby, Lord, **13**:20-21
Desch, August, **4**:27
Detroit Falcons, **8**:114-15
Detroit Lions, **1**:109
Detroit Pistons, **3**:200-01
Detroit Red Wings
vs All Stars 1950, **8**:145
vs Boston Bruins 1941, **8**:134
vs Chicago Black Hawks 1934, **8**:124-25; 1961, **8**:161
vs Montreal Canadiens 1955, **8**:150-51; 1956, **8**:155; 1966, **8**:172-73
vs New York Rangers 1944, **8**:136; 1953, **8**:148
Stanley Cup victors 1936, **8**:127; 1937, **8**:128; 1943, **8**:135; 1950, **8**:144-45; 1952, **8**:147; 1954, **8**:149; 1955, **8**:152

vs Toronto Maple Leafs 1937, **8**:127-28; 1942, **8**:134-35; 1945, **8**:137; 1948, **8**:143; 1949, **8**:143; 1963, **8**:163; 1964, **8**:167
Detroit Tigers
  vs Chicago White Sox 1922, **2**:32
  vs Cleveland Indians 1915, **2**:19; 1927, **2**:40; 1938, **2**:64; 1951, **2**:90-91; 1954, **2**:107
  vs Kansas City Athletics 1955, **2**:109
  vs Oakland Athletics 1968, **2**:149-51
  vs St. Louis Browns 1925, **2**:34; 1938, **2**:63; 1946, **2**:76-77
  vs St. Louis Cardinals 1934, **2**:54-56; 1968, **2**:152-54
Dettweiler, Helen, **5**:81
Deulberg, Franz, **10**:99
Devaney, Mike, **4**:33
de Varona, Donna, **4**:157, **12**:97-98
de Vicenzo, Roberto, **5**:132-34, 145-46
Devitt, John, **12**:62-63
Devlin, Bruce, **5**:125-26, 140
Devlin, Judy, **11**:36-37
Diamond Sculls 1947, **12**:151
DiBiasi, Klaus, **12**:82
Dickinson, Gardner, **5**:156
Dickey, Bill, **2**:51
Dicus, Chuck, **1**:68
Didi, **8**:40
Didrikson, Mildred (Babe)
  in golf, **5**:70-71, 81, 96-97
  in track and field, **4**:56-57, 66-67, 72
Diegel, Leo **5**:32-34, 42, 54
Dierking, Connie, **3**:150
Dijkstra, Sjoukje, **9**:106-07, 110-11
Dillard, Harrison, **4**:89, 91-92, 105
DiMaggio, Joe, **2**:68-69, 71-73, 81-85, 116
Dinwiddie, Marcus, **10**:44
d'Inzeo, Piero, **11**:157
d'Inzeo, Raimondo, **11**:157
Diolite, **13**:20-22
Directum I, **13**:96
discus throw, **4**:10-12; *see also* records, track and field, discus throw
disqualifications
  golf, **5**:100, 145-46
  swimming, **12**:89-91
  track and field, **4**:8-9, 24, 72-73, 116
Ditmarsia Kiel-Ratzeburger, **12**:161-62
diving. *See* Olympic diving
Divin, Karol, **9**:103
Dixon, Craig, **4**:95
Dixon, Robin, **9**:107-08
D.J., **11**:179
Djukic, Dragan, **8**:62
Dodd, Muriel, **5**:11
Dodds, Harold, **1**:47
Dodson, Doug, **13**:47
dog shows, **11**:163-80
  obedience trials, **11**:171
  popularity of, **11**:164
  small club, **11**:171

  training for, **11**:169-71
dog sledding, **9**:13, 42
Doherty, H.L., **6**:3
Doll, Bob, **3**:16-17
Dolph, Jack, **3**:83
Dominguin. *See* Gonzales, Luis Miguel
Donnacona, **13**:10
Donoghue, Steve, **13**:14
Donohue, Mark, **13**:188-89
Donovan, Arthur, **7**:71-72
Dooley, Edwin B., **7**:174, 179
Doornick, Robert, **10**:129
Dorais, Charley, **1**:7-8
Doran, Jim, **1**:109
Doraty, Ken, **8**:121
d'Oriola, Jonquieres, **11**:158
d'Oriola, Pierre, **11**:154-55
Douglas, J., **8**:12
Dowling, Brian, **1**:67
Doyle, Jimmy, **7**:78
Drake, Ted, **8**:25
Drasnin, Irv, **10**:185-90
Draves, Victoria, **12**:44-47
Dray, W., **4**:9
Dressen, Charley (Chuck), **2**:79, 93-95, 102-03
Drew, H.P., **4**:17
Drillon, Gordon, **8**:129
Drobny, Jaroslav, **6**:94-95, 104
drugs and
  bicyclists, **10**:103, 106
  football players, **1**:180-83
  horses, **11**:160-61, **8**:6, 71-72
  Olympic hockey, **9**:164
  Olympic skiing, **9**:159-60
  swimming, **12**:89-91, 100-02
  track and field athletes, **4**:162
  weight lifters, **11**:111-12
Drut, Guy, **4**:192-93
Dryden, Ken, **8**:184-85
Drysdale, Don, **2**:124-25, 149
duBief, Jacqueline, **9**:61
duck hunting, **10**:154-58
Ducret, M., **11**:118
Dudley, Stadium, **1**:12
Duenkel, Ginny, **12**:70-71
Dufek, Don, **1**:41-42
Duffey, Arthur F., **4**:4-5, 8-9
Dufton, Rowland, **11**:18
Duggan, Dorothy, **10**:4
Duke University basketball team, **3**:72
Duke University football team, **1**:30-31
Dumas, Charley, **4**:116-17
Duncan, George, **5**:21-22
Dundee, Angelo, **7**:186
Dundee, Johnny, **7**:23
Dunn, Jack, **2**:19
duPont, Margaret Osborne, **6**:83-87
Duquesne University basketball team, **3**:16-17, 50-51

Durack, Fanny, **12**:8
Durrance, Dick (Little Man), **9**:29, 31, 43
Duran, Roberto, **7**:179, 194
Durante, Eli, **8**:62
Durocher, Leo, **2**:77-79, 94-95
Durr, Françoise, **6**:158, 169
Dusak, Erv, **2**:77-78
Dutra, Olin, **5**:54, 56-57
Dwight, Roy, **8**:41-42
Dyer, Eddie, **2**:77-78
Dykes, Jimmy, **2**:41-42, 89-90

Earl, Bill, **1**:38-39
earnings. *See also* salaries
earnings, boxing, **7**:14, 160-61
earnings, golf
    Bob Hope Desert Classic 1975, **5**:181
    Brewer, **5**:134
    British Open 1966, **5**:143; 1968, **5**:155; 1974, **5**:180;
       5:191
    Crampton, **5**:176
    Cupit, **5**:123
    Floyd, **5**:189
    Goalby, **5**:146
    Hill, **5**:189
    Jacobs, **5**:134
    Lema, **5**:122, 124
    Lopez, **5**:193-94
    Masters 1965, **5**:131; 1978, **5**:192-93
    Miller (J.), **5**:174, 180-81, 183
    Nicklaus, **5**:117, 122, 124, 130, 134, 144, 161, 163, 165,
       167, 168, 176-77, 183, 184
    $1 million winners, **5**:189
    Player, **5**:113, 121, 131-32, 155, 192
    Sifford, **5**:156-57
    Stockton, **5**:189
    Trevino, **5**:146, 147, 163, 165
    United States Open 1972, **5**:167; 1973, **5**:175; 1978, **5**:195
    Walt Disney World Classic 1973, **5**:177
    Watson, **5**:190
    Weiskopf, **5**:183
earnings, tennis
    Connors 1977, **6**:195
    King 1971, **6**:175
    Laver 1969, **6**:166
    Rosewall 1970, **6**:171-72
    women's vs men's, **6**:194-95
Earp, Claud, **10**:176-77
Easterbrook, Syd, **5**:54
Eastern Intercollegiate League 1960, **11**:62
East German. *See* Germany
Eastham, George, **8**:65-66
Eastman, Ben, **4**:67-68, 73-74

Eastman, Joseph B., **2**:75
Echevarria, Guillermo, **11**:82
Eckert, William, **2**:144-45, 154-55
Ederle, Gertrude, **12**:10-18
Eddleman, Dwight, **4**:89
Eden Aristocrat, **11**:165-66
Edward VIII (Prince of Wales), **8**:18, **13**:21
Edwards, E.M. (Ted), **11**:16-17
Edwards, Glen, **1**:165
Edwards, Margaret, **12**:59
Edwards, William, **1**:88-89
Egan, Sheila, **10**:50-51
Egg, Eleanor, **4**:57
Eintrancht, **8**:44
El Capitan, **10**:116
El Cordobes. *See* Benitez, Manuel
Elder, Jack, **1**:20-21
Elder, Lee, **5**:155, 157-58, 179, 181-82
Eldredge, Pete, **10**:85
electric block signals, tobogganing, **9**:10
Elek, Schacherer, **11**:123
elephant hunting, **10**:163-64
Eliot, Charles W., **1**:174
Elizabeth, Queen Mother, **8**:27, 33
Elizabeth II, Queen of England, **8**:31, 34
El Lagarto, **12**:138-40
Elliott, Herb, **4**:129-30, 139-41
Ellis, Clarence, **1**:70-72
Ellis, Jimmy, **7**:173-74
El Ouafi, **4**:53-54
El Salvador soccer team, **8**:64-65
Elsener, Patty, **12**:44-47
Embry, Wayne, **3**:174
Emerson, Roy
    in Australian matches 1962, **6**:128
    in Davis Cup matches 1963, **6**:131
    in French matches 1962, **6**:128
    portrait of **6**:138-41
    in U.S. matches 1962, **6**:130
    Wimbledon winner 1964, **6**:135
Emery, Victory, **9**:116-17
Emily's Pride, **13**:106-07
Empire Games 1962, **12**:67
Empire Gold Cup 1947, **13**:48-49
Endeavour, **12**:139
Endeavour II, **12**:144-46
Ender, Kornelia
    at 1972 Olympics, **12**:84
    at 1976 Olympics, **12**:91-93, 96-97, 99-101
Enderle, Dick, **1**:164
Endrich, Felix, **9**:72-73
Engan, Toralf, **9**:119-20
Engel, Ingrid Kramer. *See* Kramer, Ingrid
England. *See also* Britain; British; English
England, polo team of, **10**:16-20
England, soccer in
    athletes' salary, **8**:21
    betting pools, **8**:21-22

popularity of, **8**:8-12, 22
reserve clause, **8**:65-66
riots, **8**:9
and Scottish players, **8**:15
women in, **8**:67
England soccer team of
vs Brazil 1970, **8**:68
vs Hungary 1954, **8**:35
vs Scotland 1936, **8**:22
vs United States 1950, **8**:32
World Cup victors, 1966, **8**:55-56
English Football Association Cup champions
Arsenal Gunners 1930, **8**:18; 1936, **8**:25; 1950, **8**:31-32;
1971, **8**:72-73
Blackpool 1953, **8**:34
Bolton Wanderers 1926, **8**:15
Cardiff City 1926, **8**:15
Everton 1966, **8**:53
Liverpool 1974, **8**:79-80
Manchester United 1963, **8**:51
Newcastle United 1951, **8**:33; 1952, **8**:33
Portsmouth 1939, **8**:27
Preston North End 1938, **8**:27
Sheffield United 1925, **8**:13
Southhampton 1976, **8**:85
Sunderland 1973, **8**:76-77
West Bromwich 1931, **8**:19; 1954, **8**:35
West Ham United 1940, **8**:27; 1975, **8**:84
Wolverhampton Wanderers 1949, **8**:31
English Channel swim
Abertondo 1962, **12**:67
Burgess 1911, **12**:4
Chadwick 1950, **12**:49-50
Ederle 1926, **12**:15-18
English Derby, **13**:15-16, 21-22, 53
English Pilgrim Association, **8**:4-5
English Soccer Cup champions
Aston Villa 1957, **8**:38
Bolton Wanderers 1929, **8**:18; 1958, **8**:39
Everton 1933, **8**:20
Manchester City 1934, **8**:20; 1956, **8**:37-38
Nottingham Forest 1959, **8**:41-42
Sunderland 1937, **8**:26
Ensign Hanover, **13**:103
Enterprise, **12**:131-33
ephedrine, **9**:159-60, **12**:90
equestrian events. *See* Olympic equestrian events
Erb, Dave, **13**:61
Erdelatz, Eddie, **1**:62
Ericsson, Sigvard Sigge, **9**:79-80
Eriksen, Stein, **9**:64
Eriksson, Sven, **9**:39
Erne, Frank, **7**:6
Eroshina, Radia, **9**:96-97
Errath, Christine, **9**:168
Erskine, Carl, **2**:102-04
Ertle, Harry, **7**:168
Erving, Julius, **3**:177-80, 188-89, 192-95

Escoba, **13**:7
Esposito, Phil, **8**:183-84, 189-90
Ethelinda, **13**:97
Europe, bike racing in, **10**:101-02
Europe, soccer in, **8**:43-44
European skating championship 1925, **9**:10; 1936, **9**:28-29
Europe Soccer Cup **8**:44, 50, 63
Evans, Charles, Jr., **5**:13, 15, 17-18
Evans, Lee, **4**:168-70
Evans, Robert, **7**:167
Evans, Tom, **11**:99
Evensen, Bernt, **9**:10-11
Everhardus, Herman, **1**:91
Evert, Christine
doubles with Connors, **6**:190
French Open winner 1975, **6**:186
in U.S. Open 1971, **6**:175
U.S. Open winner 1975, **6**:188-89
in Wimbledon matches 1973, **6**:180-81; 1978, **6**:201-02
Wimbledon winner 1974, **6**:182-83; 1976, **6**:191
Everton, **8**:20, 39, 53
Ewbank, Weeb, **1**:113-15, 146, 156-57
Ewell, Barney, **4**:92, 101
Ewing, Cecil, **5**:61-63
Ewry, Ray, **4**:6
Exterminator, **13**:7
Eyston, E.T., **13**:144

Fabius, **13**:61-62
Face, Elroy, **2**:125-26
Fair Play, **13**:5-6
Fales, Harold, **2**:35
Falkanger, Thorbjoern, **9**:71-72
Famose, Annie, **9**:132-33
Fane J. Onslow, **7**:119
Fangio, Juan Manuel, **13**:152, 158-59
fans
baseball, **2**:31
basketball, **3**:7, 124-26, 189-90, 197-99
football, **1**:28, 108
hockey. *See* riots, hockey
soccer, **8**:32, 43-44, 91-92; *see also* riots, soccer
Far East, **5**:3
Farkas, Andy, **1**:99
farms, hunting on, **10**:176-77
Farquhar, John, **5**:162-63
Farrell, James A., Jr., **9**:175, 177
Farrell, Jeff, **12**:66
Farrell, Johnny, **5**:39-40
Farrell, O'Neil, **9**:11

Farrell, William, **9**:100-02
Fassi, Carlo, **9**:164, 168
Fassnacht, Hans, **12**:84
Faurot, Don, **1**:51
Favell, Doug, **10**:86-87
Fazio, George, **5**:78-79
Fears, Tommy, **1**:106-08, 123
featherweight champion
    Armstrong, 1937, **7**:63
    Chocolate 1932, **7**:44-45
    Dundee, 1922, **7**:23
    Kilbane 1912, **7**:11
    Moore 1959, **7**:131
    Pep 1949, **7**:92-93
    Ramos 1963, **7**:148-49
    Robertson 1964, **7**:159
    rough bout 1951, **7**:107
    Saddler 1948, **7**:91; 1950, **7**:97-99; 1951, **7**:106-07
Feistmantl, Josef, **9**:113
Feldman, Lew, **7**:44-45
Feller, Bob, **2**:60, 64, 68-69, 90-91, 95-97, 139
Fellowes, Cornelius, J., **8**:103
Felsch, Oscar, **2**:25-28, 32
Felt, Irving Mitchell, **6**:145
fencing, **11**:118-27
    and boxing **7**:122-23
    championships, **11**:118, 120, 122-26
    electrical recorder, **11**:123
    Olympic, **11**:118, 121-27
    popularity of, **11**:118-20
Fendt, Josef, **9**:154
Fenstemaker, Leroy, **1**:51
Fergerson, Mable, **4**:185
Ferguson, John, **8**:180-82
Ferguson, Tom, **10**:134, 136
Ferrari car, **13**:159, 162-63
Ferrari, Enzo, **13**:170
Ferrier, Jim, **5**:77-78
Ferris, Daniel, **4**:72
Ferris, Samuel, **4**:71
Feuerbach, Al, **4**:184-85
Ficker, Bill, **12**:174-75
Fick, Peter, **12**:33
field hockey, **10**:33-35
figure skating
    as ballet, **9**:126-27
    European contest 1925, **9**:10; 1936, **9**:28-29
    Ice Palace tournament 1921, **9**:7
    popularity of, **9**:2, 6
    see also national figure skating champions; North American figure skating contest; Olympic figure skating Champions, pairs; Olympic figure skating, scoring; world figure skating champions; world figure skating champions, pairs
Filatov, Sergei, **11**:157
Filchock, Frank, **1**:101-02, 105, 123, **10**:75
Filion, Herbe, **13**:117
Filkey, Helen, **4**:43

Fillol, Ubaldo, **8**:96-97
films
    boxing, **7**:9-11
    football, **1**:10-11
    golf, **5**:47
    horse-race, **13**:28
Findlay, Alexander, **5**:5
Fingers, Rollie, **2**:187-88
Finland, fencers of, **11**:125
Finland, gymnasts of, **11**:129
Finland, Olympic skating team of, **9**:8
Finland, Olympic ski team of, **9**:32-33, 71, 162
Finland, second place in Winter Olympics 1924, **9**:9
Finland, wrestling team of, **11**:83-84
Finley, Charles O., **2**:187-88
Finsterwald, Dow, **5**:107, 116-17, 124
Fire Glow, **13**:97
Firethorn, **13**:27-28
Firpo, Luis Angel, **7**:24-26
Fischer, Johnny, **5**:61-63
Fischl, Frank, **1**:41-42, 45
fishing. *see* wood, field and stream activities
Fish, Jenny, **9**:125
Fishwick, Diana, **5**:40
Fisk, Carlton, **2**:179-80
Fiske, William, **9**:12-13, 25
Fitch, Horatio M., **4**:39
Fitzgerald, Bob, **9**:48-49
Fitzsimmons, Robert, **7**:4-6
Fitzsimmons, Sunny Jim, **13**:35-36
fixing
    basketball games, **3**:22, 37-39, 41-46, 63-66
    boxing matches, **1**:81-82, 134-35
    World Series 1919, **2**:25-28, 32
    wrestling matches, **11**:95, 99
Flaherty, Ray, **1**:95-96, 121
Flanagan, J.J., **4**:8, 9, 12-13
Fleckman, Martin, **5**:144-45
Fleischer, Hilde, **4**:76-77
Fleischer, Nat, **7**:144
Fleitz, Bev Baker, **6**:108
Fleming, Peggy, **9**:111, 120-22, 124, 126-27, 137-38
Fleming, Reggie, **8**:160
Fliegel, Hy, **3**:15
Flock, Tim, **13**:154, 160
Flood, Curt, **2**:157, 167-68
Flowers, Tiger, **7**:26, 32
Floyd, Ray, **5**:158, 188-89
fly-casting, **10**:157-59, 163, 166
Flying Scot, **12**:32-33
Flynn, Leon, **7**:37
flyweight championship, **7**:148
Foldberg, Dan, **1**:42, 45
Fontinato, Lou, **7**:153
Foolish Pleasure, **13**:78-79
football, college. *See* college football
football, English. *See* soccer
football and society, **1**:172-86

anthropology, **1**:185-86
drug use, **1**:183
racism, **1**:179-80, 182
ritual, **1**:185-86
subsidies, athletic, **1**:177-78
football, professional, **1**:84-171
All American Football Conference, **1**:99-100, 103
American Football League, **1**:88, 92, 117, 128-29
antitrust laws and, **1**:112-13
blacks in, **1**:179-80, 182
body guards, **1**:143-46
coaching, **1**:110
computers in, **1**:132-33
defense, **1**:134-35
electronics in, **1**:110, 132-33
free agents, **1**:160-61
gambling, **1**:101-02, 124-26, 133, 179
goal posts, **1**:159
kickoffs, **1**:159
mergers, **1**:97, 99
National-American Football League, **1**:103
National Football League. *See* National Football
    League
passes, **1**:89, 121-23, 148
penalties, **1**:159
and public opinion, **1**:151
radio broadcast of, **1**:108
records. *See* records, professional football
recruiting, **1**:174-78
rules, **1**:89, 159-60
salaries, **1**:115, 126-27
strike of players, **1**:149, 160, 163-64
sudden death, **1**:95, 159
Super Bowl 1969, **1**:139-41; 1971, **1**:150-51; 1972,
    1:151-53; 1973, **1**:153-54; 1974, **1**:157-58; 1975, **1**:161-63;
    1976, **1**:165-66; 1977, **1**:167-68; 1978, **1**:168-69; 1979,
    1:169-71
Supreme Court ruling on, **1**:112-13
on television, **1**:108, 125, 139, 154-55
union, **1**:136
and U.S. Senate, **1**:154-55
World Football Championship 1940, **1**:95-96; 1942,
    1:96-97
World Football League, **1**:155, 158-60, 164-65
see also college football; football and society
Forbes, Norene, **12**:28
Ford, Alan, **12**:43-44
Ford, Danny, **1**:80-81
Ford, Doug, **5**:101, 104-05
Ford, Henry, **13**:179
Ford, Whitey, **2**:132-33, 152
Ford Hanover, **13**:103
Ford-Lotus car, **13**:170, 175
Ford Mark IV, **13**:179
Fordham University football team, **1**:31-32
Foreman, George
    vs Ali 1974, **7**:185-86
    heavyweight champion 1973, **7**:181

in Olympics 1968, **7**:173
Forest Hills tennis matches. *See* United States tennis
    matches
Formigli, Francesco, **11**:142-43
Formo, Ivar, **9**:167
Forrester, Bill, **12**:91-92
Fort Wayne Pistons, **3**:119, 124, 126-29, 142
Forward Pass, **13**:70-72
Fosbury, Dick, **4**:172
Foss, Frank, **4**:29-30
Foster, Bob, **7**:172-73
Foster, Marjorie, **10**:45-46
Foster, Rodney, **5**:162-63
Fox, Billy, **7**:134-35
Foxx, Jimmy, **2**:44
Foyt, A.J., **13**:166-67, 173-74, 187-88, 195-96
Frame, Freddy, **13**:138
France, Shirley May, **12**:49-50
France, bicyclists of, **10**:97-98, 100-01
France, equestrian team of, **11**:162
France, fencers of, **11**:125
France, mountain climbers of, **10**:111
France, Olympic hockey team of, **9**:8
France, soccer team of, **8**:19
France, tennis in, **6**:40-42, 48, 53; *see also* French tennis
    matches champions
France, yachting team of, **12**:136
Francis, Bevo, **3**:49
Franke, Nikki Tomlinson, **11**:127
Franklin and Marshall College football team, **1**:178
Franklin, Sidney, **11**:140
Fraser, Dawn, **12**:63-64, 66-67
Fraser, Gretchen, **9**:53
Fraser, Leo, **5**:156
Fraser, Neale, **6**:119-20, 125-27, 131
Frazier, Joe
    vs Ali 1974, **7**:183-84, 186-88
    vs Foreman 1973, **7**:181
    heavyweight champion 1970, **7**:173-74; 1970, **7**:176-78
    in Olympics 1964, **7**:159-60
Frazier, Walt, **3**:73-74, 164-65, 168-69
free agents
    baseball, **2**:141-42, 184-85, 187-89
    basketball, **3**:144
    football, **1**:160-61
    hockey, **8**:200-01
Freebooter, **13**:54-55
Freeman, David, **11**:34
Freeman, Ron, **4**:168-69
Freisinger, Leo, **9**:35-36
French hard court tournament 1930, **6**:48
French tennis matches champions
    Evert 1975, **6**:186
    Lacoste 1927, **6**:37-38
    Laver 1962, **6**:128
    Lenglen 1920, **6**:17-18
    Rosewall 1953, **6**:97-98
Friar, Margaret, **8**:40

Frick, Ford, **2**:76, 80, 91, 127-28, 141, 144
Friedlund, J. Arthur, **1**:103
Frisch, Frank, **2**:38
Fritz, Ken, **1**:80-81
Fromm, John, **4**:146
Frossi, Annibale, **7**:26
Frush, Danny, **7**:23
Fry, Joan, **6**:30
Fry, Shirley, **6**:93-94, 104, 112-13
Fulham soccer team, **8**:84
Fullam, Frank, **7**:85-86
Fullmer, Gene, **7**:127-28, 148
Funseth, Rod, **5**:192-93
Furgol, Ed, **5**:75, 94-96
Furillo, Carl, **2**:102-04, 124-25
Furlong, Frank, **13**:25
Furman University basketball team, **3**:50
Furniss, Bruce, **12**:93, 96, 103
Furuhashi, Hironoshin, **12**:49
Fusina, Chuck, **1**:82-83
Futch, Eddie, **7**:187

Gabrielsen, Jim, **5**:162-63
Gage, Richard, **10**:177
Gaby, F.R., **4**:48
Gagnon, Johnny, **8**:117-18
Gailly, Etienne, **4**:100
Gale IV, **12**:157-58
Galehouse, Dennis, **2**:185-86
Galento, Tony, **7**:67-68
Galiffa, Arnold, **1**:40-42
Galitzen, Mickey Riley, **12**:23-24, 29-30
Gallagher, Art, **12**:149-51
Gallant Fox, **13**:19-23
Gallant Knight, **13**:20-21
Gallant Man, **13**:63-64
Gallinger, Don, **8**:142
Galloway, Jim, **10**:66-67
gambling in
    baseball, **2**:79
    basketball, **3**:22, 38, 122-23
    football, **1**:101-02, 124-26, 133, 179
    hockey, **8**:142
    horse-racing, **13**:30, 36-37
    see also betting
Gamecock Duke of Wales, **11**:167-68
game preserves, **10**:159-60
Gammoudi, Mohamed, **4**:153, 167-68
Ganakas, Gus, **3**:98
Gandil, Arnold, **2**:25-28, 32
Gans, Joe, **7**:6-7
Garcia, Rod, **1**:73-74

Gardiner, Bert, **8**:130
Gardner, Cal, **8**:144
Garland, Charles S., **6**:12, 14
Garmisch bobsled race 1953, **9**:72-73
Garrels, John C., **4**:15
Garrett, Mike, **1**:148
Garrett, Robert, **4**:2, 4
Garrincha, Little Bird, **8**:53-54
Garvey, Ed, **1**:160, 163-64
Gaspar, Phil, **1**:30-31
Gater Bowl, **1**:80-81
Gatewood, Tom, **1**:71-72
Gaudin, J., **11**:121
Gavilan, Kid
    vs Robinson 1949, **7**:95-96
    welterweight champion 1951, **7**:102, 104-05; 1953, **7**:114
Gay, A., **8**:7
Geesink, Anton, **11**:98
Gehrig, Adeline, **9**:118
Gehrig, Lou, **2**:44-46, 50-51, 64-67
Gehrig, Mrs. Lou, **1**:99
Geijssen, Carolina, **9**:127-28
Genereux, George, **10**:49
Genter, Steve, **12**:86, 91
Genung, Ed, **4**:60, 62-63
Geoffrion, Bernie, **8**:169, 160-61
George V, King of England, **8**:15, 18, 20, **13**:21
George, Pete, **11**:107-08
George VI, King of England, **8**:27, 33, **13**:21
Georgette, Franco, **10**:99
George, W.G., **4**:25-26
Georgia Tech football team, **1**:18, 54-55, 179-80
Geraghty, Agnes, **12**:13
Gerald, Rob, **1**:78
Gerber, Samuel, **7**:78
Germany, aquatic team of, **12**:92-102
Germany, bobsled team of, **9**:64, 70-71, 167-68
Germany, crew team of, **12**:161
Germany, equestrian team of, **11**:140, 149, 156-58, 160-62
Germany, ski team of, **9**:31-32
Germany, soccer team of, **8**:25, 36-37, 55-56, 82-83
Germany, toboggan team of, **9**:112, 136
Germany, yachting team of, **12**:140-41
Geronimo, Cesar, **2**:168-69
Gerschwiler, Hans, **9**:45, 50-51, 54-55, 59-60
Gervin, George, **3**:200-01
Gesell, Gerhard, **4**:199
Gestring, Marjorie, **12**:37
Ghana Boxing Authority, **7**:159
Ghezzi, Vic, **5**:68-70
Giacomin, Ed, **8**:195
Giammalva, Sam, **6**:114
Giardello, Joey, **7**:167-68
Gibb, Roberta, **4**:162
Gibson, Althea
    in golf, **5**:189
    in tennis, **6**:87
    in U.S. matches 1956, **6**:113

U.S. matches winner 1957, **6**:117-18; 1958, **6**:120-21
in Wightman Cup matches 1957, **6**:118-19
Wimbledon winner 1957, **6**:117
Gibson, Bob, **2**:140-41, 152-54
Gibson, Josh, **2**:161-62
Gifford, Frank, **1**:113-15
Gilbert, A.C., **4**:9
Giles, Marvin, **5**:162-63
Giles, Warren C., **2**:91, 100, 127, 141
Giletti, Alain, **9**:73
Gilgo Beach surfing championship, **12**:108-09
Gill, Barney, **1**:58
Gilliam, Junior, **2**:104
Gillian, John, **1**:162-63
Gilmore, Artis, **3**:184
Gimondi, Felice, **10**:104
Ginther, Richie, **13**:171
Gionfreddo, Al, **2**:81-85
Giordani, Claudia, **9**:161-62
Gitshaw, C.W., **4**:21-23
Giusti, Dave, **2**:168
Givens, Jack, **3**:106-07
Gladieux, Bob, **1**:65-66
Glasgow Rangers, **8**:75
Glass, Harry, **9**:86-87
Glazer, Gene, **9**:125-26
gliding, **10**:122-24
Goalby, Bob, **5**:121
Goggin, Willie, **5**:54-55
Goitschel, Christine, **9**:107-08, 111-12, 115
Goitschel, Marielle, **9**:107-08, 111-12, 115, 129-30, 132-33
Gola, Tom, **3**:49, 51, 127
Goldberger, Arthur J., **2**:167-68
Gold Cup 1934, **12**:138-39; 1935, **12**:140; 1961, **12**:163
Golden, Johnny, **5**:33-34
Golden State Warriors, **3**:185-86
Goldstein, Ruby, **7**:142-44
golf
  advantage of playing, **6**:88-90
  amateur, **5**:4, 8, 44-46
  American Professional Golfers, **5**:156
  and apartheid, **5**:134, 179
  ball, **5**:11, 17-19, 26, 50, 99, 143
  betting in, **5**:138
  as big business, **5**:136-39
  blacks in. *See* blacks and golf
  and Britain, **5**:33-34, 40-41, 54, 61-63, 162-63
  British Open. *See* British Open Golf Tournament
    winners
  caddies, **5**:108-09
  club, **5**:17, 26, 157
  country clubs, **5**:15-16, 136-39, 185-87; *see also* specific
    clubs
  courses, **5**:138-39, 148-54
  disqualifications in, **5**:100, 145-46
  earnings in. *See* earnings, golf
  equipment, **5**:60, 105, 136-37
  films, **5**:47
  gains in U.S., **5**:7-8, 14
  Hall of Fame, **5**:81
  history of, **5**:2, 14
  Ladies' PGA championship, **5**:111, 189-94
  Los Angeles Open 1950, **5**:75-76; 1969, **5**:156-57
  manners, **5**:8
  Masters Golf Tournament. *See* Masters Golf Tourna-
    ment; Masters Golf Tournament winners
  men golfers vs women golfers 1922, **5**:24
  on moon, **5**:162
  National Amateur Golf Championship 1930, **5**:44-46
  professional, **5**:4, 14
  Professional Golfers' Association. *See* Professional
    Golfers' Association; Professional Golfers; Associa-
    tion Tournament winners records. *See* records, golf
  regulations, **5**:4, 7, 14, 139-40, 157
  Ryder Cup championship, **5**:33-34, 54
  Scottish Open Golf Tournament 1910, **5**:7
  in South Africa, **5**:134
  styles, **5**:8
  on television, **5**:156
  tournament regulation, **5**:77, 156
  United Golfers' Association Tournament 1968, **5**:155-56
  and United States. *See* United States and golf; United
    States Open Golf Tournament winners
  Walker Cup championship, **5**:40-41, 61-63
  Walt Disney World Classic 1973, **5**:176-77
  Weismuller in, **12**:49
  women in, *See* women, in golf
  Women's Metropolitan Golf League, **5**:5-6
  women's national golf tournament, **5**:81-86
  women's open golf tournament, **5**:74, 96-97, 106, 128
Gonzales, Luis Miguel, **10**:140-44
Gonzales, Richard (Pancho), **6**:83-86, 115-16
Gonzalez, Manny, **7**:160
Goodell, Brian, **12**:94-96, 103-05
Goodfellow, Eddie, **7**:127-28
Goodman, Johnny, **5**:61-63
Goodrich, Gail, **3**:71, 173, 176-77
Goolagong, Evonne
  in U.S. matches 1974, **6**:184-85; 1975, **6**:188-89
  in Wimbledon matches 1972, **6**:176; 1973, **6**:182; 1975,
    6:186-87; 1976, **6**:191
goose hunting, **10**:193-94
Gordon, Ed, **4**:62
Gordon International Medal, **9**:6, 27
Gorman, Charley, **9**:10-11
Gorman, Tom, **8**:103, 120
Gorshkov, Aleksandr, **9**:151, 154
Gossard, G.D., **1**:177
Goss, Eleanor, **6**:24-25, 28
Gossick, Sue, **12**:76-77
Gotch, Frank, **11**:79-80
Gottselig, Johnny, **8**:115-16
Gould, Jay, **11**:4, 8, 10
Gould, Shane, **12**:84-87
Gourdin, E. O., **4**:35-36
Gourdnine, Simon, **3**:186-87

Graboski, Joe, **3**:126-27
Gracie, Bob, **8**:118-19
Graczyk, Jean, **10**:103
Graebner, Clark, **6**:150-51
Grafstrom, Gillis, **9**:20-21
Graham, Billy, **7**:104-05
Graham, Otto, **1**:101, 105-09
Granatelli, Andy, **13**:185
Grand Prix. *See* auto racing, Grand Prix
Grange, Felix, **11**:56-57
Grange, Harold (Red), **1**:13, 87-89
Grant, Bud, **1**:161
Grant, Jerry, **13**:188-89
Grant, Robert III, **11**:16-19
Granville, **13**:29-30
Grasegger, Kaethe, **9**:29-30
Gray, Gilbert, **12**:135-36
Gray, Pete, **2**:75
Grayson, Bobby, **2**:25-27
Graziano, Rocky
    middleweight champion 1947, **7**:80-81
    vs Zale 1946, **7**:77-78; 1948, **7**:84-85
Great Britain. *See* Britain; England
Greb, Harry, **7**:26
Greeks, ancient, **4**:2-4, 10-12
Green, Al, **12**:34-36
Green, Charlie, **5**:162-63
Green, Hubert, **5**:190, 192-93
Green, Ted, **8**:180-82
Green Bay Packers
    vs Baltimore Colts 1965, **1**:127
    vs Dallas Cowboys 1968, **1**:135-36
    vs Kansas City Chiefs 1967, **1**:130-32
    Lambeau on, **1**:104
    Lombardi as coach, **1**:116, 138-39
    vs New York Giants 1938, **1**:94
    vs Oakland Raiders 1968, **1**:137
    vs Philadelphia Eagles 1960, **1**:119-20
Greenberg, Hank, **2**:63-66, 76-77, 128-9
Greene, Abe J., **7**:74, 83
Greene, Bert, **5**:158
Greene, Cornelius, **1**:74
Greene, Nancy, **9**:123, 132-33
Greenleaf, Ralph, **11**:53, 56, 58-62
Greenlee, W.A. (Gus), **2**:162-64
Green Speed, **13**:118
Greer, Hal, **3**:171
Gregg, Peter, **13**:192-193
Gregg, Steve, **12**:91-92
Gretel, **12**:163-66
Gretel II, **12**:174-75
Greyhound, **13**:101-02, 116
Grider, Dallas, **1**:63-64
Grier, Bobby, **1**:54-55, 179
Griese, Bob, **1**:66, 151-54, 156-57
Griffin, Archie, **1**:74-75
Griffin, Frank, **8**:35
Griffin, Marvin, **1**:179-80

Griffith, Calvin, **2**:128
Griffith, Emile
    vs Benvenuti 1967, **7**:170
    middleweight champion 1966, **7**:166-67
    vs Paret 1961, **7**:141-42
    purse of, **7**:160
    welterweight champion 1961, **7**:140; 1962, **7**:142-44;
        1963, **7**:151
Griffith, John, **1**:86, 178
Griffith, R.W., **1**:177-78
Grinham, Judy, **12**:59
Grishin, Yevgeni, **9**:76-78, 112
Grissom, Marv, **2**:108
Groenningen, **9**:127
Grogan, Jimmy, **9**:73
Gros, Piero, **9**:167
Grout, Jack, **5**:170-71
Grove, Robert, **2**:43
Groza, Alex, **3**:32, 34-35, 42-45
Groza, Lou, **1**:101, 105-09, 113
Grudzien, Josef, **7**:173
Gucker, Tom, **11**:128-29
Guenel, Joe, **8**:72
Guerin, Eric, **13**:56-57
Gulack, George, **11**:128
Guldahl, Ralph, **5**:64
Gullett, Don, **2**:168-69, 182-83
Gunn, Watts, **5**:28
guns
    hunting, **10**:151-52, 157
    see also shooting
"Guns of Autumn, The" (Drasnin), **10**:185-90
Gunter, Henry, **3**:63, 65
Gurney, Dan, **13**:177, 179, 185
Guseva, Klara, **9**:92
Gustafson, Bill, **1**:40-41
Gustafsson, Toini, **9**:125, 130, 136
Gustavson, Linda, **12**:77-78
Guthrie, Jane, **13**:194, 196-97
gymnastics, **4**:109; **11**:128-37

Haas, Charles, **5**:61-63
Haas, Christl, **9**:115
Haase, Helge, **9**:90-91
Hackenschmidt, George, **11**:78-79
Hackett, Bobby, **12**:94-95
Haden, Pat, **1**:74
Haddix, Harvey, **2**:123
Haegg, Gunder, **4**:89
Hagenlacher, Erich, **11**:57
Hagen, Walter
    British Open Golf Tournament 1922, winner, **5**:21-22;
        1924, winner, **5**:26-27; 1926, third place, **5**:29-30;
        1928, winner, **5**:38-39; 1929, winner, **5**:39-40

portrait of, **5**:37-38
Professional Golfers' Association Tournament 1921, winner, **5**:21, 1923, second place, **5**:25-26; 1925 winner, **5**:30; 1926, winner, **5**:32; 1927, winner, **5**:36-37
in Ryder Cup competition 1927, **5**:33-34; 1933, **5**:54
in top 5 poll, **5**:173
United States Open Golf Tournament 1914, winner, **5**:13
World's Golf Classic 1922, second place, **5**:23
Hahn, Archie, **4**:8
Hahn, Lloyd, **4**:37, 42-43, 45-47, 49
Haines, George, **12**:72-75, 85
Haines, Marjorie, **11**:154
Hainsworth, George, **8**:117
Hairston, Happy, **3**:176
Hakaoh soccer team, **8**:15-16
Hakulinen, Veikko, **9**:76, 95-96
Halas, George, **1**:51, 137-38
Hall, Gary, **12**:89, 95-96
Hall, Kaye, **12**:79-80
Hallahan, Willie, **2**:48-49
Hall of Fame
    baseball, **2**:57, 161-65
    basketball, **3**:183
    boxing, **7**:118-19
    golf, **5**:81
Halpin, Matt, **4**:17, 19-21
Haluska, Jim, **1**:49
Hamalainen, Kalevi, **9**:98
Hambletonian Stakes, **13**:105
Hambletonian Stakes winners
    Blaze Hanover 1960, **13**:109
    Calumet Butler 1931, **13**:98
    Emily's Pride 1958, **13**:106-07
    Green Speed 1977, **13**:118
    Greyhound 1935, **13**:101
    Hanover's Bertha 1930, **13**:97-98
    Lord Jim 1934, **13**:99-100
    Mary Reynolds 1933, **13**:98-99
    Steve Lobell 1976, **13**:118
    Titan Hanover 1945, **13**:102-03
Hames, Richard, **10**:66
Hamill, Dorothy, **9**:160-61, 164, 168
Hamilton, Brutus, **4**:30
Hamilton, Tom, **1**:25-26, 38-39, 47
Hamilton-Miller, Dudley J.V., **10**:12-14
Hamm, Edward, **4**:47
Hammond, John S., **8**:104
Hampden, **13**:45-46
Hampson, Tom, **4**:62-63
handball
    Association Championship, **11**:21
    popularity of, **11**:16
handball champions (AAU)
    Banuet 1930, **11**:15
    Hershkowitz 1949, **11**:18-19; 1953, **11**:19
    Jacobs 1956, **11**:20
    Platak 1940, **11**:18
    Sandler 1969, **11**:24

Schmidt 1930, **11**:13
Schwartz-Seaman 1926, **11**:10
hang-gliding, **10**:126-29
Hanover's Bertha, **13**:97-98
Hanratty, Terry, **1**:65-66
Hansen, Fred, **4**:155-57
Hansenne, Marcel, **4**:92, 94, 97-98
Hapes, Merle, **1**:101-02, 105
Harada, Masahika (Fighting), **7**:148
Hard, Darlene
    in U.S. matches 1958, **6**:120-21; 1962, **6**:130
    U.S. matches winner 1960, **6**:126-27
    Wightman Cup winner 1963, **6**:134
    in Wimbledon matches 1957, **6**:117; 1959, **6**:124
Harding, Warren G., **2**:30
Hardy, Jim, **12**:174-75
Harlan, Bruce, **12**:43-44, 46-47
Harlem children, **3**:179-80
Harlem Globetrotters, **3**:119
Harmsworth Trophy Regatta 1921, **12**:121; 1930, **12**:129; 1933, **12**:137
Harrelson, Bud, **2**:159
Harridge, Will, **2**:75-76
Harriman, E. Roland, **13**:105
Harris, Franco, **1**:161-63, 166, 170-71
Harris, Ronie, **7**:173
Harris, Ted, **8**:180
Harrison, Reggie, **1**:166
Harroun, Ray, **13**:125, 150
Hartack, William, **13**:63-64
Hart, Albert E., Jr., **11**:160
Hart, Doris
    in French matches 1953, **6**:97-98
    in U.S. matches 1946, **6**:81-82; 1949, **6**:85-86; 1952, **6**:96-97; 1953, **6**:102-03
    U.S. matches winner 1955, **6**:110-11
    in Wimbledon matches 1948, **6**:83; 1953, **6**:100; 1954, **6**:104
Hart, Ed, **4**:175-76
Hart, Marvin, **7**:6
Henderson, Paul, **7**:189
Hendley, Bob, **2**:142
Heneage, Harry R., **1**:178
Henie, Sonja
    European figure skating champion 1936, **9**:28-29
    in Olympics 1928, **9**:12; 1932, **9**:21-22, 24; 1936, **9**:34, 38-39
    portrait of, **9**:14-15
    in professional skating, **9**:39-41
    world champion 1930, **9**:15-16; 1931, **9**:16; 1934, **9**:27
Henkel, Karl, **5**:55
Henne, Ernst, **10**:89
Henne, Jan, **12**:77-78
Hennessey, Tom, **11**:72
Henning, Anne, **9**:147-48
Henning, Harold, **5**:156-57
Henricks, Joe, **12**:55-56
Henry, F.S., **11**:152

Henry, George, **5**:158
Henry, Kenneth, **9**:64-65
Hepburn, George, **3**:4
Hepburn, Ralph, **13**:142-43
Herber, Maxi, **9**:30, 37
Herbert, H.L., **10**:16
Herberts, Sailor, **8**:109
Herewithem, J.P., **11**:166-67
Herman, Dave, **1**:145-46, 156
Herman, Robert R., **8**:53, 58
Hernandez, Emilio, **7**:199
Herndon, Mack, **3**:59-60
Herrmann, August, **2**:22
Hershkowitz, Vic, **11**:18-19, 21
Hertz, John D., **13**:15, 17
Hertz, Mrs. John D., **13**:17-18, 43-45
Herz, Wilhelm, **10**:89
Hettich, Urban, **9**:159
Heuga, James, **9**:118-19, 122-23, 128-29
Heuss, Theodor, **8**:36-37
Hewson, Brian, **4**:115
Hewitt, Bill, **1**:91
Hextall, Bryan, **8**:133
Hickcox, Charles, **12**:78-79, 84
Hicks, Art, **3**:63, 65
Hicks, Betty, **5**:96-97
Hicks, Thomas J., **4**:7
Hicks, Wayne, **8**:161
Higashi I., **1: 11**:78
Higgins, Johnny, **12**:41-42
Higbe, Kirby, **2**:72, 84
Hill, A.G., **4**:28-29
Hill, Benny, **13**:134
Hill, Dave, **5**:160-61, 189
Hill, Dorothy Poynton. *See* Poynton, Dorothy
Hill, George E.B., **9**:27, 35, 42
Hill, Graham, **13**:171, 175-77
Hill, Harry, **1**:45
Hill, Jerry, **1**:139-40
Hill, Jim, **10**:50
Hill, Mel, **7**:131
Hill, Phil, **13**:162-65, 167-68
Hill, Winston, **1**:156
Hillhouse, Art, **3**:12
Hillman, H.L., **4**:8
Hills, Ralph G., **4**:36
Hines, Jim, **4**:163-64
Hinterseer, Ernst, **9**:91, 94-95
Hinterseer, Hans, **9**:152-53
Hirsch, Elroy, **1**:123
Hirsch, Mary, **13**:25
Hitchcock, Tommy, **10**:24-25, 27
Hites, Sandor, **8**:58
Hitler, Adolf
    and boxing, **7**:59
    at 1937 Olympics, **12**:142
    and soccer, **8**:25
    and track and field events, **4**:76, 78-84, 101-02

Hlavaty, Jana, **9**:157
Hoad, Lewis, **6**:97, 106-10, 112-14
hockey, professional ice, **8**:102-206
    All Star hockey team, **7**:141, 145
    blacks in, **8**:145
    compensation rule, **8**:200-01
    Dominion championship, **8**:102
    fans, **8**:150-51, 155
    fights. *See* hockey, mélées
    free agents, **8**:200-01
    gambling, **8**:142
    goalie mask, **8**:159, 163-64
    goaltending, **8**:138-39, 163-64
    injuries, **8**:122, 124, 180
    league mergers, **8**:204-05
    Madison Square Garden rink, **8**:103-06
    mélées, **8**:114, 118, 122, 134, 140, 180-82; *see also*
        hockey, riots, violence
    minor leagues, **8**:200
    National Hockey League. *See* National Hockey League
    penalties, **8**:114, 125, 153, 160
    pension, **8**:141
    players, **8**:156, 200-01
    Players' Emergency Fund, **8**:186
    play-off system, **8**:112
    radio broadcast of **8**:104
    records. *See* records, hockey
    referees, **8**:120, 168-69, 194-95
    riots, **8**:150-51, 155
    rules. *See* rules, hockey
    salaries, **8**:102, 188-89, 191-92, 200
    Soviet Union Team, **8**:189-90
    Stanley Cup champions. *See* Stanley Cup champions
    sticks, **8**:173
    training, **8**:103
    and United States, **8**:103
    violence, **8**:153-54, 175-79, 186-87, 194-95; *see also*
        hockey, mélées, riots
    and women reporters, **8**:196
    World Hockey Association, **8**:185-86, 188-90, 204-05
    see also field hockey; Olympic hockey
Hodge, Charlie, **8**:170
Hodges, Gil, **2**:93, 111-13, 156-57
Hodges, Thomas, **10**:185
Hodgson, George, **4**:20
Hoeckert, Gunnar, **4**:82-83
Hoff, Charles, **4**:54
Hoffman, George, **11**:129
Hoffman, John, **1**:104
Hofheinz, Roy, **8**:58
Hogan, Ben
    British Open Golf Tournament 1953, winner, **5**:92-93
    car crash, **5**:71
    at Los Angeles Open 1950, **5**:75-76
    Masters Golf Tournament 1951, winner, **6**:82-83; 1953,
        winner, **5**:87-88; 1954, second place, **5**:93-94; 1955,
        second place, **5**:97-98;1946, winner, **5**:70
    in top 5 poll, **5**:173

United States Open Golf Tournament 1950, winner, **5**:78-80; 1951, winner, **5**:83-84; 1953, winner, **5**:90-92; 1954, second place, **5**:94-96

Hogan, Frank
   and basketball investigation, **3**:38-39, 42, 63-66
   and boxing investigation, **7**:134, 144

Hogue, Paul, **3**:64, 67-68

Hohne, Christoph, **4**:167-68

Holderness, Ernest, **5**:40-41

Holdorf, Willi, **4**:158-59

Holland, Bill, **13**:148-50

Holland, Stephen, **12**:94-95

Holland, bicyclists in, **10**:99-100

Holland, soccer team of, **8**:13, 82-83, 96

Holland, swim team of, **12**:38-40

Holland, yachting team of, **12**:136, 140-41

Hollett, Bill, **8**:133

Holman, Marshall, **11**:75

Holman, Nat, **3**:8, 47, 49-50, 113, 116

Holm, Eleanor
   dropped from Olympic team 1936, **12**:32-33
   at 1932 Olympics, **12**:24-25, 28
   records 1930, **12**:22; 1934, **12**:31
   spectator at 1936 Olympics, **12**:36, 38

Holmenkollen ski festival 1954, **9**:74

Holmes, Julie, **9**:140

Holmes, Larry, **7**:198-99

Holtzman, Ken, **2**:188

Holum, Dianne, **9**:125, 128, 148-49

Holy Cross basketball team, **2**:29-30, 194

Holzman, Red, **3**:168-69

Homans, Gene, **5**:44-46

Homburger, Henry, **9**:25

Honduras soccer team, **8**:64-65

Hood, Frederick E. (Ted), **12**:180-81

Hoogerhyde, Russell, **10**:5

Hooton, Burt, **2**:192, 194

Hoover, Dick, **11**:69

Hoover, Herbert, **1**:25

Hopkins, Allen, **11**:66

Hopman, Harry, **6**:75-76, 138-41

Hoppe, Willie, **11**:47, 50-56, 58-62

Horemans, Edouard, **11**:53-54, 57

Horner, Joseph, **4**:15-16

Horn, Ted, **13**:141-43

Hornung, Paul, **1**:119-20, 124-27, 138

Hornsby, Rogers, **2**:33-34, 36-40, 42

horse, bullfighters, **10**:138-39

horse, polo. *See* pony, polo

horse racing, **13**:2-119
   Belmont Park, **13**:2-5, 16-17
   Belmont Stakes winners. *See* Belmont Stakes winners
   Double Decade Pace 1960, **13**:110
   and drugs, **13**:6, 71-72
   film, **13**:28
   Freehold Special race 1968, **13**:115
   gambling, **13**:30, 36-37
   Golden Gate Mile 1950, **13**:55-56

   Grand National Steeplechase, **13**:54-55, 80
   Hambletonian Stakes, **13**:105; *see also* Hambletonian Stakes winners
   Hanover Colt Stake No. 1, 1968, **13**:115
   Harbor Hill Steeplechase 1956, **13**:62-63
   International Trot 1963, **13**:111-12
   jockeys, **13**:17, 25, 72-73
   Kentucky Derby winners. *See* Kentucky Derby winners
   Kentucky Futurity winners. *See* Kentucky Futurity winners
   Little Brown Jug race, **13**:103, 108-09
   Messenger Stakes, **13**:108, 110-11, 114-15
   pacers, **13**:94-119
   Preakness winners. *See* Preakness winners
   records. *See* records, horse-racing
   Review Futurity 1965, **13**:114
   rules. *See* rules, horse racing
   Sanford Memorial 1919, **13**:9
   Saratoga (The Travers) 1930, **13**:23
   steeplechase, **13**:16-17, 54-55, 80
   Super Bowl, **13**:117
   totalisator, mechanised, **13**:20
   triple crown winners. *See* triple crown winners
   trotters, **13**:94-119
   Washington Park race, 1955, **13**:59-61
   and women, **13**:25, 72-73
   Yonkers Futurity 1955, **13**:105

horseshoe pitching, **10**:7-10

horse shows, **11**:140-62
   jumps, **11**:148-49
   military horsemanship, **11**:140, 142-43, 151
   see also National Horse Show

Horsley, Jack, **12**:81

Hosket, Bill, **3**:160

Hostin, Louis, **11**:106

Hotchkiss, Hazel, **6**:3

Houser, Clarence, **4**:36, 41, 48

Houston Aeros, **8**:191-92

Houston Astrodome, **2**:145

Houston Oilers, **1**:128

Houston Rockets, **3**:196-97

Houston University basketball team, **3**:75-76

Howard, Charles S., **13**:34-35

Howe, Gordie
   portrait of, **8**:165-67
   record 1953, **8**:148; 1956, **8**:154; 1960, **8**:160; 1963, **8**:164-65
   salary, **8**:191-92

Howell, Jim Lee, **1**:94

Howell, Millard, **1**:26-27

Howe, Syd, **8**:136

Howley, Chuck, **1**:151-52

Hoyt, Monty, **9**:102

Hubbard, DeHart, **4**:35, 43

Hubbell, Carl, **2**:46-48, 61

Huber, Hans, **7**:160

Huber, Hubert, **9**:134

Huddersfield Town soccer team, **8**:18, 27

Huffman, John R., **11**:123-24
Huggett, Brian, **5**:119-20, 132-34
Hugsted, Peter, **9**:57-58
Hull, Bobby, **8**:173
   record 1962, **8**:161-62; 1966, **8**:171-72; 1971, **8**:183
   in WHA, **8**:188-89
Hulsemann, Sylvie, **12**:106
Humane Society of the United States, **10**:132-33
Hungary fencers, **11**:126-27
Hungary, soccer team
   vs Brazil 1954, **8**:36; 1966, **8**:54-55
   vs England 1954, **8**:35
   vs Germany 1954, **8**:36
   vs Italy 1938, **8**:27
   Olympic victory 1952, **8**:34; 1964, **8**:52
Hungary swim team, **12**:53-54
Hungary table tennis team, **11**:43
Hungary water polo team, Olympic
   1932, **12**:31
   1952, **12**:55
   1956, **12**:57, 60-61
   1964, **12**:71
Hunt, Lamar, **1**:29; **8**:87
Hunt, Steve, **8**:89
Hunter, Francis, **6**:47
Hunter, Jim (Catfish), **2**:148
hunting. *See* wood, field and stream activities
Hurst, Geoff, **8**:56
Hussey, Francis, **4**:41-42
Hutchison, Jack, **5**:19-22
Hutson, Don, **1**:27, 43, 121-23
Hyde, Fillmore Van S., **11**:6-7, 9-10
hydroplane, **12**:121; *see also* Gold Cup; President's Cup
Hyndman, Bill, **5**:162-63
Hyvarinen, Antti, **9**:86-87

Iannicelli, Thomas, **11**:15, 18
ice fishing, **10**:161
Ice Palace Tournament 1921, **9**:7
Igaya, Chiharu (Chick), **9**:79-80
Iliad, **13**:21-22
Illini, Harry, **3**:40-41
Illinois University basketball team, **3**:40-41
Illinois University football team, **1**:13
Ilman, Gary, **12**:69
Imbach, Joseph, **4**:37, 39
Immerfall, Dan, **9**:160
Imogene V., **11**:168

India, cricket in, **10**:59-60
India, field hockey team of, **10**:33-35
India, tennis in, **6**:185
Indiana Pacers, **3**:178-79, 184-85
Indiana University basketball team, **3**:7-8, 48, 101-02
Indiana University soccer team, **8**:85
Indians, American, **10**:82-83, 86-87
Indonesia, badminton in, **11**:37
Indonesia, soccer team of, **8**:38
injuries
   bicycling, **10**:102
   bullfighting, **10**:140, 142-44
   football, **1**:25, 143-46
   hockey, **8**:122, 124, 180
   hunting, **10**:162
   motorcycling, **10**:88
   ski, **9**:140-41
In Memoriam, **13**:14-15
Inokuma, Isao, **11**:97
International Amateur Swimming Federation (FINA), **12**:62
international boat race 1920, **12**:116-18
International Boxing Club, **7**:119, 128-29, 140-41
International Luge Federation contest 1968, **9**:133
International Rowing Festival 1978, **12**:186
International Union of American Skating Champions, **9**:2
Inter of Milan, **8**:50, 56-57
Intrepid, **12**:172-75
Iowa State wrestling team, **11**:104
Iowa University football team, **1**:12-13
Ireland, **4**:13, **8**:16
Irish, Ben, **13**:13
Irishtocrat, **11**:180
Iron Constitution, **13**:82-83
Iron Liege, **13**:63-64
Irvin, Dick, **8**:149
Irwin, Hale, **5**:194-95
Isias, Fernando, **10**:7
Iso-Hollo, Volmari, **4**:69-70, 85
isometrics, **11**:113
Israeli deaths, **4**:180
Italy, bobsled team of, **9**:128
Italy, bicyclists of, **12**:62
Italy, equestrian team of, **11**:157
Italy, fencers of, **11**:118, 125
Italy, gymnasts of, **11**:128
Italy, hockey team of, **9**:50
Italy, military ski patrol team of, **9**:37
Italy, soccer in, **8**:13, 26-27, 41
Italy, soccer team of
   vs Austria 1934, **8**:21; 1937, **8**:26
   vs Brazil 1970, **8**:69
   Olympic victory 1936, **8**:26
   vs United States 1934, **8**:21; 1952, **8**:33
   World Cup championship 1934, **8**:21; 1938, **8**:27
Italy, water polo team of, **12**:48, 67
Ivan, Tommy, **8**:20
Ivey, Mitchell, **12**:81

Jabbar, Kareem Abdul-
　vs Boston Celtics 1974, **3**:191-92
　vs Houston Rockets 1968, **3**:75-76
　in NCAA championship 1967, **3**:74-75; 1969, **3**:79
　vs Philadelphia 76ers 1970, **3**:166-68
　on racial bias, **3**:78
　subsidies to, **3**:186-88
　varsity career of, **3**:72-76
Jack, Beau, **7**:102-03
Jacklin, Tony, **5**:160-61, 164-65, 172-73
Jackson, Arnold, **4**:19-20
Jackson, Donald, **9**:103
Jackson, Harvey, **8**:118-20, 138
Jackson, Henry, **2**:158
Jackson, Joe, **2**:25-28, 32
Jackson, Marjorie, **4**:106
Jackson, Reggie, **2**:176, 188, 192-95
Jackson, Tony, **3**:57-58
Jacobs, Helen
　in French hard court tournament 1930, **6**:48
　in U.S. matches 1928, **6**:44-45; 1936, **6**:66-69
　U.S. matches winner 1932, **6**:55-56; 1933, **6**:59-61
　in Wightman Cup matches 1933, **6**:58-59
　in Wimbledon matches 1929, **6**:45; 1935, **6**:64-65
Jacobs, Hirsch, **13**:65
Jacobs, Irving, **11**:13
Jacobs, Jim, **11**:20-21
Jacobs, Michael, **7**:83
Jacobs, Tommy, **5**:126-28, 134-35
Jacoby, Fred, Jr., **12**:148
Jaffee, Irving, **9**:11-12, 16-19, 94
jai alai, **11**:27-30
Jalkanen, Kalle, **9**:32-33
Jamerson, Wilbur, **1**:46
James, Larry, **4**:168-69
Jameson, Betty, **5**:81-86, 99-100
Jamestown, **13**:24
Jamie K., **13**:56-57
Jamison, Al, **1**:57
Jamison, H.B., **4**:4
Janiro, Tony, **7**:134
Janowicz, Vic, **1**:75
January, Don, **5**:144-45, 188-89
Jany, Alex, **12**:44-45, 47
Japan, sumo wrestling in, **11**:93-94
Japan, swim team of, **12**:34, 41-42, 49
Japan, table tennis team of, **11**:40
Japan, volleyball team of, **11**:45-46
Jarrett, Eleanor Holm. See Holm, Eleanor
Jarvinen, Akilles, **4**:69-70
Jarvinen, Matti, **4**:66
Jaworski, Chet, **3**:15
Jazy, Michel, **4**:140-41
Jeannette, Joe, **7**:12
Jefferson, Bernie, **1**:29
Jeffries, James, **7**:4-6, 9-11, 14
Jelinek, Josef, **8**:76
Jenkins, Charley, **4**:124-25, 127, **12**:55

Jenkins, David, **9**:74, 80-82, 96-97
Jenkins, Hayes Alan, **9**:73-75, 77-78, 80-82, 88-89
Jenkins, Rodney, **11**:161-62
Jenner, Bruce, **4**:194-95
Jensen, Knud Enemark, **10**:103
Jensen, Zoe Ann, **12**:52
Jenssen, Leif, **11**:112
Jernberg, Sixten, **9**:82-83, 89-90, 113-14
Jessen, Ruth, **5**:128
Jessup, Marion Zinderstein, **6**:23, 28
Jewtraw, Charles, **9**:7-8
Jim Dandy, **13**:23
Jimenez, Julio, **10**:106
jiu jitsu, **11**:78
Jochim, Alfred, **11**:128
Johannesen, Knut, **9**:97-98, 117
Johansson, Ingemar, **7**:131-33, 135-38
Johansson, Irma, **9**:96-97
Johncock, Gordon, **13**:195-97
Johns Hopkins University lacrosse team, **10**:81, 83, 85-87
Johnson, Ban, **2**:8-9, 13, 21-22, 32
Johnson, Bascom, **4**:5-6
Johnson, Bernard, **10**:126
Johnson, Bill, **10**:90
Johnson, Butch, **1**:168
Johnson, Ching, **8**:110
Johnson, Cornelius, **4**:75-77
Johnson, Derek, **4**:121-23
Johnson, Don, **11**:74
Johnson, Harold, **7**:146, 150
Johnson, Harvey, **1**:101
Johnson, Jack
　deterioration of, **7**:12
　heavyweight champion 1908, **7**:7-8; 1909, **7**:8-9; 1910,
　　7:9-11
　vs Willard 1915, **7**:12
Johnson, Larry (Boston Shorty), **11**:64
Johnson, Lyndon, **1**:70
Johnson, Rafer, **4**:118, 125, 128, 138-40
Johnson, Ralph, **3**:73-74
Johnson, Robert (Junior), **13**:164-65
Johnson, Walter, **2**:16-17, 32, 35, 138-40
Johnson, Wallace F., **6**:20-21
Johnston, Charley, **7**:107, 119
Johnston, Harrison, **5**:40-41
Johnston, William M.
　All Comers' Tournament winner 1915, **6**:8
　in Davis Cup matches 1927, **6**:40-42
　in U.S. matches 1920, **6**:15; 1922, **6**:23-24; 1923, **6**:26-27;
　　1924, **6**:29; 1925, **6**:31-32; 1926, **6**:35-37
Johnstown, **13**:35-36
Joliat, **8**:115-18
Jolly, Herbert, **5**:33-34
Jones, Ann Haydon, **6**:146-47, 150-51, 158, 163-64
Jones, Ben, **13**:49-51
Jones, Caldwell, **3**:195
Jones, Carlmon, **1**:180
Jones, Doug, **7**:146

Jones, Deacon, **1**:143, 145, **4**:137
Jones, Edgar, **1**:101
Jones, Greg, **9**:167
Jones, Hayes, **4**:146, 151
Jones, Howard, **1**:18, 24-25
Jones, John Paul, **4**:19-20, 26
Jones, L.M. (Biff) **1**:179
Jones, Lou, **4**:127
Jones, Parnelli, **13**:171-72
Jones, Robert Trent, **5**:148-54
Jones, Robert Tyre, Jr., **5**:17, 19
   and Augusta National Golf Course, **5**:52-53
   British Open 1926, winner, **5**:29-30; 1927, winner, **5**:35-36; 1930, winner, **5**:41-42
   as idol of Nicklaus, **5**:168-71
   in Masters Golf Tournament 1934, **5**:55
   National Amateur Championship 1925, winner, **5**:28; 1930, winner, **5**:44-46
   retirement of, **5**:47-49
   in top 5 poll, **5**:173
   United States Open Golf Tournament 1922, second place, **5**:22-23; 1923, winner, **5**:24-25; 1925, second place, **5**:27-28; 1926, winner, **5**:30-32; 1930, winner, **5**:42-44
   in Walker Cup competition 1930, **5**:40-41
Jones, Sam, **3**:149-50
Jordan, Don, **7**:140
Jordan, Kathy, **6**:199
Jorgensen, Spider, **2**:81-82
Joy, Andy, **12**:159
Jsmayr, Rudolf, **11**:105-06
Juantorena, Alberto, **4**:189-90, 193-94
Juday, Steve, **1**:63-64
judo, **11**:44-45, 81, 95, 97-99
Juison, George, **13**:15
Jupiter, **12**:136
Jurgensen, Sonny, :121-22

Kabos, Endro, **11**:123
Kahanamoku, Duke, **4**:20, **12**:5-8, 14
Kaiser, Dave, **1**:55
Kakousis, Herikles, **4**:8
Kaline, Al, **2**:113-14, 149-51
Kallakorpi, Aulis, **9**:86-87
Kangasniemi, Kaaro, **11**:111
Kankkonen, Veikko, **9**:106-07, 119-20
Kansas City Athletics, **2**:109, 147-48
Kansas City Chiefs, **1**:128, 130-32, 148
Kansas City Royals baseball team, **2**:189-90
Kansas City Royals basketball team, **3**:175
Kansas City Steers, **3**:143
Kansas State basketball team, **3**:56

Kansas University basketball team, **3**:43-44, 53-55
Kapitonov, Viktor, **10**:103
Kaplan, Harry, **7**:138
Kapp, Joe, **1**:160-61
Kapus, Franz, **9**:84-85
karate, **11**:95-96, 102
Karch, Sargent, **1**:164
Karr, Billy, **1**:89-91
Karras, Alex, **1**:124-26
Kasaya, Yukio, **9**:144
Kaserer, Monika, **9**:153
Kastenman, Petrus, **11**:155
Kathleen, **12**:159
Kauffman, Cynthia, **9**:132
Kauffman, Ronald, **9**:132
Kaufman, Beth, **12**:72-73
Kavanaugh, Ken, **1**:103-04
kayaks, **12**:178
Kaye, Danny, **2**:185
Kazantsev, Vladimir, **4**:106-07
Kearns, Jack, **7**:96
Keating, Ed, **1**:158, 64-65
Keeling, Butch, **8**:112, 121-22
Keene, James, **13**:2-6
Kefauver, Estes, **2**:124, **7**:134, 139-41
Keino, Kipchoge, **4**:172, 178-79, 182-83
Kelleher, Robert, **6**:156-58
Keller, Erhard, **9**:130-31
Keller, Jack, **4**:62-63
Kelley, Larry, **10**:74
Kellmeyer, Fern Lee (Peachy), **6**:135
Kellogg, Junius, **3**:37-38
Kellum, Bill, **1**:41-42
Kelly, Dan, **4**:17
Kelly, Jack, Jr., **12**:151, 159
Kelly, Jack, Sr., **12**:118
Kelso, **13**:69-70
Keltner, Ken, **2**:85-86
Kemps, Mario Alberto, **8**:96
kendo, **11**:96
Kenilworth race 1920, **13**:11-12
Kennedy, John, **4**:150
Kennedy, Joseph, **8**:27
Kennedy, J. Walter, **3**:145-46, 148, 156-58, 173, 183
Kennedy, Robert, **7**:141
Kennedy, Ted, **8**:143
Kentucky Colonels, **3**:178-79, 184-85
Kentucky Derby winners
   Affirmed 1978, **13**:85-86
   Assault 1946, **13**:45-46
   Carry Back 1960, **13**:67-68
   Citation 1948, **13**:49-51
   Count Fleet 1943, **13**:41
   Dancer's Image 1968, **13**:70-71
   Exterminator 1918, **13**:7
   Forward Pass 1968, **13**:71-72
   Gallant Fox 1930, **13**:20-21
   Iron Liege 1957, **13**:63-64

Johnstown 1939, **13**:35-36
Omaha 1935, **13**:26-27
Omar Khayyam 1917, **13**:7
Regret 1915, **13**:7
Reigh Count 1928, **13**:17-19
Seattle Slew 1977, **13**:80-82
Secretariat 1973, **13**:73-74
Sir Barton 1919, **13**:8
Swaps 1955, **13**:58-59
Tim Tam 1958, **13**:65-66
War Admiral 1937, **13**:30-31
Whirlaway 1941, **13**:38-40
Zev 1923, **13**:12-15
Kentucky Futurity winners
  Ayres 1964, **13**:114
  Emily's Pride 1958, **13**:107
  Ethelinda 1923, **13**:97
  Ford Hanover 1951, **13**:103
  Lindy's Pride 1969, **13**:116
  Nevelle Pride 1968, **13**:116
  Speedy Scot 1963, **13**:112
  Super Bowl 1972, **13**:117
Kentucky University basketball team
  vs Alabama 1954, **3**:49
  game-fixing, **3**:42-45
  NCAA champions 1948, **3**:32; 1951, **3**:41; 1958, **3**:56;
    1978, **3**:106-07
  vs Oklahoma A & M 1949, **3**:34-35
  vs Rhode Island 1945, **3**:26
  Rupp as coach, **3**:47
  vs Seattle 1968, **3**:56
  vs Utah 1947, **3**:28-29
Kentucky University football team, **1**:46
Kenya, hunting in, **10**:191-92
Kenyoh, Mel, **13**:185
Keogh, Frankie, **13**:11
Keon, Dave, **8**:164
Kerr, Johnny, **3**:146
Kerslake, Bill, **11**:94
Kessing, O.O., **1**:103
Ketchel, Stanley, **7**:7-9
Kidd, William Winston, **9**:118-19, 125-26, 128-29, 139
Kiefer, Adolph, **12**:40-42
Kielty, Dorothy, **5**:74
Kiesling, Walter, **1**:97
Kight, Lenore, **12**:28, 30-31, 41-42
Kiick, Jim, **1**:158-59, 164-65
Kilbane, John, **7**:11
Killy, Jean-Claude, **9**:122-23, 128-29, 133-35
Kilmarnock of Scotland, **8**:45-46
Kilmer, Willis Sharp, **7**:13
Kilrea, Hec, **8**:127-28
Kim, Nelli, **11**:132-35
Kimihara, Kenji, **4**:171-72
Kiner, Ralph, **2**:87, 174
King, Billy Jean Moffitt
  doubles with Riessen, **6**:190
  earnings of 1971, **6**:175
  portrait of, **6**:147-49
  vs Riggs 1973, **6**:180
  U.S matches winner 1967, **6**:150-51; 1971, **6**:174-75;
    1974, **6**:184-85
  in U.S. Open 1968, **6**:160
  in Wimbledon matches 1963, **6**:133; 1969, **6**:163-64;
    1970, **6**:167-69
  Wimbledon matches winner 1962, **6**:128; 1966, **6**:143;
    1967, **6**:146-47; 1968, **6**:157-58; 1972, **6**:176; 1973,
    6:180-81; 1975, **6**:186-87
  on World Tennis Team, **6**:179
King, Don, **7**:193-94, 198-99
King, Micki, **12**:84
King, Morris, **3**:144
King, Robert, **4**:45
King, Ron, **3**:83-84
King Cole, **13**:39
King Pepper, **11**:165-66
Kingpetch, Pone, **7**:148
Kingscote, A.R.F., **6**:14
Kinney, Jeff, **1**:72
Kinsella, Walter, **11**:6, 10-11
Kinsey, Dan, **4**:36-37
Kinsey, Howard, **6**:43
Kiphuth, Robert, **12**:62, 64
Kirby, Gustavus, **9**:11
Kirk, Grayson, **1**:47
Kirkpatrick, Charles, **8**:4
Kissinger, Henry, **8**:82-84
Kitamura, Kusuo, **12**:29
Kite, Tom, **5**:162-63
Kiviat, Abel, **4**:19-20
Kiyokawa, Maseji, **12**:29, 40
Klamforth, Dick, **10**:89
Klammer, Franz, **9**:153
Kleberg, R.J., **13**:47-48
Klein, Dick, **3**:152
Kluszewski, Ted, **2**:110-11
Knape, Ulrika, **12**:88
Knight, Bobby, **3**:101-02
Knodle, Robert, **11**:105
Knox, Ronnie, **1**:55
Koceski, Leo, **1**:42
Koch, Bill, **9**:153, 167
Kodes, Jan, **6**:174-75, 180-82, 190-91
Koehler, Thomas, **9**:113, 136
Kohlemainen, Hannes, **4**:26, 33-34
Kohno, Mitsuro, **11**:43
Kojac, George, **12**:22
Kok, Ada, **12**:80-81
Kolb, Claudia, **12**:78, 81
Koll, Bill, **11**:87
Komenich, Milo, **3**:19
Konno, Ford, **12**:51-54
Kono, Tommy, **11**:107, 110
Koosman, Jerry, **2**:151-52, 156-57, 159
Koppisch, Walter, **1**:86
Korbut, Olga, **11**:131-35

Koufax, Sandy, **2**:138-39, 142-44
Konrads, John, **12**:66-67
Kosichkin, Viktor, **9**:95-96, 98, 114
Koulakova, Galina, **9**:144, 146-47, 149, 159-60
Kovacs, Frank, **6**:77
Kovatch, John, **1**:29
Kowalcyk, Walt, **1**:55
Koy, Ted, **1**:70
Krachen, Jack, **7**:54
Kraenzlein, A.C., **4**:5-8, 15
Kralzert, Billy, **5**:192-93
Kramer, Frank L., **10**:95, 97
Kramer, Ingrid, **12**:62-65, 67, 69, 77
Kramer, Jerry, **1**:138-39
Kramer, John (Jack), **6**:81-82, 86
Kramer, Walter, **11**:34-35
Kramer, Wille, **4**:17
Kranepool, Ed, **2**:135
Krauss, Barry, **1**:82-83
Krauss, Harry, **7**:163-64
Kreiner, Kathy, **9**:164, 166-67
Krovopouskov, Viktor, **11**:127
Krueger, Al, **1**:30-31
Krueger, Ken, :144
Krulewitch, Melvin, **7**:150
Kuck, John, **4**:44-46
Kuckhahn, Karl, **1**:41-42
Kucsis, Charles, **5**:61-63
Kuhn, Bowie, **2**:154-55, 161, 165-66, 175, 184-85, 187-88
Ku Klux Klan, **7**:168, **10**:66
Kulikov, Yevgeny, **9**:160
Kunnert, Kevin, **9**:196-97
Kurland, Bob, **3**:25, 27, 46
Kurtsinger, Charley, **13**:30-35
Kurtz, Frank, **12**:29-30, 42
Kurynov, Alexander, **11**:110
Kusolinski, Janusz, **4**:59
Kusserow, Lou, **1**:40-41
Kuts, Vladimir, **4**:124-26
Kuznetsov, Vasily, **4**:138
Kyle, Alex, **5**:61-63

labor union, **1**:136
Lacey, A.J., **5**:54
Lach, Elmer, **8**:149
Lackie, Ethel, **12**:13-14
Lacoste, René, **6**:36-38, 40-43
lacrosse, **10**:80-87
Ladewig, Marion, **11**:69, 72-73
Lafforgue, Maurice, **9**:42
Lafleur, Guy, **8**:203
LaGuardia, Fiorello, **2**:66-72
Laguna, Ismael, **7**:161

Lahore, **13**:7
Lajoie, Napoleon, **2**:12
Lake Placid Sno-Birds meet 1941, **9**:43-44
Lambeau, Curly, **1**:104
Lambert, Ward (Piggy), **3**:113, 117
Lamonica, Daryle, **1**:137
LaMotta, Jake
    and boxing investigation, **7**:81-82
    fixing of 1947 bout, **7**:134-35
    middleweight champion 1949, **7**:93
    vs Robinson 1951, **7**:101
LaMotta, Joseph, **7**:134
Landis, Kenesaw Mountain, **2**:30-32, 75
Landon, Dick, **4**:28
Landry, Tom, **1**:135, 151-53, 166, 168
Landy, John, **4**:113-15, 124
Lane, F.W., **4**:4
Langer, Ludy, **12**:5-6
Langford, Sam, **7**:12
Lansdell, Grenville, **1**:30-31
Lanzi, Mario, **4**:80
Lantschner, Gustav, **9**:31
Lapchick, Joe, **3**:113-16, 118
Larned, William, **6**:3-4
LaRoche, Chet, **11**:24
Larrabee, Mike, **4**:157-58
Larsen, Don, **2**:116-19, 121-22
Larsen, Ernest, **4**:126-27
Larson, Lance, **12**:62-63
Larsson, Artur, **9**:35
Larsson, Goran, **12**:49-50
Larsson, Gunnar, **12**:86-87, 89
Larva, Harry, **4**:50
LaSalle College basketball team, **3**:49
Lassiter, Ike, **1**:146
Lassiter, Luther, **11**:63-64
Laund, Loyalty, **11**:165-66
Launi, Marcello, **8**:58
Laurin, Lucien, **13**:74-77
Lavagetto, Cookie, **2**:81-82, 85
Lavelli, Dante, **1**:101, 106, 123
Lavelli, Tony, **3**:34
Laver, Rod
    Australian matches winner 1960, **6**:125; 1962, **6**:128
    vs Connors 1975, **6**:185
    in French matches 1962, **6**:128
    pro tournaments, **6**:145
    in U.S. matches 1960, **6**:126-27
    U.S. matches winner 1962, **6**:130; 1969, **6**:166
    in Wimbledon matches 1959, **6**:122-24
    Wimbledon winner 1961, **6**:127; 1962, **6**:129; 1968, **6**:157; 1969, **6**:164-65
Lawrence, Andrea Mead, **9**:63, 65-66, 68, 75-76
Law, Vernon, **2**:125-26
Laws, Joe, **1**:91
Layden, Elmer, **1**:13, 15-16, 96, 100
Layne, Bobby, **1**:109
Layne, Floyd, **3**:39

Layton, Johnny, **11**:59
Lazzeri, Tony, **2**:60
Leach, Johnny, **11**:39
lead shots, **10**:190-91
Leahy, Frank, **1**:34, 43-44
Lebanon Valley College football team, **1**:177
Lebel, Aldrine, **9**:74
Lebel, Leo, **9**:74
Lechner, Erica, **9**:133
Lecoq, Louis, **13**:130
LeDoux, Scott, **7**:193
Lee, Cornelius S., **5**:26
Lee, Robin, **9**:27-28, 37, 41-42
Lee, Sammy, **12**:43, 45-47, 53
Lee Axworthy, **13**:97
Leeds soccer team, **8**:76-77
LeGendre, Robert, **4**:35
LeGoff, Jack, **11**:161
Lehane, Jan, **6**:125
Lehigh University football team, **1**:178
Lehtinen, Lauri, **4**:67-69
Leicester City soccer team, **8**:31, 47-48, 51
Leitner, Mathias, **9**:94-95
Leland Stanford Jr. University, **1**:13; *see also* Stanford University
Lemaire, Jacques, **8**:190, 203
Lema, Tony, **5**:122, 124, 132-34, 140
Lemm, Wally, **1**:182
Lemon, Bob, **2**:107-08
Lenglen, Suzanne
    Cannes matches winner 1926, **6**:32-33
    French matches winner 1921, **6**:17-18
    victories of, **6**:34
    in Wimbledon matches 1920, **6**:14
    Wimbledon winner 1919, **6**:2; 1921, **6**:18; 1922, **6**:21-22; 1923, **6**:24; 1925, **6**:30
Lenin Peak, **10**:120-21
Leonard, Benny, **7**:20-23
Leonard, Jackie, **7**:140-41
Leonard, J. Richard, **11**:18
Leonard, Sugar Ray, **7**:191-92
Lesage, François, **11**:143
Leslander, Klas, **9**:92
Leswick, Tony, **8**:145, 149
Levegh, Pierre, **13**:157
Levinsky, Battling, **7**:20
Levis, Joseph, **11**:123
Lewis, Ed (Strangler)
    headlock of, **11**:82
    vs Munn 1925, **11**:83
    retirement, **11**:87
    in wrestling championships, **11**:81-84
    vs Zbyszko 1919, **11**:80-81
Lewis, Frank, **11**:86
Lewis, Herb, **8**:128
Lewis, J. Norman, **2**:105
Lewis, Reg, **8**:31
Lewis, Ted, **7**:15

Lewis, Tommy, **1**:50-51
Liddell, Eric H., **4**:39
Lieder, Craig, **3**:87-88
light heavyweight champions
    Foster 1968, **7**:172-73
    Johnson 1962, **7**:162
    Loughran 1927, **7**:39
    Moore 1952, **7**:112
    Pastrano 1963, **1**:150
    Rosenbloom 1930, **7**:41
    Tunney 1922, **7**:20
lightweight champion
    Ambers 1939, **7**:69-70
    Armstrong 1938, **7**:66-67
    Brown 1956, **7**:124
    Canzoneri 1930, **7**:42; 1931, **7**:42-43
    controversy about 1966, **7**:167-68
    Duran 1972, **7**:179; 1978, **7**:194
    Laguna 1965, **7**:161
    Leonard 1919, **7**:15; 1922, **7**:22-23
    Ortiz 1962, **7**:145
    Ross 1933, **7**:45
Lilienthal, Otto, **10**:128
Lilly, Bob, **1**:151-52
Lincoln Road, **13**:65-66
Linder, Carl, **4**:31
Lindley, Grace Carter, **9**:43
Lindsay, Ted, **8**:143-45, 156
Lindy's Pride, **13**:116
Lipton, Thomas, **12**:116-18, 131-33
Lisciotti, Larry, **11**:66
Liscombe, Carl, **8**:135
Liston, Charles (Sonny)
    vs Ali 1964, **7**:155-59; 1965, **7**:161-63
    background of, **7**:147-48
    heavyweight champion 1962, **7**:146-47
    and racketeers, **7**:139
Little, Lou, **1**:25-26, 49-51, 91
Litwhiler, Danny, **2**:74
Liverpool soccer team, **8**:31-32, 72-73, 79-80
Livie, Bruce, **1**:108
Llanoria, **12**:153-54, 156
Lloyd, Christine Evert. *See* Evert, Christine
Lloyd, Marion, **11**:121-22
Locke, Bobby, **5**:81, 113
Locke, Dorothy, **11**:122
Lofthouse, Nat, **8**:34, 39
Logan, John, **11**:100-02
Logan, Johnny, **2**:124-25
Lomakin, Trofim, **11**:107
Lombardi, Vic, **2**:78, 82-85
Lombardi, Vince, **1**:116, 138-39
Lom, Benny, **1**:18
Lonborg, Jim, **2**:146-47
Londos, Jim, **11**:85-86, 103
Longboat, Tom, **4**:13
Long, Dale, **2**:115
Long, Dallas, **4**:146, 148, 155-57

Longden, Johnny, **13**:41-42, 62
Long Island University basketball team, **3**:10, 12, 15-18, 38-39
Long Island University soccer team, **8**:58
Loomis, Frank, **4**:27
Lopez, Al, **2**:109-11
Lopez, Hector, **2**:132-33
Lopez, Nancy, **5**:193-94
Lord Boswell, **13**:46-47
Lord Jim, **13**:99-100
Lorenzen, Fred, **13**:178
Lorz, Fred, **4**:7
Los Angeles Aztecs, **8**:83-84
Los Angeles Dodgers
  vs Atlanta Braves 1974, **2**:171-72
  vs Chicago Cubs 1965, **2**:142-43
  vs Milwaukee Braves 1959, **2**:124-25
  vs Minnesota Twins 1965, **2**:143-44
  move from Brooklyn, **2**:120-21
  vs New York Yankees 1977, **2**:192-95
  vs Oakland Athletics 1974, **2**:176-78
  vs Philadelphia Phillies 1968, **2**:149
  vs St. Louis Cardinals 1962, **2**:133
  vs San Francisco Giants 1962, **2**:134
Los Angeles Kings, **8**:183-84
Los Angeles Lakers
  vs Atlanta Hawks 1972, **3**:173
  vs Baltimore Bullets 1971, **3**:173
  vs Boston Celtics 1962, **3**:144; 1963, **3**:145-46; 1965, **3**:151-52; 1966, **3**:155; 1968, **3**:162; 1969, **3**:162-63
  Chamberlain on, **3**:162
  vs Houston Rockets 1977, **3**:196-97
  NBA champions
  vs New York Knicks 1970, **3**:168-70; 1973, **3**:178
  vs Philadelphia Warriors 1961, **3**:142
  record 1971, **3**:173; 1972, **3**:176
  vs Seattle Supersonics 1972, **3**:176
  vs Syracuse Nationals 1961, **3**:142
Los Angeles Rams, **1**:105-08, 144-45
Los Angeles Toros, **8**:62
Los Angeles Wolves, **8**:62-63
Lothrop, Jim, **10**:129
Lott, George M., Jr., **6**:54-55
Lotus-Ford car, **13**:170, 175
Loughran, Beatrix, **9**:12, 15
Loughran, Tommy, **7**:39
Louis, Joe
  Army exhibition fights, **7**:74
  vs Baer 1935, **7**:54-56
  vs Carnera 1935, **7**:53-54
  vs Charles 1950, **7**:99-100
  in Hall of Fame, **7**:118-19
  heavyweight champion 1937, **7**:60-62; 1938, **7**:65-66; 1939, **7**:67-68, 1941, **7**:71-72; 1946, **7**:74-77; 1947, **7**:82-83; 1948, **7**:85-87
  vs Marciano 1951, **7**:108-09
  on racketeers, **7**:141
  retirement of, **7**:87

  vs Schmeling 1936, **7**:56-59
Louisville University basketball team, **3**:59
Loukola, Toivo, **4**:52
Loveland, Helge, **4**:30
Lovellette, Clyde, **3**:43-44, 46
Lovelock, Jack, **4**:81-82
Loyola University basketball team, **3**:15-16, 50
Lubanski, Ed, **11**:72
Lucas, Jerry, **3**:61-62, 64, 144
Luchow, Morgens, **11**:125
Luckman, Sid, **1**:95-99, 102
Lueg, Weiner, **4**:107-08
luge races
  International Luge Federation contest 1968, **9**:133
  see also Olympic toboggan race
Luisetti, Hank, **3**:12, 14, 118
Lujack, Johnny, **1**:35-36, 103-04, 179
Lu, Liang Huan, **5**:164-65
Lumley, Harry, **8**:143
Lundquist, E.H., **4**:50
Lunn, Bob, **5**:160-61
Lusis, Janis, **4**:165-66
Luton Town soccer team, **8**:41-42
Lycett, Randolph, **6**:14, 18
Lynch, Joe, **7**:21-22
Lynn, Fred, **2**:180-84
Lynn, Janet, **9**:140, 144-46
Lysak, Steve, **12**:153-54
Lytle, Rob, **1**:168-69

Maas, Jan, **12**:136
McAfee, George, **1**:30-31
McArdle, Pete, **4**:151
MacArthur, Douglas, **4**:150-51
McArthur, K.K., **4**:21-23
Macauley, Ed, **3**:31
McAuley, Ken, **8**:136
McCaffery, Burt, **8**:113
McCall, Scott, **1**:29-30
McCarthy, Joe, **2**:64-67, 85-86
McCarty, Luther, **7**:11-12
Maccioli, Mike, **1**:43-44
McClain, Ted, **3**:184
McClure, Jimmy, **11**:38
McClure, Wilie, **7**:139
McConn, C.M. **1**:178
McCormick, Patricia, **10**:140
McCoy, Al, **7**:13
McCulley, Al, **1**:38-39
McDaniel, Mildre, **4**:127
McDermott, Donald, **9**:64
McDermott, Terry, **9**:112, 130-31
MacDonald, Dave, **13**:173-74

MacDonald, Florence, **4**:50
MacDonald, Irene, **12**:57
McDonald, Pat, **4**:29, 35-36
McDonald, Paul, **1**:79-80
MacDonald, Ramsay, **8**:19-20
MacDonald, Scott, **5**:162-63
MacDonald, Tommy, **1**:119-23
MacDonald, Torbert, **1**:154-55
McFarlane, Willie, **5**:27-28
McGee, Max, **1**:130
McGinnis, George, **3**:184, 194-95
McGinnity, Joe, **2**:6-7
McGlothlin, Jim, **2**:146
McGrath, Jack, **13**:153
McGrath, M.J., **4**:13, 22
McGraw, John, **2**:14-16, 20-21, 38, 48-49
McGraw, Tug, **2**:170
McGuire, Al, **3**:102-04
McGuire, Edith, **4**:157-58, 162
McGuire, James, **8**:58
McKane, Kathleen, **6**:24, 30-31
McKay, Clarence H., **11**:2-3
McKay, John, **1**:74
Mack, Connie, **2**:48-49, 60, 89-90
Mackbee, Earsell, **1**:148
McKean, Miriam, **9**:42
McKechnie, Deacon Bill, **2**:68-69
McKee, J.Edwin, **7**:171-72
McKee, Tim, **12**:86-87
McKenley, Herbert, **4**:96-97
MacKenzie, Alister, **5**:40-41, 52-53
McKenzie, Don, **12**:77
MacKenzie, Stuart, **12**:159
Mackey, John, **1**:149
McKinley, Chuck, **6**:127, 131-33
McKinney, Frank, **12**:66
McLean, Robert, **9**:6
Mackmull, Jack, **1**:40-42
MacKnowski, Steve, **12**:153-54
McLain, Dennis Dale, **2**:149-54
McLane, Jimmy, **12**:44-48, 51-52, 55
McLarnin, Jimmy, **7**:46-47, 49-50
McLeod, Fred, **5**:18
McLoughlin, M.E., **6**:5-6, 8
McMahon, James, (Junie), **11**:69-70
McMillan, Kathy, **4**:187
McMillan, Roy, **2**:135-36
McMilland, Jim, **3**:173, 187
McMillen, Bob, **4**:107-08
MacMitchell, Leslie, **4**:88
McMullin, Fred, **2**:25-28, 32
McMurtry, William, **8**:195
McNally, Dave, **2**:156-57, 184-85
McNamara, Reggie, **10**:95, 98
McNeil, Fred, **1**:167
MacPhail, Larry, **2**:76, 79
MacPhail, Lee, **2**:185
McPherson Oilers, **3**:10-11

McQuinn, George, **2**:77, 84
McShane, James, **7**:135
McTigue, Mike, **7**:39, 167
McVea, Sam, **7**:12
Madison, Helene, **12**:22-24, 29-31
Madison Square Garden
    basketball at, **3**:9-10, 40-42, 112; *see also* National
        Basketball Association champions
    hockey rink, **8**:103-06
    professional tennis tournament at, **6**:145
    6-day bicycle race, **10**:95, 97-99
    skating rink, **9**:10
Maehata, Hideko, **12**:36
Maentyranta, Eero, **9**:110-11
Mager, Norman, **3**:36-37
Maglie, Sal, **2**:107-08, 116-17
Magnani, Dante, **1**:99, 121-23
Magnuson, Waren, **2**:158
Mahaffey, John, **5**:177
Mahan, Larry, **10**:131-33
Maher, Bill, **12**:170
Mahmoud, **13**:53
Mahovlich, Frank, **8**:190
Mahre, Phil, **9**:158-60
Maier, Fred Anton, **9**:133
Maki, Wayne, **8**:180
Mako, Gene, **6**:73-74
Malaya badminton team, **11**:35
Mallory, Molla
    analysis of playing of, **6**:10-11
    in French matches 1921, **6**:17-18
    as umpire, **6**:12
    in U.S. matches 1923, **6**:24-25; 1924, **6**:28
    U.S matches winner 1921, **6**:19; 1922, **6**:22-23; 1926,
        6:34-35
    in Wimbledon matches 1922, **6**:21-22
Malott, Deane, **1**:47
Malone, Moses, **3**:182-83
Manchester, Rex, **12**:169-70
Manchester City soccer team, **8**:15, 20, 37-38
Manchester United soccer team
    air crash of, **8**:39
    vs Aston Villa 1957, **8**:38
    vs Bolton Wanderers 1958, **8**:39
    English Soccer Cup victors 1963, **8**:51
    European Soccer Cup victors 1968, **8**:63
    vs Southampton 1976, **8**:85
Mandel, Carola, **10**:49
Mandel, Frank, **1**:197
Mandelstam, Rodney, **6**:135
Manders, Jack, **1**:89, 91-93, 95-96
Manero, Tony, **5**:59-60
Mangrum, Lloyd, **5**:68-72, 78-79, 87-88, 94-96
Manhattan College basketball team, **3**:37-38
Maniaci, Joe, **1**:95-96
Mann, Graham, **12**:160-61
Mann, Shelly, **12**:59
Manning, Madeline, **4**:170

Manolete, **10**:140-42

Man o' War, **13**:9-12, 53-54

Mantha, George, **8**:117

Mantha, Silvio, **8**:113-17

Mantle, Mickey, **2**:100-01, 115-16

Marathon, Boston, **4**:44, 162

Marathon, New York, **4**:200-01

marathon, Olympic

  collapse of runners, **4**:40-41

  criticism of, **4**:31

  rules, **4**:25

  see also marathon winners, Olympic; records, track and

    field, marathon

marathon, 144-hour, **4**:55

marathon winners, Olympic

  Bikela 1964, **4**:160

  Cabrera 1948, **4**:98

  Hayes 1908, **4**:13-14

  Hicks 1904, **4**:7

  Kolehmainen 1920, **4**:31

  McArthur 1912, **4**:21-23

  Ouafi 1928, **4**:53-55

  Shorter 1972, **4**:182-83

  Son 1936, **4**:86-87

  Wolder 1968, **4**:171-72

  Zabala 1932, **4**:70-72

  Zatopek 1952, **4**:108-09

marathons. *See* Olympic ski race champions, marathon;

  snowshoe marathon

Maravich, Pete, **3**:77, 80

Marble, Alice, **6**:66-69

March, Harry, **1**:86, 89, 92

March, Mush, **8**:125

Marciano, Rocky

  heavyweight champion 1951, **7**:108-09; 1952, **7**:110-11;

    1954, **7**:117-18; 1955, **7**:120-22

  retirement of, **7**:124

Margaret Rose, Princess of England, **8**:33

Marichal, Juan, **2**:134, 145

Marine Corps, **1**:13

Marion, Marty, **2**:77-78

Maris, Roger, **2**:129-30

Marks, Geoff, **5**:162-63

Marmon car, **13**:125

Marquard, Rube, **2**:13-14

Marquette University basketball team, **3**:102-04

Marquette University football team, **1**:29-30

Marr, Dave, **5**:125-26

Marsh, David, **5**:162-63

Marshall, Mike, **2**:176-78

Marshall, Thurgood, **7**:178

Marshall University basketball team, **3**:73-74

Martella, Dan, **11**:15

martial arts, **11**:78-104

Martin, Alfred Manuel (Billy), **2**:102-04, 192-93, 195-96

Martin, Juan Carlos, **8**:47

Martingale, **13**:12-13

Mary, Queen Mother of England, **8**:20

Maryland University lacrosse team, **10**:84-85, 87

Maryland University soccer team, **8**:46-47, 50

Mary Reynolds, **13**:98-99

Marzani, Danny, **13**:55

Marzi, Gustavo, **11**:122-23

Mastenbrook, Rita, **12**:34, 38, 41

Masters Golf Tournament

  black players in, **5**:181-82

  earnings of players 1963, **5**:122; 1965, **5**:131; 1978,

    5:192-93

  record purse 1963, **5**:122

Masters Golf Tournament winners

  Burke 1956, **5**:98-99

  Demaret 1950, **5**:77-78

  Ford 1957, **5**:101

  Goalby 1968, **5**:145-46

  Hogan 1951, **5**:82-83; 1953, **5**:87-88

  Middlecoff 1955, **5**:97-98

  Nicklaus 1953, **5**:122; 1965, **5**:130-31; 1966, **5**:134-35;

    1972, **5**:165-66; 1975, **5**:182-83

  Palmer 1958, **5**:104-05; 1960, **5**:107; 1962, **5**:116-17; 1964,

    5:125-26

  Player 1961, **5**:111-13; 1974, **5**:178-79; 1978, **5**:192-93

  Snead 1949, **5**:71-72; 1952, **5**:85-86; 1954, **5**:93-94

Masterson, Bernie, **1**:93

Masterson, Bob, **1**:99

matadors. *See* bullfighting

Matal, Red, **1**:25

Mateer, Diehl, **11**:21

Mateo, Miguel, **10**:145

Matford, Vic, **11**:163-64

mathematics, **3**:61

Mathews, Eddie, **2**:124-25

Mathewson, Christy, **2**:6-8, 11-12, 14-15, 22, 41, 138-40

Mathias, Bob, **4**:96-98, 107-08

Mathiesen, Oscar, **9**:6

Mathisen, Charles, **9**:36

Matson, Ollie, **4**:106

Matson, Randy, **4**:155, 160-61, 163-64

Matt, Alfred, **9**:134

Matthes, Roland, **12**:78-79, 81-82, 86-88, 91-93, 101

Matthews, Stanley, **8**:34, 42

Matthews, Vince, **4**:179-82

Mauermayer, Gisela, **4**:79-80

Maxim, Joey, **7**:109

Mayberry, John, **2**:184

Mayer, Dick, **5**:94-96

Mays, Carl, **2**:25

Mays, Rex, **13**:143-44, 146

Mays, Willie, **2**:107-08, 129

Meadows, Earle, **4**:80-81

Medica, Jack, **12**:31, 37, 40-42

Medved, Alexander, **11**:100

Meggysey, Dave, **1**:180-83

Mehlhorn, Bill, **5**:22-23, 30-34

Mehrtens, Warren, **13**:45-48

Melchiorre, Gene, **3**:42

Mellor, Charles, **4**:31

Melnyk, Steve, **5**:162-63
Meminger, Dean, **3**:181
Memphis State University basketball team, **3**:54-55
Mercedes car, **13**:154
Merckx, Eddy, **10**:107
Meredith, J.E., **4**:18-19
mergers, basketball league, **3**:113, 118, 170, 191-92
  basketball league, **3**:113, 118, 170, 191-92
  in football, **1**:97, 99
  hockey league, **8**:204-05
  soccer league, **8**:58, 63
Meriwether, Delano, **4**:174
Merkle, Fred, **2**:9-12, 14
Merlin, Andre, **6**:57
Merrill, Gretchen Van Zandt, **9**:44-45
Mesbah, Mohammed Ahned, **11**:106
Meserve, Cyndi, **3**:100-01
Messersmith, Andy, **2**:184-85
Messing, Shep, **8**:75-76, 89
Metcalfe, Ralph, **4**:60-61, 64, 78
Metreveli, Aleksandr, **6**:135, 180-81
Metropolitan All Stars, **3**:10-11
Metropolitan Basketball Writers' Association, **3**:13
Metz, Nick, **8**:133
Mexican All-Stars, **8**:35
Mexican Baseball League, **2**:86-87
Mexico, bullfighters of, **10**:140
Mexico, equestrian team of, **11**:151-53
Mexico, soccer team of, **8**:20
Meyer, Debbie, **12**:77-81
Meyer, L.D. (Monk), **1**:28-30
Meyer, Louis, **13**:134, 138-39, 141
Meyers, Margaret, **9**:125-26
Miami Dolphins, **1**:151-54, 157-59
Michael, Karl, **12**:61-62
Michaels, Cynthia, **10**:29
Michigan State basketball team, **3**:98
Michigan State football team
  vs Notre Dame 1966, **1**:64-66
  vs UCLA 1956, **1**:55; 1966, **1**:63-64
Michigan State soccer team, **8**:52
Michigan University basketball team, **3**:70-71
Michigan University football team
  vs Army 1949, **1**:41-42
  Big 10 rating 1926, **1**:16
  football revenue of, **1**:9
  vs Illinois 1924, **1**:13
  vs Ohio State 1921, **1**:10; 1977, **1**:77-78; 1978: 80-81
  slush funds for athletes, **1**:177
  vs Stanford 1972, **1**:73-74
Middlecoff, Cary, **5**:72-74, 97-99
middleweight champions
  Basilio 1957, **7**:129-30
  Benvenuti 1967, **7**:170
  Cerdan 1948, **7**:90-91
  Flowers 1926, **7**:26
  Graziano 1947, **7**:80-81
  Griffith 1966, **7**:166-67

  Ketchel 1908, **7**:7
  LaMotta 1949, **7**:93
  Maxim 1952, **7**:109
  Monzon 1970, **7**:176; 1976, **7**:190-91
  Robinson 1950, **7**:100-01, 1951, **7**:101, 105-06; 1955, **7**:122; 1957, **7**:127-28; 1958, **7**:130-31
  Tiger 1962, **7**:148
  Turpin 1951, **7**:103
  Valdez 1974, **7**:184-85
  Walker 1926, **7**:32
  Zale 1946, **7**:77-78; 1948, **7**:84-85
Midkiff Seductive, **11**:164-65
Miguelin. *See* Mateo, Miguel
Mikan, George, **3**:24-26, 116-18, 120, 157
Mikita, Stan, **8**:173, 191
Mikkelsen, Roy, **9**:27
Mikulak, Mike, **1**:91
Milbank, Samuel, **11**:172
Milburn, Devereux, **10**:15, 27
Milburn, Rod, **4**:174, 179-80
Mildren, Jack, **1**:72
Mileti, Nick, **1**:155
Milford, David, **11**:19
military horsemanship, **11**:140, 142-43, 151
Mill, Andy, **9**:153-54
Miller, Al, **13**:141
Miller, Allen, **5**:162-63
Miller, Bill, **4**:64
Miller, Creighton, **1**:136
Miller, Joe, **8**:110-11
Miller, Johnny

  Bob Hope Desert Classic winner 1975, **5**:180-81
  British Open Golf Tournament 1976, winner, **5**:187-88
  earnings, **5**:174, 180-81, 183
  Masters Golf Tournament 1975, second place, **5**:182-83
  record, **5**:174-75
  United States Open Golf Tournament 1973, second place, **5**:175-76; 1973, winner, **5**:174-75

Miller, L.J., **10**:45
Miller, Marvin, **2**:188-89
Miller, Ray, **7**:107
Miller, Red, **1**:168-69
Mills, William M., **4**:153
Milne, Ross, **9**:103
Milnes, Fred, **8**:7
Milton, Tonny, **13**:132-33
Milwaukee Braves
  vs Brooklyn Dodgers 1954, **2**:106
  vs Chicago Cubs 1957, **2**:120
  vs Los Angeles Dodgers 1959, **2**:124-25
  move from Boston, **2**:100
  move to Atlanta, **2**:141
  vs New York Yankees 1957, **2**:121-23
  vs Philadelphia Phillies 1963, **2**:135
  vs Pittsburgh Pirates 1959, **2**:123
  vs San Francisco Giants 1961, **2**:129
Milwaukee Brewers, **2**:158

Milwaukee Bucks, 159
  vs Boston Celtics 1974, **3**:181-82
  vs Chicago Bulls 1971, **3**:171
  Embry as manager, **3**:174
  NBA title 1971, **3**:172
  vs Philadelphia 76ers 1970, **3**:166-68; 1971, **3**:171
Minahan, Edmond J., **4**:7
Minneapolis Lakers
  vs Boston Celtics 1959, **3**:135-36
  vs Fort Wayne Pistons 1950, **3**:119
  NBA champions 1948, **3**:116; 1950, **3**:119; 1952, **3**:120;
    1953, **3**:120-22; 1954, **3**:123
  vs New York Knicks 1949, **3**:117-18; 1960, **3**:141
  vs Washington Capitols 1949, **3**:118
Minneapolis-St. Paul football club, **1**:118
Minnesota North Stars, **8**:206
Minnesota Twins
  vs Boston Red Sox 1967, **2**:146-47
  vs California Angels 1974, **2**:174
  vs Los Angeles Dodgers 1965, **2**:143-44
  vs Oakland Athletics 1968, **2**:148
Minnesota University football team, **1**:28-29
Minnesota Vikings, **1**:148, 157-58, 161-63
Minotaur, **12**:163
Mintz, Barney, **1**:27-28
Miss America, **12**:118-20
Miss America II, **12**:121
Miss America IX, **12**:133-34
Miss America X, **12**:137
Miss Bardahl, **12**:169-70
Miss Budweiser, **12**:169-70
Miss Century 21, , **12**:163
Misstep, **13**:17-19
Mitchell, Abe, **5**:54
Mitchell, Bobby, **5**:165-66
Mittermaier, Rosi, **9**:161-64, 167
Miyazaki, Yasuji, **12**:23
Mize, Johnny, **2**:103
Moakley, John, **4**:16
Modell, Arthur B., **1**:165
Moe, Don, **5**:40-41
Moe, Karen, **12**:89-90
Moe, Per Ivar, **9**:114
Moegle, Dickey, **1**:50-51
Moffitt, Billie Jean. *See* King, Billie Jean Moffitt
Molesworth, Keith, **1**:89-92
Molinas, Jack, **3**:122-23
Momsen, Tony, **1**:42
Monday, Rick, **2**:186-87
Mondou, Pierre, **8**:205
Monk, Alice, **4**:57
monster fishing, **10**:181-84
Montague, Russell, **5**:11-13
Montana, Joe, **1**:79-80
Mont Blanc, **10**:116
Montgomery, Bill, **1**:25-26, 29-30, 68
Montgomery, Jim, **12**:93, 96-99
Monti, Eugenio, **9**:100, 107-08, 117, 128, 133, 136-37

Montreal Canadiens
  vs Boston Bruins 1931, **8**:115
  vs Chicago Black Hawks 1931, **8**:115-17; 1952, **8**:147-48;
    1960, **8**:160; 1973, **8**:190
  vs Detroit Red Wings 1937, **8**:127-28; 1952, **8**:147; 1954,
    8:149; 1955, **8**:150-52
  vs Montreal Maroons 1927, **8**:107
  Morenz on, **8**:116-17
  vs New York Rangers 1947, **8**:140; 1954, **8**:148
  Prince of Wales Cup victors 1925, **8**:104-06
  Stanley Cup victors 1924, **8**:103; 1930, **8**:113-14; 1931,
    8:118; 1944, **8**:137; 1946, **8**:137-38; 1953, **8**:149; 1956,
    8:155; 1957, **8**:156-57; 1958, **8**:158; 1959, **8**:159; 1960,
    8:160; 1965, **8**:169-70; 1966, **8**:172-73; 1968, **8**:174;
    1969, **8**:180; 1970, **8**:184-85; 1973, **8**:191; 197 , **8**:201-02;
    1977, **8**:203-04; 1978, **8**:205-06
  vs Toronto Maple Leafs 1945, **8**:137; 1947, **8**:141; 1951,
    8:145-47; 1961, **8**:161; 1967, **7**:173-74
Montreal Royals, **2**:80
Montreal Maroons
  vs Montreal Canadiens 1927, **8**:107
  vs New York Rangers 1928, **8**:109-12
  vs Ottawa Senators 1926, **8**:106
  Stanley Cup victors 1926, **8**:106-07; 1935, **8**:126
  suspension from NHL, **8**:130
  vs Toronto Maple Leafs 1932, **8**:118-19
Monzon, Carlos, **7**:190-91
Moody, Helen
  in Cannes matches 1925, **6**:32-33
  French hard court tournament winner 1930, **6**:48
  injury of, **6**:58-61
  tennis of, **6**:100-01
  in U.S. matches 1922, **6**:22-23; 1933, **6**:59-61
  U.S. matches winner 1923, **6**:24-25; 1923, **6**:28; 1925,
    6:30-31; 1927, **6**:39-40; 1928, **6**:44-45; 1929, **6**:45-46;
    1931, **6**:52-53
  Wimbledon winner 1927, **6**:38-39; 1929, **6**:45; 1930,
    6:48-49; 1935, **6**:64-65
moon, golf on, **5**:162
Moore, Archie
  light heavyweight champion 1952, **7**:112
  vs Marciano 1955, **7**:120-22
  vs Patterson 1956, **7**:125-26
Moore, Bernie, **1**:48
Moore, Bobby, **8**:55-56, 84
Moore, Charley, **4**:102
Moore, Davey
  death of, **7**:148-49
  featherweight champion 1959, **7**:131
  vs Ramos 1963, **7**:148-49
Moore, Dickie, **8**:149
Moore, Joe, **9**:10
Moore, Ken, **4**:181
Moore, Lou, **13**:134
moose hunting, **10**:159-60
Moran, Gertrude (Gussie), **6**:92
Moreno, Henry, **13**:56-57
Morenz, Howie, **8**:107, 113-14, 116-18

Morerod, Lise-Marie, **9**:160
Morlock, Max, **8**:36-37
Morozova, Olga, **6**:182-83
Morrall, Earl, **1**:139-40, 143, 150
Morris, Glenn, **4**:82, 84
Morris, Ron, **4**:141
Morrison, Allie, **11**:83-84
Morrison, Herbert, **8**:33
Morrow, Bobby, **4**:116-18, 120-21, 131
Mortanges, Pahudde, **11**:143
Mortimer, Stanley G., **11**:3-6, 8, 11, 13-14
Morton, Craig, **1**:150-51
Mosbacher, Emil Bus, **12**:163-66, 172-73
Mosconi, Willie, **11**:62-63, 65-66
Moscrip, Monk, **1**:27
Moses, Ed, **4**:189-90
Mosienko, Bill, **8**:147
Mosk, Stanley, **5**:113
Moss, Edward, **6**:47
Moss, Stirling, **13**:154, 161, 163, 165
Motherwell soccer team, **8**:20
Motley, Marion, **1**:106-08, 123
Moto Cross races, **10**:91-93
motorboats
    description of, **12**:127-28
    jet-propelled, **12**:156-59, 171-72
    popularity of racing, **12**:154
    records, **12**:133
    speed of, **12**:114-15
    women in, **12**:134-35
motorcycle racing, **10**:88-94
Motor Racing Drivers' Association of America, **13**:125-26
motor scooters, and hunting, **10**:165-66
Mottridge, Edith, **12**:38, 41
Moukhine, Lev, **7**:126
mountain climbing, **10**:109-21
mountain lion hunting, **10**:153
Mountbatten, Philip, **8**:31, 34
Mount Eiger, **10**:116
Mount Everest, **10**:111-14
Mount Rainier, **10**:117-19
Mowers, Johnny, **8**:135
Moyers, Leroy, **13**:70
Mueller, Peter, **9**:163
Mullen, John A., **7**:133-34
Mulligan, Martin, **6**:129
Mulliken, William, **12**:64-65
Mulloy, Gardnar, **6**:90-92, 96-97
Mundy, Harry, **13**:170
Muncey, Bill, **12**:163
Munn, Wayne (Big), **11**:83
Murchison, Clint, Jr., **1**:118
Murchison, Ira, **4**:117-18
Murchison, Loren, **4**:33-35
Murdoch, Murray, **8**:113
Murphy, Bob, **5**:180-81
Murphy, Eddie, **9**:16-18
Murphy, Jimmy, **13**:131-33

Murphy, Johnny, **2**:78
Murphy, Mike, **4**:17, 19, 21, 26
Murray, Charles, **1**:97
Murray, Jack, **3**:8
Murray, "Red", **2**:14-15
Musial, Stan, **2**:104-05, 109-11, 116
Mussolini, Benito, **8**:21, 26-27
Musson, Ron, **12**:169-70
Mustonen, Kaija, **9**:127-28
Mutch, George, **8**:27
Mutters, M., **8**:12
My Gallant, **13**:77
My Request, **13**:49-51
Myrha, Steve, **1**:113-15
Myrra, J., **4**:27, 34

Naber, John, **12**:91-93, 96-99, 102-03
Nadig, Marie Therese, **9**:142-43, 146
Nagel, Judy Ann, **9**:129-30
Nagle, Kelvin, **5**:119-20, 131-32
Nagle, W.J., **9**:41
Nagurski, Bronco, **1**:93, 99
Naismith, James, **3**:2, 11, 14-15
Nakama, Keo, **12**:42-43
Namath, Joe, **1**:126, 139-46, 156-57
Nambu, Chuker, **4**:66
Napoles, Jose, **7**:188
Nardiello, Vincent, **7**:85, 107
NASA, **10**:128
Nash, Tony, **9**:107-08
Nashua, **13**:57-61
Nastase, Ilie
    conduct of, **6**:194
    vs Connors 1977, **6**:195
    in Davis Cup matches, 1969, **6**:165
    U.S. Open winner 1972, **6**:177
    in Wimbledon matches 1972, **6**:176-77; 1976, 192
Natchez, **13**:47-49
National Amateur Athletic Union. *See* Amateur Athletic Union
National Association for Stock Car Auto Racing, **13**:170, 182-83, 187
National Association of Audubon Societies, **10**:152
National Association of Basketball Coaches, **3**:96-97
National Association of Minor Baseball Leagues, **2**:4
National Association of Professional Baseball Players, **2**:157
National Association of Professional Basketball Leagues, **3**:113
National Basketball Association
    Chicago team, **3**:136
    and Erving, **3**:177-78
    fine of Washington Bullets by, **3**:196-97
    and Hawkins, **3**:163-64

and Haywood, 3:172
home games, 3:197-99
Kennedy as president of, 3:145-46
merger with ABA, 3:170, 191-92
new teams in, 3:156, 159, 166
O'Brien as commissioner of, 3:183-84
pact with players, 3:178
player dispute with, 3:157-58
playoff money increased, 3:159
and Porter, 3:82-83
and race relations, 3:135
rivalry with ABA, 3:160
strike threatened, 3:148
subsidies to stars, 3:186-88
and zone defense, 3:199-200
National Basketball Association champions
    Boston Celtics 1953, 3:130-31; 1959, 3:135-36; 1960,
        3:140-41; 1962, 3:144; 1964, 3:149; 1965, 3:151-52;
        1966, 3:155; 1968, 3:162; 1969, 3:162-63; 1974, 3:181-
        82; 1976, 3:190-91
    Golden State Warriors 1975, 3:185
    Los Angeles Lakers 1972, 3:176-77
    Milwaukee Bucks 1971, 3:172
    Minneapolis Lakers 1950, 3:119; 1952, 3:120; 1953, 3:120-
        22; 1954, 3:123
    New York Knicks 1970, 3:168-70; 1973, 3:178
    Philadelphia 76ers 1967, 3:158
    Philadelphia Warriors 1956, 126-27
    Rochester Royals 1951, 3:119-20
    Saint Louis Hawks 1958, 3:133-35
    Syracuse Nationals 1955, 3:124
    Washington Bullets 1978, 3:202-03
National Basketball League championship, 3:116-17
National Boxing Association
    freezing of titles, 7:74
    Johnson as world champion, 7:146
    safety code, 7:83
    title contenders, 7:74
National Collegiate Athletic Association, and basketball
    expansion of tournament, 3:84
    and Madison Square Garden games, 3:40
    and Porter, 3:82-83
    and rules, 3:8, 46
National Collegiate Association, basketball champions
    California 1959, 3:58-59
    Cincinnati 1961, 3:63-64; 1962, 3:67-68
    Holy Cross 1947, 3:29-30
    Illinois 1951, 3:40-41
    Indiana 1953, 3:48; 1976, 3:101-02
    Kansas 1952, 3:43-44
    Kentucky 1948, 3:32; 1951, 3:41; 1958, 3:56; 1978,
        3:106-07
    LaSalle 1954, 3:49
    Marquette 1977, 3:102-04
    New York University 1950, 3:36-37
    North Carolina 1974, 3:97-98
    Ohio 1960, 3:61
    San Francisco 1955, 3:51; 1956, 3:52

    Stanford 1942, 3:19
    Texas Western 1966, 3:71-72
    UCLA 1964, 3:68-69; 1967, 3:74-75; 1968, 3:77, 1969,
        3:79; 1970, 3:80; 1971, 3:81-82; 1972, 3:83-84; 1973,
        3:88-89; 1975, 3:99-100
    Utah 1944, 3:21
    Wisconsin 1941, 3:18
    Wyoming, 1943, 3:19
National Collegiate Athletic Association, and football,
    1:15, 47, 68-70, 184-85
National Collegiate Athletic Association, lacrosse cham-
    pionship, 10:84-87
National Collegiate Athletic Association, soccer champions
    Navy 1964, 8:52
    St. Louis University 1959, 8:43; 1960, 8:46-47; 1962,
        8:50; 1970, 8:70; 1974, 8:79
    San Francisco 1967, 8:58; 1976, 8:75
National Collegiate Athletic Association, and swimming
    championship 1969, 12:84; 1977, 12:102-5
    dead start system, 12:14
    rules, 12:6
National Collegiate Athletic Association, and track and
    field, 4:55, 150-51, 161-62, 199-200
National Collegiate Athletic Association, wrestling tourn-
    ament. See college, wrestling
national figure skating champions
    Albright 1953, 9:74; 1965, 9:88
    Button 1945, 9:44; 1960, 9:61
    Fleming 1966, 9:120-21
    Hoyt 1962, 9:102
    Jenkins (Hayes) 1954, 9:74; 1956, 9:88-89
    Lee 1935, 9:28; 1937, 9:41-42
    Lynn 1971, 9:140
    Petkevich 1971, 9:140
    Turner 1929, 9:14
    Wood 1968, 9:138
    Vinson 1929, 9:14; 1933, 9:27; 1935, 9:28
National Football League
    admission of new teams, 1:118
    and Baltimore club, 1:108
    championship 1943, 1:97-99; 1950, 1:105-6; 1951,
        1:106-8; 1953, 1:109
    and Cleveland club, 1:93
    and drugs in football, 1:183
    Eastern-Western divisions of, 1:104-05
    and Hapes-Filchock scandal, 1:101-02
    and Layden, 1:96, 100
    merger with AFL, 1:128-29
    merger with All-American Conference, 1:103
    player plan, 1:92
    player-reserve system, 1:160-61
    players as labor union, 1:136
    players' strike, 1:160, 163-64
    Rozelle as comissioner of, 1:117-18
    stocking plan, 1:165
    suspension of players, 1:124-26
    and WFL, 1:164-65

National Hockey League
  franchises of, **8**:107, 120, 170-71, 182, 193-94
  gambling probe by, **8**:142
  and Howe, **8**:191-92
  St. Louis Eagles' defranchising, **8**:126-27
  suspension of Montreal Maroons, **8**:130
  and violence, **8**:195
  and WHA, **8**:185-86, 192, 204-05
National Hockey League Players' Association, **8**:156, 200-01,
National Horse Show, **11**:140, 142-48, 150-52, 158-59, 162
National Hot Rod Association, **13**:183-84
nationalism, and soccer, **8**:92-96
National League. *See* baseball, National League
National League of Professional Baseball Clubs, **2**:4, 157-58
national regatta, **12**:149-51
National Rifle Association, **10**:185, 194-95
national rowing championship, **12**:170
national ski championship, **9**:43
national ski jump contest, **9**:27
Native Dancer, **13**:56-57
Nave, Doyle, **1**:30-31
Navratilova, Martina, **6**:186, 201-02
Navy crew, **12**:121-22, 124-25, 156, 161-62
Navy football team, **1**:36-39, 44-45, 60-62
Nazaruk, Mike **13**:150-51
Nazis, **5**:55, 7:50, **11**:86
Nazlimov, Vladimir, **11**:126-27
Neal, Richard, **1**:164
Neale, Earle, **1**:97
Nebraska University football team, **1**:13, 33, 72
Needless, **13**:61-62
Negley, William, ,**10**:163-64
Negrea, Gheorghe, **7**:126
Negroes. *See* blacks
Nehmer, Meinhard, **9**:167-68
Neilson, Sandra, **12**:86
Nella Dillon, **13**:97
Nelson, Byron, **5**:64-65, 68-70, 126
Nelson, Cindy, **9**:157
Nelson, Edmund (Gunner), **13**:160-61
Nelson, Marjorie Jackson, **4**:114
Nelson-Mitchell bowling team, **11**:67
Nepela, Ondrej, **9**:151-52
Neri, Romeo, **11**:128
Nesseth, Don, **7**:140-41
Netherlands, the. *See* Holland
Nettles, Graig, **2**:188, 190
Neumann, Paul, **3**:150
Neun, Johnny, **2**:40
neurosurgeons and knockouts, **7**:138
Neusel, Walter, **7**:50
Nevele Pride, **13**:116
Neville, Dave, **9**:39
Newcastle United soccer team, **8**:33, 79-80
Newcombe, Don, **2**:88-89, 93
Newcombe, John,
  in Davis Cup matches 1963, **6**:131

in U.S. matches 1966, **6**:144; 1973, **6**:182
  U.S. matches winner 1967, **6**:150-51
  in Wimbledon matches 1968, **6**:158; 1969, **6**:164-65
  Wimbledon winner 1967, **6**:146; 1971, **6**:173-74
  on World Tennis Team, **6**:179
New England Whalers, **8**:190
Newman, Harry, **1**:89-91
New Orleans Jazz, **3**:200-01
New Orleans Saints, **1**:130
Newton, Al, **1**:180
Newton, A.L., **4**:7
New York Americans, **8**:129
New York Celtics, **3**:112-13
New York Cosmos, **8**:76, 84-85, 88-90
New York Generals, **8**:62
New York Giants, baseball team
  vs Boston Braves 1916, **2**:20-21
  vs Boston Red Sox 1912, **2**:14-16
  vs Brooklyn Dodgers 1934, **2**:53-54; 1951, **2**:94-95
  vs Chicago Cubs 1908, **2**:9-12; 1912, **2**:13-14
  vs Cincinnati Reds 1937, **2**:61
  vs Cleveland Indians 1954, **2**:107-08
  Hornsby trade, **2**:39-40
  and Marquard, **2**:13-14
  move to San Franciso, **2**:119-20
  vs Philadelphia Athletics 1905, **2**:6-8
  vs Philadelphia Phillies 1952, **2**:97
  vs Pittsburgh Pirates 1949, **2**:87
  vs St. Louis Cardinals 1933, **2**:46-48; 1954, **2**:104-05
New York Giants football team, **1**:87-92, 94, 113-15, 120
New York Islanders, **8**:192, 196-99
New York Jets, **1**:139-43, 156-57
New York Knicks, **3**:113-16
  vs Boston Celtics 1958, **3**:132-33; 1960, **3**:139
  vs Chicago Stags 1946, **3**:114
  vs Cincinnati Royals 1969, **3**:164-65
  vs Los Angeles Lakers 1970, **3**:168; 1972, **3**:176-77
  vs Minneapolis Lakers 1949, **3**:117-18; 1952, **3**:120; 1953, **3**:120-22
  NBA champions 1970, **3**:168-70; 1973, **3**:178
  vs Philadelphia Warriors 1960, **3**:139
  vs Rochester Royals 1951, **3**:119-20
  vs San Francisco Warriors 1963, **3**:146
New York Marathon, **4**:200-01
New York Mets
  vs Baltimore Orioles 1969, **2**:156-57
  vs Chicago Cubs 1973, **2**:170
  vs Philadelphia Phillies 1964, **2**:136-37
  vs St. Louis Cardinals 1964, **2**:140-41; 1969, **2**:155-56; 1974, **2**:173-74
  vs San Diego Padres 1970, **2**:159
  vs San Francisco Giants 1964, **2**:135-36
New York National League basketball club, **2**:4, 6
New York Nationals, **8**:16-17
New York Nets, **3**:188-89, 192-94
New York Rangers, **8**:103
  vs Boston Bruins 1929, **8**:112-13; 1939, **8**:130-32; 1972, **8**:187-88

Boucher on, **8**:136
vs Chicago Black Hawks 1952, **8**:147
vs Detroit Red Wings 1937, **8**:128; 1944, **8**:136; 1950, **8**:144-45; 1953, **8**:148
vs Montreal Canadiens 1925, **8**:104-6; 1947, **8**:140; 1953, **8**:148
vs Montreal Maroons 1928, **8**:109-10
vs St. Louis Blues 1974, **8**:195
Sanderson on, **8**:193
Stanley Cup victors 1928, **8**:110-12; 1933, **8**:121-22; 1940, **8**:133-34;
vs Toronto Maple Leafs, 1932, **8**:119-20
New York Soccer Club, **8**:9-10, 71
New York University basketball team
. vs CCNY 1934, **3**:9; 1947, **3**:27-28
vs Cincinnati 1960, **3**:61
vs Notre Dame 1948, **3**:30
Notre Dame game cancelled, **3**:9
vs Ohio 1945, **3**:23-24
St. Louis 1948, **3**:31
New York University fencing team, **11**:125-26
New York University football team, **1**:177
New York Yankees baseball team
vs Boston Americans 1908, **2**:8
vs Boston Red Sox 1949, **2**:87-88; 1951, **2**:92-93; 1956, **2**:116; 1961, **2**:129-30
vs Brooklyn Dodgers 1941, **2**:72-73; 1947, **2**:81-85; 1953, **2**:102-04; 1955, **2**:111-13; 1956, **2**:116-19
Gehrig on, **2**:64-67
vs Kansas City Royals 1976, **2**:189-90
vs Los Angeles Dodgers 1977, **2**:192-95
Martin as manager of, **2**:195-96
vs Milwaukee Braves 1957, **2**:121-23
vs Philadelphia Athletics 1936, **2**:60
vs Pittsburgh Pirates 1960, **2**:125-26
player purchase, **2**:187-88
Ruth purchase, **2**:23
vs St. Louis Cardinals 1926, **2**:36-38
vs Washington 1908, **2**:8-9
vs Washington Senators 1953, **2**:100-01; 1956, **2**:115-16
New York Yankees football team, **1**:101
Nicklaus, Jack
and American Professional Golfers, **5**:156
British Open Golf Tournament 1966, winner, **5**:142-43; 1968, second place, **5**:154-55; 1970, winner, **5**:161-62; 1972, second place, **5**:187-88; 1977, second place, **5**:190-91
and civil rights demonstration, **5**:158
earnings of, **5**:117, 122, 124, 130, 134, 144, 161, 163, 165, 167-68, 176-77, 183-84
hard hits of, **5**:119
Masters Golf Tournament 1963, winner, **5**:122, 1964, second place, **5**:125-26; 1965, winner, **5**:130-31; 1966, winner, **5**:134-35; 1972, winner, **5**:165-66; 1975, winner **5**:182-83
and new golf rules, **5**:139-40
portrait of, **5**:168-72
Professional Golfers' Association Tournament 1962,

third place, **5**:121; 1963, winner, **5**:124; 1964, **5**:128-30; 1973, winner, **5**:176; 1975, winner, **5**:185-86
record, **5**:130-31
in top 5 poll, **5**:173
in United States Amateur Golf final 1959, **5**:106-7; 1961, **5**:114-16
United States Open Golf Tournament 1960, second place, **5**:109-11; 1962, winner, **5**:117-19; 1967, winner, **5**:144-45; 1968, second place, **5**:146-47; 1971, second place, **5**:163; 1972, winner, **5**:166-67; 1973, fourth place, **5**:175-76
Walt Disney World Classic 1973, **5**:176-77
Nichols, Bob, **5**:128-30
Nieder, Bill, **4**:133-34
Niederhoffer, Victor, **11**:26
Nielsen, Kurt, **6**:98, 107
night game
baseball, **2**:56, 62-63
football, **1**:17
soccer, **8**:15
Nikandrov, Yuri, **10**:50
Niles, Nathaniel, **9**:6-7, 14-15
Nilson, Laila Schou, **9**:29-31
Nilsson, Jonny, **9**:103
Nimbus, **13**:53
Nitschke, Ray, **1**:138
Nixon, Richard, **1**:68, 154, 182, **11**:74
Noll, Chuck, **1**:166
Nolting, Ray, **1**:95-96
Nones, Franco, **9**:124
Norbis, Ana Marie, **12**:77
Norelius, Martha, **12**:12, 14, 20, 28
Norkay, Tensing, **10**:114
Norris, James D., **7**:119, 128-29, 139
North American figure-skating contest, **9**:44-45
North American ski contest, **9**:60-61
North American Soccer League, **8**:53, 57, 64, 86-89
college draft, **8**:75
foreigners in, **8**:90
franchises, **8**:71, 79
and International Football Federation, **8**:96
new format of, **8**:90
North American Soccer League champions
Atlanta Chiefs 1968, **8**:64
Los Angeles Aztecs 1975, **8**:83-84
New York Cosmos 1973, **8**:76; 1977, **8**:89-90
Tampa Bay Rowdies 1975, **8**:85
North, Andy, **5**:194-95
North Carolina University basketball team, **3**:27, 55, 75-76, 97-98
Northcott, Baldy, **8**:126
Northwestern University basketball team, **3**:10
Northwestern University football team, **1**:28-29
Northwestern University soccer team, **8**:7-8
Norton, B.I.C., **6**:18
Norton, Ken, **7**:189
vs Ali 1973, **7**:182-83; 1976, **7**:192-93
vs Holmes 1978, **7**:198-99

and WBC, **7**:196
Norton, Ray, **4**:142-43
Norway, ski team of, **9**:7-9
Norway, soccer team of, **8**:25
Norway, Winter Olympics winner, 1924, **9**:9; 1928, **9**:12-13; 1952, **9**:71-72
Norway, yachting team of, **12**:123, 141
Nosakova, Eliska, **11**:129
Notre Dame College basketball team, **3**:10, 30, 86-88, 95-96
Notre Dame college crew, **12**:169-70
Notre Dame College football team
   vs Army games disbanded, **1**:178-79
   vs Army 1913, **1**:7-8; 1929, **1**:20-22; 1946, **1**:35-36; 1957, **1**:52-53
   vs Michigan 1966, **1**:64-66
   vs Nebraska 1924, **1**:13
   vs Oklahoma 1957, **1**:57-58
   vs Purdue 1950, **1**:43-44
   records, **1**:15, 23-24, 44
   vs Stanford 1925, **1**:15-16
   vs Texas 1970, **1**:70-71; 1971, **1**:71-72
   T formation of, **1**:34
   travels of, **1**:8
   vs USC 1931, **1**:23-24; 1978, **1**:79-80
Nottingham Forest soccer team, **8**:41-42
Novikova, Elena, **11**:126
Noyelle, Andre, **10**:100
Noyes, Albertina, **9**:120
Nunes, Leo, **11**:120
Nuremberg Soccer Club, **8**:37
Nurmi, Paavo, **4**:37-41, 49, 51-52, 58, 87, 101
Nuthall, Betty, **6**:39-40
Nyilas, Tiber, **11**:125-26

Oakland Athletics
   vs Detroit Tigers 1968, **2**:149-51
   vs Los Angeles Dodgers 1974, **2**:176-78
   vs Minnesota Twins 1968, **2**:148
   move from Kansas City, **2**:147-48
   voided player sale, **2**:187-88
Oakland Clippers, **8**:63
Oakland Raiders, **1**:137, 139, 146, 167-68
Oberst, Eugene, **4**:34
Obert, Carl, **11**:24
O'Bolger, Diego, **10**:146-47
O'Brien, Jim, **1**:150-51
O'Brien, Johnny, **3**:47
O'Brien, Lawrence, **3**:183-84, 196-97
O'Brien, Parry, **4**:112-13, 123-24, 133
O'Callaghan, Patrick, **4**:60-61
Ochoa, Francisco Fernandez, **9**:150
O'Connor, Christy, **5**:132-34
O'Day, Hank, **2**:9-10
O'Day, George, **12**:163
O'Donnell, Eddie, **13**:131
Oerter, Al, **4**:141-42, 148-50, 154-56, 164

Ogutu, Matthew, **10**:191
Ohio State basketball team, **3**:16-18, 23-24, 27, 61, 76
Ohio State football team
   Hayes as coach of, **1**:47
   vs Michigan 1921, **1**:10; 1977, **1**:77-78; 1978, **1**:80-81
   vs USC 1975, **1**:74
Oh, Sadaharu, **2**:191
Oimet, Francis, **5**:9-11, 13, 17-18, 40-41
Oimoen, Casper, **9**:27
Okeson, Walter, **1**:33-34
Okker, Tom, **6**:160-62
Oklahoma A & M basketball team, **3**:24-27, 34-35
Oklahoma A & M wrestling team, **11**:86
Oklahoma State wrestling team, **11**:97
Oklahoma University football team, **1**:57-58, 72, 184-85
Oldfield, Barney, **13**:123, 130
Olinski, Jerry, **8**:153
Oliver, Ed, **5**:70, 87-88
Olmedo, Alex, **6**:121-24
Olsen, Zoe Ann, **12**:44,46
Olson, Carl (Bobo), **7**:100-01, 122
Olympic aquatic events
   1920, **12**:9
   1924, **12**:12-14
   1928, **12**:20-21
   1932, **12**:23-31
   1936, **12**:32-42
   1948, **12**:43-48
   1952, **12**:50-55
   1956, **12**:55-61
   1960, **12**:62-67
   1964, **12**:67-71
   1968, **12**:76-82
   1972, **12**:84-91
   1976, **12**:91-102
Olympic archery, **10**:5-6
Olympic basketball
   1936, **3**:9, 11
   1948, **3**:33-34
   1952, **3**:45-46
   1956, **3**:52-53
   1960, **3**:62
   1964, **3**:69
   1968, **3**:78
   1972, **3**:85-86
Olympic bicycle racing, **10**:97-101, 104, 106-07
Olympic bobsled race winners
   Bott 1948, **9**:49
   Britain 1964, **9**:107-08
   East Germany 1976, **9**:167-68
   Canada 1964, **9**:116-17
   Fishbacher 1948, **9**:49
   Italy 1968, **9**:128
   Monti 1968, **9**:136-37
   Switzerland 1936, **9**:34; 1956, **9**:84-85; 1972, **9**:149
   United States 1928, **9**:12; 1932, **9**:21-22, 25; 1936, **9**:36-38; 1948, **9**:57-58
   West Germany 1962, **9**:64, 70-71

Olympic boxing
    Bobick in 1972, **7**:179-81
    Frazier in 1964, **7**:159-60
    United States gold medal 1932, **7**:44; 1952, **7**:110; 1956, **7**:126; 1960, **7**:139; 1968, **7**:173; 1976, **7**:191-92
Olympic canoe race
    1948, **12**:153-54
    1952, **12**:156
    1956, **12**:159
    1960, **12**:161
    1968, **12**:174
    1972, **12**:177
Olympic carbine championship, **10**:46
Olympic clay-pigeon shoot, **10**:50, 52
Olympic diving
    Capilla·victory 1956, **12**:60
    Chandler victory 1976, **12**:94
    Gossick victory 1968, **12**:76
    McCormick victory 1952, **12**:52; 1956, **12**:57
    Poynton victory 1932, **12**:28-29, 1936, **12**:38-41
    scoring rules, **12**:60
    United States in 1932, **12**:29-30; 1936, 34-40; 1948, **12**:46-47; 1952, **12**:51; 1956, **12**:61-62
Olympic equestrian events, **11**:140-62
Olympic fencing, **11**:118, 121-27
Olympic field hockey, **10**:33
Olympic figure skating champions
    Albright 1956, **9**:82-83
    Button 1948, **9**:51-52, 54-55; 1952, **1**:57-59
    Curry 1976, **9**:161
    Dijkstra 1964, **9**:110-11
    Fleming 1968, **9**:126
    Hamill 1976, **9**:164, 168
    Heiss 1960, **9**:93-94
    Henie 1928, **9**:12; 1936, **9**:38-39
    Jenkins (David) 1960,.**9**:96-97
    Jenkins (Hayes) 1956, **9**:80-82
    Schafer 1932, **9**:20-21
    Schnelldorfer 1964, **9**:116
    Schuba 1972, **9**:146
    Schwarz 1968, **9**:133-34
    Scott 1948, **9**:56-57
Olympic figure skating champions, pairs
    Baier-Herber 1936, **9**:35-36
    Belousova-Protopopov 1964, **9**:104; 1968, **9**:131-32
    Gorshkov-Pakhomova 1976, **9**:154
    Oppelt-Schwarz 1956, **9**:84
    Paul-Wagner 1960, **9**:89-90
    Rodnina-Ulanov 1972, **9**:147
    Rodnina-Zaitsev 1976, **9**:156
Olympic figure skating, scoring of, **9**:96
Olympic Games, **1**:12
    1896 (Athens), **4**:2-4
    1900 (Paris), **4**:4-7
    1904 (St. Louis), **4**:7-8
    1908 (London), **4**:12-14
    1912 (Stockholm), **4**:17-23

    1920 (Antwerp), **4**:27-32
    1924 (Colombes), **4**:34-42
    1928 (Amsterdam), **4**:44-55
    1932 (Los Angeles), **4**:59-72
    1936 (Berlin), **4**:76-87
    1948 (London), **4**:89-101
    1952 (Helsinki), **4**:102-12
    1956 (Melbourne), **4**:117-28, **12**:61
    1960 (Rome), **4**:133-45
    1964 (Tokyo), **4**:153-60, **12**:70
    1968 (Mexico City), **4**:163-72
    1972 (Munich), **4**:174-83
    1976 (Montreal), **4**:187-96
Olympic gymnastics, **11**:128-36
Olympic hockey
    Canada in 1920, **9**:7; 1924, **9**:9; 1932, **9**:23-24; 1936, **9**:31; 1952, **9**:69
    Czechoslovakia in 1976, **9**:164. 167
    dispute about 1948, **9**:48, 57-59
    Finland in 1976, **9**:160, 167
    France in 1924, **9**:8
    Poland in 1976, **9**:164
Olympic judo, **11**:44-45, 97-98
Olympic kayak race 1972, **12**:178
Olympic luge race. *See* Olympic toboggan race champions
Olympic pistol shooting, **10**:43-44, 46, 49
Olympic polo, **10**:20
Olympic Regatta
    1920, **12**:118
    1928, **12**:127-28
    1948, **12**:153-54
Olympic riflery, **10**:38-40, 43-44, 48-51
Olympic rowing
    1924, **12**:123
    1936, **12**:141
    1948, **12**:152-53
    1956, **12**:159
    1960, **12**:161-62
    1964, **12**:168
    1968, **12**:173
    1972, **12**:177-78
    1976, **12**:181
Olympic rugby, **10**:72-74
Olympic running deer shoot, **10**:43, 45, 49
Olympic sailing
    monotypes in, **12**:135
    1932, **12**:135-36
    1952, **12**:156
Olympic ski course, **9**:105
Olympic ski jump champions
    Aschenbach 1976, **9**:156-57
    Beloussov 1968, **9**:136-37
    Bergmann 1952, **9**:71-72
    Engan 1964, **9**:119-20
    Hyvarinen 1956, **9**:86-87
    Kankkonen 1964, **9**:106-07
    Kasaya 1972, **9**:144-45

Ruud 1932, **9**:22-23; 1936, **9**:39
Schnabl 1976, **9**:168
Thoma 1960, **9**:92
Olympic ski race champions
  Beiser 1948, **9**:53
  Berthod 1956, **9**:82
  Biebl 1960, **9**:90-91
  Boyarskikh 1964, **9**:113
  Cochran 1972, **9**:148-49
  Colliard 1956, **9**:78-79
  Cranz 1932, **9**:29-30
  Eriksen 1952, **9**:64
  Fraser 1948, **9**:54-55
  Goitschel (Christine) 1964, **9**:107-08
  Goitschel (Marielle) 1964, **9**:111-12; 1968, **9**:129-30
  Greene 1968, **9**:132-33
  Groenningen 1968, **9**:127
  Grow 1976, **9**:167
  Haas 1964, **9**:115
  Hakulinen 1956, **9**:76
  Hemmi 1976, **9**:160-61
  Hinterseer 1960, **9**:94-95
  Killy 1968, **9**:125-26, 128-29, 134-35
  Klammer 1976, **9**:153
  Kreiner 1976, **9**:164, 166-67
  Larsson 1936, **9**:35
  Lawrence 1952, **9**:63, 68
  Mittermaier 1976, **9**:157, 161-63
  Nadig 1972, **9**:142-43, 146
  Ochoa 1972, **9**:150
  Reichert 1956, **9**:75-76
  Russi 1972, **9**:145
  Ruud 1936, **9**:29
  Sailer 1956, **9**:79-80, 83-84
  Staub 1960, **9**:91-92
  Stiegler 1964, **9**:118-19
  Vuarnet 1960, **9**:92-93
  Wehling 1976, **9**:159
  Zimmermann 1964, **9**:104-05
Olympic ski race champions, cross-country
  Bajukov 1976, **9**:157-58
  Boyarskikh 1964, **9**:114
  Brenden 1952, **9**:66-67; 1956, **9**:78-79
  Finland 1952, **9**:71
  Gustafsson 1968, 125, 130, 136
  Hakulinen 1960, **9**:98
  Hamalainen 1960, **9**:98
  Jernberg 1960, **9**:89-90
  Koulakova 1972, **9**:144, 146-47, 149
  Leslander 1960, **9**:92
  Maentyranta 1964, **9**:110-11
  Nones 1968, **9**:124
  Saveliev 1976, **9**:153
  Soviet Union 1956, **9**:84-85; 1964, **9**:116-17; 1972, **9**:150
  Takola 1976, **9**:156-57
  Vedenine 1972, **9**:142
  Videman 1952, **9**:71
Olympic ski race champions, marathon

Jernberg 1956, **9**:82-83; 1964, **9**:113-14
Sweden 1936, **9**:39
Olympic ski race champions, military patrol
  Italy 1936, **9**:37
  Norway 1928, **9**:10
  Switzerland 1948, **9**:59
Olympic ski race champions, relay
  Finland 1936, **9**:32-33; 1952, **9**:71; 1976, **9**:162
Olympic soccer
  1924 Uruguay vs Holland, **8**:12
  1936 Peru vs Austria, **8**:26
  1952 U.S. vs Italy, **8**:33
  1952 Yugoslavia vs Soviet Union, **8**:34
  1956 Soviet Union victory, **8**:38
  1960 Yugoslavia victory, **8**:46
  1964, Hungary victory, **8**:52
Olympic speed-skating champions, 1500-meter
  Andersen 1952, **9**:66-67
  Antson 1964, **9**:115
  Grishin 1956, **9**:78
  Holum 1972, **9**:146-47
  Mathiesen 1936, **9**:36
  Mikhailov 1956, **9**:78
  Mustonen 1968, **9**:127-28
  Schenk 1972, **9**:144-45, 150
  Shea 1932, **9**:18
  Skoblikova 1960, **9**:91-92; 1964, 106-07
  Storholt 1976, **9**:166
  Stepanskaya 1976, **9**:153-54
  Verkerk 1968, **9**:133-34
Olympic speed-skating champions, 500-meter
  Ballangrud 1936, **9**:33-34
  Grishin 1956, **9**:76-77
  Helgesen 1948, **9**:48-49
  Henning 1972, **9**:147-48
  Henry 1952, **9**:64-65
  Jewtraw 1924, **9**:7-8
  Keller 1968, **9**:130-31; 1972, **9**:142-43
  Kulikov 1976, **9**:160
  McDermott 1964, **9**:112
  Shea 1932, **9**:16-18
  Skoblikova 1964, **9**:104-05
  Titova 1968, **9**:125-26
  Young 1976, **9**:154-55
Olympic speed-skating champions, 5000-meter
  Andersen 1952, **9**:65-66
  Ballangrud 1928, **9**:10-11; 1936, **9**:34
  Jaffee 1932, **9**:16-18
  Kosichkin 1960, **9**:95-96
  Schenk 1972, **9**:142-43
  Shilkov 1956, **9**:77-78
  Thunberg 1924, **9**:7-8
Olympic speed-skating champions, 1000-meter
  Geijssen 1968, **9**:128
  Guseva 1960, **9**:92
  Mueller 1976, **9**:163-64
  Skoblikova 1964, **9**:106-10
  Young 1976, 155-56

Olympic speed-skating champions, 10,000 meter
    Andersen 1952, **9**:67
    Ericsson 1956, **9**:79-80
    Formo 1976, **9**:167
    Jaffee 1928, **9**:11; 1932, **9**:18-19
    Johannesen 1960, **9**:97-98
    Schenk 1972, **9**:145-46, 150
    Seffarth 1948, **9**:52
Olympic speed-skating champions, 3000-meter
    Averina 1976, **9**:158
    Baas-Kaiser 1972, **9**:149
    Schut 1968, **9**:129
    Skoblikova 1964, **9**:110-11
Olympic toboggan race champions
    Austria 1964, **9**:113-14
    East Germany 1968, **9**:136
    Fendt 1976, **9**:154
    West Germany 1964, **9**:112-13
Olympic trapshooting, **10**:42-43, 45
Olympic volleyball, **11**:44-46
Olympic water skiing, **12**:110
Olympic weight lifting, **11**:105-08, 110-12
Olympic wrestling, **11**:83-84, 86-87, 92-95, 99-100, 103
Olympic yacht race
    1924, **12**:123
    1932, **12**:136
    1936, **12**:140-41
    1956, **12**:159
    1960, **12**:163
    1964, **12**:168-69
    1968, **12**:174
Omaha, **13**:26-29
O'Malley, Walter F., **2**:127
Omar Khayyam, **13**:7
Omwake, Howard, **1**:178
O'Neill, Brian, **8**:186
O'Neill, Frankie, **13**:12
Oosterhuis, Peter, **5**:180
Oppelt, Kurt, **9**:84
Orantes, Manuel, **6**:188-89
Orban, Alex, **11**:126-27
Ordonez, Antonio, **10**:142-44
Ord, Tommy, **8**:89-90
Oregon University basketball team, **3**:16
Original Celtics, **3**:113-14, 116
Orlich, Dan, **10**:51
O'Rourke, Charlie, **1**:96-97
Orr, Bobby, **8**:175-79, 182
Ortega y Gasset, José, **10**:176
Ortiz, Carlos
    vs Laguna 1965, **7**:161
    lightweight champion 1962, **7**:145
    vs Ramos 1966, **7**:167-68
Ortmann, Charley, **1**:41-42
Osborne, Harold, **4**:35, 40
Osborne, Margaret. *See* duPont, Margaret Osborne
O'Shea, Kevin, **3**:30
Ostler, Andreas, **9**:70-71

O'Toole, Jim, **2**:132
Ottawa Senators, **8**:106, 109, 120
Ott, Melvin, **2**:61
Otto, Jim, **1**:145-46
Our Native, **13**:75-76
Out of their League (Meggysey and Scott), **1**:182-83
Overton, Johnny, **4**:26
Owen, Maribel. *See* Vinson, Maribel
Owen, Mickey, **2**:72-73, 86-87
Owen, Steve, **1**:135
Owens, Jesse, **4**:75-81, 101-02, 154
Oxford University crew race, **12**:136
Oxford University rugby team, **10**:77-79
Oyakawa, Yoshinobu, **12**:53-54
Oyama, Masutatsu, **11**:95-96

pacers, **13**:94-119
Pacheco, Tommy, **7**:138
Pack, Rod, **10**:125
paddle tennis, **10**:36-37
Paddock, Charles, **4**:27-28, 30, 32, 34-37
Padgham, Alfred, **5**:54
Pafko, Andy, **2**:93
Page, Estelle Lawson, **5**:63
Page, George, **9**:31
Paige, Satchel, **2**:151, 161-65
Paille, Marcel, **8**:159
Pakhomova, Ludmila, **9**:151, 154
Pakistan, field hockey team of, **10**:34-35
Pakistani squash racquets players, **11**:20
Pak, Mrs. Yung Sun, **11**:43
Palace club, **3**:112
Palermo, Frank (Blinky), **7**:135, 139
Palestine, soccer in, **8**:16
Palfrey, Sarah, **6**:58-59, 79
Palin, **13**:100-02
Palmer, Arnold
    British Open Golf Tournament 1961, winner, **5**:113-14; 1962, winner, **5**:119-20
    earnings, **5**:117, 119, 122-24
    Masters Golf Tournament 1958 winner, **5**:104-05; 1960 winner, **5**:107; 1961, second place, **5**:111-13; 1962, winner, **5**:116-17; 1964, winner, **5**:125-26; 1965, second place, **5**:130-31
    popularity of, **5**:158
    Professional Golfers' Association Tournament 1964, third place, **5**:128-30
    in top 5 poll, **5**:173
    United States Open Golf Tournament 1960, winner, **5**:109-11; 1962, second place, **5**:117-19, 1963, third place, **5**:123-24; 1966, second place, **5**:140-42; 1967, second place, **5**:144-45; 1972, third place, **5**:166-67
Pan American Sports Organization, **10**:66
Papanicolaou, Christos, **4**:173
Paprocky, Raymond, **3**:65
Papyrus, **13**:13-14
Paraguay soccer team, **8**:19

Parent, Bernie, **8**:192, 199-200
Parenti, Michael, **3**:65
Paret, Benny (Kid),
  brain operation, **7**:142-43
  death of, **7**:144
  vs Griffith 1961, **7**:140; 1962, **7**:142-44
  welterweight champion 1961, **7**:141-42
pari-mutuel, **13**:36-37
Parise, Jean-Paul, **8**:189
Park, Willie, **5**:2, 4
Parke, J.C., **6**:14
Parker, Bruce, **12**:106
Parker, Frank, **6**:75-76, 78-79, 81
Parker, Jack, **4**:84-85
Parseghian, Ara, **1**:70-72
Parsons, Benny, **13**:194
Parsons, Eli B., **4**:12
Passeau, Claude, **2**:68
Pastore, John, **1**:154
Pastrano, Willie, **7**:150, 160
Patera, Ken, **11**:112
Paterno, Joe, **1**:82-83
Paterson Football Club, **8**:9-10
Patrick, Frank, **8**:124
Patrick, Lynn, **8**:130
Patterson, Armstrong, **8**:17
Patterson, Floyd, **7**:138
  vs Ali 1965, **7**:163-65
  heavyweight champion 1956, **7**:125-26; 1960, **7**:135-38
  vs Johansson 1959, **7**:131-33
  vs Liston 1962, **7**:146-47
Patterson, Gerald, **6**:14, 22
Patterson, Gerry, **10**:87
Patton, George F., Jr., **4**:20
Patton, Mel, **4**:94-95
Paul, Robert, **9**:89-90
Pavesi, Carlo, **11**:125
Paxson, Jim, **3**:48
Payson, Mrs. Charles Shipman, **2**:127
Pazesi, Attilio, **10**:100
Pazos, R. Angel, **8**:51
Peabody, Charles C., **11**:4
Pearce, Robert, **11**:84
Pearson, David, **13**:193-94
Pearson, Drew, **1**:166
Pearson, Stanley W., **11**:4, 8, 19-20
Pedersen, Sue, **12**:77-78
Pelkey, Arthur, **7**:11-12
Pélé, **8**:40-41, 53-55
  drawing power of, **8**:87-88
  vs Inter of Milan 1966, **8**:56-57
  kicking of, **8**:74
  in NASL championship 1977, **8**:89
  on New York Cosmos, **8**:84-85
  portrait of, **8**:77-78
  record 1969, **8**:65
  retirement, **8**:73
  in World Cup championship 1970, **8**:68-70

Pell, Clarence .C., Jr., **11**:15, 18-19
Pell, Clarence C., Sr.
  portrait of, **11**:14-15
  in racquets championships, **11**:3-6, 8, 13-14
  Tuxedo Gold Racquet winner 1927, **11**:11; 1930, **11**:13; 1936, **11**:15
Pell, T.R., **6**:7-8
Pelle, Stephen, **11**:128
Penacho, Larry, **12**:108
Pender, Mel, **4**:163
Pendley Calling of Blarney, **11**:167-68
Pennel, John, **4**:152, 161
Pennink, Frank, **5**:61-63
Pennock, Herbie, **2**:45-46
Pennsylvania State basketball team, **3**:2, 5
Pennsylvania State football team, **1**:12, 16, 82-83, 177
Pennsylvania State soccer team, **8**:7-9
Pep, Willie
  featherweight champion 1949, **7**:92-93
  loss of license, **7**:107
  vs Saddler 1948, **7**:91; 1950, **7**:97-99; 1951, **7**:106-07
Perillat, Guy, **9**:125
Perini, Lou, **2**:100
Perkins, Phil, **5**:51-52
Perry, Don, **11**:129
Perry, Fred, **6**:57, 61-63, 65-69
Peru, **8**:26, 51
Peschel, Randy, **1**:68
Peters, Gordon, **5**:61-63
Peters, Jimmy, **8**:140
Peterson, Ann, **12**:79
Peterson, Ben, **11**:103
Peterson, John, **11**:103
Peters, Reeves, **1**:48
Peter Volo, **13**:96
Petkevich, John Misha, **9**:140, 149
Petrik, Larisa, **11**:131
Pettit, Bob, **3**:112, 132-35, 148, 150
Petty, Lee, **13**:162
Petty, Mary Lou, **12**:41
Petty, Richard, **13**:168-69, 187, 190-91, 193-94
Peugeot car, **13**:129
Peyton, Kim, **12**:93, 99
Pflug, Monika, **9**:148-49
Pfnuer, Franz, **9**:31-32
phenylbutazone in horses, **13**:72
Philadelphia Athletics
  vs Boston Red Sox 1941, **2**:72
  vs Chicago Cubs 1929, **2**:41-42
  vs Cleveland Indians 1925, **2**:34
  vs New York Giants 1905, **2**:6-8
  vs New York Yankees 1936, **2**:60
  retirement of Mack, **2**:89-90
  vs Washington Senators 1926, **2**:35; 1932, **2**:44
Philadelphia Eagles, **1**:96-97, 102, 119-20
Philadelphia Flyers
  vs Montreal Canadiens 1976, **8**:201-02

vs New York Islanders 1974, **8**:192, 1975, **8**:197-99
Stanley Cup victors 1974, **8**:193; 1975, **8**:199-200
violence of, **8**:194-95
Philadelphia Phillies
  vs Brooklyn Dodgers 1949, **2**:87-88; 1950, **2**:88-89; 1951, **2**:93
  vs Chicago Cubs 1976, **2**:186-87
  vs Cincinnati Reds 1935, **2**:56
  vs Los Angeles Dodgers 1968, **2**:149
  vs Milwaukee Braves 1963, **2**:135
  vs New York Giants 1952, **2**:97
  vs New York Mets 1964, **2**:136-37
  vs St. Louis Cardinals 1974, **2**:172-73
Philadelphia 76ers
  vs Boston Celtics 1965, **3**:151; 1968, **3**:160
  Chamberlain bought by, **3**:150
  Erving acquisition, **3**:192-94
  vs Milwaukee Bucks 1971, **3**:171
  NBA champions 1967, **3**:158
  vs Portland Trail Blazers 1977, **3**:194-95
Philadelphia Warriors
  BAA champions 1947, **3**:116
  vs Chicago Packers 1962, **3**:142
  vs Chicago Stags 1947, **3**:116
  vs Los Angeles Lakers 1961, **3**:142
  NBA champions 1956, **3**:126-27
  vs New York Knicks 1960, **3**:139
  vs St. Louis Hawks 1960, **3**:137
Philbin, Gerry, **1**:139
Phillips, Bill, **8**:106-07
Phillips, Chester, **11**:128-29
Phillips, Eddie, **1**:71-72
Phillips 66ers, **3**:77-78
Phoenix Suns, **3**:159, 163-64, 189-91
Pierce, Palmer, **1**:86
Pietrosante, Nick, **1**:52-53, 58
Pietrzykowski, Ziggy, **7**:139
Piller, George, **11**:123
Pimlico Racetrack, **13**:19
Pincay, Laffit, Jr., **13**:73-74, 77
Pinegrade Perfection, **11**:166-67
ping pong. *See* table tennis
Pipp, Wally, **2**:64-66
Pirie, Gordon, **4**:125
pistol shooting, **10**:43-44, 46, 49-50
Pitou, Penny, **9**:90-91, 93-94, 97
Pittsburgh Crawfords, **2**:162-64
Pittsburgh Nationals, **2**:6
Pittsburgh Penguins, **8**:196-67
Pittsburgh Pirates
  vs Brooklyn Dodgers 1956, **2**:115
  vs Chicago Cubs 1938, **2**:63-64; 1975, **2**:178
  vs Cincinnati Reds 1972, **2**:168-69
  vs Milwaukee Braves 1959, **2**:123
  vs New York Giants 1949, **2**:87
  vs New York Yankees 1960, **2**:125-26
Pittsburgh Steelers
  vs Dallas Cowboys, 1976, **1**:165-66; 1979, **1**:169-71

franchise trade, **1**:96
merger with Cardinals, **1**:99
merger with Eagles, **1**:97
vs Minnesota Vikings 1975, **1**:161-63
Pittsburgh University football team, **1**:17-18, 54-55
Plante, Jacques, **8**:155, 163-64
Planutis, Gerry, **1**:55
Platak, Joe, **11**:18
platform tennis, **10**:37
Player, Gary
  British Open Golf Tournament 1959, winner, **5**:106; 1968, winner, **5**:154-55; 1974, winner, **5**:180
  donation of Masters purse 1965, **5**:131-32
  earnings, **5**:113, 121, 131-32, 155, 192
  Masters Golf Tournament 1961, winner, **5**:111-13; 1962, second place, **5**:116-17; 1965, second place, **5**:130-31; 1974, winner, **5**:178-79; 1978, winner, **5**:192-93
  portrait of, **5**:179
  Professional Golfers' Association Tournament 1962, winner, **5**:121; 1969, second place, **5**:158
  South African racial ban, **5**:134
  United States Open Golf Tournament 1965, winner, **5**:131-32
Pleau, Larry, **8**:190
Plekan, Walter, **11**:18
Plum, Fred, **10**:42
pocket billiards. *See* billiards
Podoloff, Maurice, **3**:122-23, 135, 145-46
Podres, Johnny, **2**:111-13, 134
Pogozheva, Tamara, **12**:76
Pollay, Heinz, **11**:149
polo, **10**:15-32
  auto, **10**:15-16
  indoor, **10**:23-24
  college, **10**:32
  Coronation Cup 1973, **10**:32
  East West championship, **10**:27-28
  high society, **10**:30-31
  history of, **10**:15
  National Tournament, **10**:15, 28
  Olympic, **10**:20
  pony, **10**:21-23
  in U.S., **10**:16
  World Cup, **10**:16-20, 26-27
Polo Grounds, **8**:9-10
Pompoon, **13**:30-33
Pond, Ducky, **1**:86
pony, polo, **10**:21-23
Ponzi, Andrew, **11**:60-61
pool, **11**:48
  halls, **11**:54-55
  see also billiards
Pope, Paula Jean Myers, **12**:65
Popke, Billy, **7**:7
Poppe, Henry, **3**:37-38
Porsche Carrera, **13**:192-93
Portago, Alfonso de (Marquis), **13**:160-61

Porter, Bill, **4**:95-96
Porter, Howard, **3**:81-82
Porter, Odis A., **12**:133-34
Portland Timbers, **8**:85
Portland Trail Blazers, **3**:194-95
Portsmouth soccer team, **8**:18, 20, 27
Posposil, Frantisek, **9**:164
Potter-Nelson, **2**:76-77
Poulidor, Raymond, **10**:104
Poulous, Leah, **9**:154-56
Powell, Renée, **5**:189-90
powerboats. *See* motorboats
Power, Jimmy, **13**:54
Powers, Connie, **11**:69
Powers, Richie, **3**:189
Poynter, Dan, **10**:127
Poynton, Dorothy, **12**:28-29, 37
Pratt, Walter (Babe), **8**:137
Pratt Institute, **3**:100-01
Pravda, Christian, **9**:99
Preakness winners
    Affirmed 1978, **13**:87-89
    Assault 1946, **13**:46-47
    Bold Venture 1936, **13**:29-30
    Citation 1948, **13**:51-52
    Count Fleet 1943, **13**:42
    Gallant Fox 1930, **13**:19-20
    Man o'War 1920, **13**:9
    Native Dancer 1953, **13**:56-57
    Omaha 1935, **13**:27-38
    Seabiscuit 1938, **13**:34-35
    Seattle Slew 1977, **13**:82-83
    Secretariat 1973, **13**:75-76
    Sir Barton 1919, **13**:8
    War Admiral 1937, **13**:32-33
    Whirlaway 1941, **13**:39
Prefontaine, Steve, **4**:174, 180
Preiss, Ellen, **11**:122
President's Cup, **12**:157-58, 169-70
Press, Irina, **4**:150, 157, 159
Press, Tamara, **4**:137, 149-50, 158-59
Preston North End soccer team, **8**:26-27, 35
Primeau, Joe, **8**:118, 120, 127
Priestner, Cathy, **9**:154
Prince of Wales Cup, **8**:104-06
Princeton University basketball team, **3**:70
Princeton University football team, **1**:9, 11
Princeton University soccer team, **8**:8-9
Price, Katherine, **13**:67-68
Prinstein, Myer, **4**:5-6, 8
Proell, Annemarie, **9**:142, 146, 153
Professional Basketball League of America, **3**:116
Professional Drivers' Association, **13**:187
Professional Golfers' Association, **5**:14-15
    and American Professional Golfers, **5**:156
    and civil rights demonstration, **5**:158
    and Ladies' Professional Golf Association, **5**:191-92
    and racial restrictions, **5**:71, 85, 113, 134

tournament operation, **5**:77
Professional Golfers' Association Tournament winners
    Hagen 1921, **5**:21; 1925, **5**:30; 1926, **5**:32
    Hogan 1946, **5**:70
    Nicklaus 1963, **5**:124; 1973, **5**:176; 1975, **5**:184-85
    Nichols 1964, **5**:128-30
    Player 1962, **5**:121
    Sarazen 1934, **5**:54-55
    Snead 1951, **5**:84
    Stockton 1976, **5**:188-89
Prothro, Tommy, **1**:63-64
Protopopov, Oleg, **9**:104, 121, 131-32, 138
Providence College basketball team, **3**:59-60
Psychic Bid, **13**:27-28
Pugh, Tom, **11**:21
punch drunk boxers, **7**:138
Pung, Jacqueline, **5**:99-100
Purdue University football team, **1**:43-44, 66
Pyle, Charles C., **1**:88
Pyle, Mike, **1**:136
Pyles, Rudd, **9**:139

Quarrie, Don, **4**:190-91
Quarry, Jerry, **7**:175-76
Quebec hockey team, **8**:102
Quigg, Joe, **3**:55
Quinn, Mike, **8**:46-47
Quist, Adrian, **6**:75-76

raccoon hunting, **10**:156
Race King, **13**:4-5
Racer, **13**:28-29
racing
    auto, **12**:157, **13**:120-98
    bicycle, **10**:95-108
    boat, **12**:114-86
    horse, **13**:2-119
    motorcycle, **10**:88-94
    see also specific Olympic events; records, track and
        field, specific races
racing cars
    Grand Prix design, **13**:170
    jet-powered, **13**:172-73, 176-77
    stock, **13**:170, 184
    two-man, **13**:136
    see also specific cars
racketeers and boxing, **7**:133-35, 139-41
racquetball, **11**:31-33
racquets champions
    Atkins 1954, **11**:19-20; 1960, **11**:21
    Grant 1937, **11**:16-17; 1939, **11**:17-18; 1950, **11**:19; 1953,
        11:19
    Mortimer 1923, **11**:6; 1930, **11**:13-14
    Pell (Sr.) 1917, **11**:3-4; 1921, **11**:4-5; 1925, **11**:8

Shaw 1901, **11**:2-3
Soutar 1922, **11**:5
see also Tuxedo Gold Racquet championship
racquets doubles championship, **11**:4, 8, 18
Rademacher, Peter, **7**:126
radio broadcasting of
  auto races, **13**:136
  baseball, **2**:35
  football, **1**:18, 31-32
  hockey, **8**:104
  see also television
Ragan, Dave, **5**:124
Rahn, Helmut, **8**:36-37
Rainbow, **12**:139
Ralston, Den, **6**:131, 142-43, 145
Ralston, John, **1**:73-74
Ramey, H.E., **4**:12
Ramey, Nancy Jane, **12**:59
Ramos, Sugar
  featherweight champion 1963, **7**:148-49
  vs Ortiz 1966, **7**:167-68
  vs Robertson 1964, **3**:159
Ramsey, Frank, **3**:135-36
Randolph, Leo, **7**:191
Range, Don, **8**:46-47
Ranger, **12**:144-46
Rankin, Juey, **5**:193-94
Rawls, Betty, **5**:81, 99-100
Rawls, Katherine, **12**:26, 31, 37
Ray, Carleton, **10**:164
Ray, Edward, **5**:9-11
Ray, Joie, **4**:26, 29, 33-34, 39-40, 44-45, 53-54
Ray, Ted, **5**:33-34
Raybestos Brakettes softball team, **10**:67-69
Rayborn, Calvin, **10**:91
Raye, Jimmy, **1**:65-66
Rayner, Charley, **8**:145
Reagan, Frank, **1**:59
Real Madrid, **8**:44
Reardon, Kenny, **8**:140, 144
records, archery, **10**:4-6
records, auto racing
  AAA race 1924, **13**:133
  Andretti 1969, **13**:185
  Breedlove, 1963, **13**:172-73; 1965, **13**:176-77
  Campbell, 1935, **13**:139-41
  Clark 1965, **13**:175-76
  Corum 1924, **13**:133
  Culver City race 1926, **13**:134
  Delage car 1914, **13**:127-29
  De Palma 1915, **13**:129-30
  Donohue 1972, **13**:188-89
  Eyston 1938, **13**:144
  Frame 1932, **13**:138
  hot rod 1956, **13**:159
  at Indianapolis 500 1936, **13**:141
  Jones 1963, **13**:171-72
  at Le Mans race 1953, **13**:151-52; 1967, **13**:179

Meyer 1928, **13**:134; 1933, **13**:138-39
Moss 1955, **13**:154
Murphy 1922, **13**:131-32
Oldfield 1910, **13**:123
Pan American Road Races 1953, **13**:152
Roberts 1956, **13**:159
Rose 1948, **13**:148-50
stock car 1955, **13**:154
Unser 1939, **13**:146
Wallard 1951, **13**:150-51
Yarborough 1973, **13**:190
records, barrel-jumping 1955, **9**:74
records, baseball, batting
  Aaron 1957, **2**:122
  averages falling 1968, **2**:151-52
  Cobb 1910, **2**:12
  DiMaggio 1941, **2**:71
  Hornsby 1922, **2**:33; 1924, **2**:34; 1926, **2**:38
  Lajoie 1910, **2**:12
  Lazzeri 1936, **2**:60
  Mantle 1953, **2**:100-01
  Ruth 1920, **2**:23
  Sisler 1922, **2**:33
  Stennett 1975, **2**:178
  Terry 1930, **2**:43
  Williams 1941, **2**:72
  Wilson 1930, **2**:43
records, baseball, home runs,
  Aaron 1974, **2**:171-72
  Banks 1955, **2**:111
  Cobb 1925, **2**:34
  and designated hitter rule, **2**:179
  Gehrig 1932, **2**:44
  Kiner 1949, **2**:87
  Long 1956, **2**:115
  major league 1921, **2**:31
  Mantle 1956, **2**:115-16
  Maris 1961, **2**:129-30
  Musial 1954, **2**:104-05
  Oh 1977, **2**:191
  Ruth 1926, **2**:36-38; 1927, **2**:40-41; 1934, **2**:51-52
  Schmidt 1976, **2**:186-87
  York 1937, **2**:61
records, baseball, pitching
  Bunning 1964, **2**:136-37
  Cain 1952, **2**:95-97
  Carlton 1969, **2**:155-56
  Cheney, 1962, **2**:133
  Dean (D.) 1933, **2**:49
  Dean (P.) 1934, **2**:52-53
  Drysdale 1968, **2**:149
  Feller 1938, **2**:64; 1940, **2**:68; 1951, **2**:90-91
  Gibson 1968, **2**:152-54
  Hunter 1968, **2**:148
  Johnson 1913, **2**:16-17; 1921, **2**:32
  Koufax 1965, **2**:142-43
  Larsen 1956, **2**:116-19
  Robertson 1922, **2**:32

Ryan fastball, **2**:172
Seaver 1970, **2**:159
Shore 1917, **2**:21
records, basketball; *see also* records, college basketball
Archibald 1972, **3**:178
Baylor 1959, **3**:137; 1960, **3**:141
Boston Celtics 1959, **3**:135; 1962, **3**:143
Chamberlain 1960, **3**:137, 139; 1961, **3**:142; 1962, **3**:142-43; 1963, **3**:146; 1966, **3**:153; 1972, **3**:174
Cousy 1953, **3**:120
Gervin 1978, **3**:200-01
Havlicek 1976, **3**:188
Kerr 1963, **3**:146
Los Angeles Lakers 1971, **3**:173; 1972, **3**:176
Mikan 1949, **3**:117-18; 1952, **3**:120
Milwaukee Bucks 1970, **3**:166-68
Minneapolis Lakers 1955, **3**:125
Pettit 1964, **3**:148, 150
Russell 1957, **3**:131; 1960, **3**:137
Saint Louis Hawks 1957, **3**:132
Schayes 1958, **3**:132; 1960, **3**:137; 1961, **3**:142
Thompson 1978, **3**:200-01
West 1969, **3**:162-63
Yardley 1958, **3**:133
records, bicycling, **10**:95, 97-98
records, billiards, **11**:47-48, 50, 58-60, 62-63
records, bobsledding 1932, **9**:21-22; 1946, **9**:36-37
records, bowling, **11**:67-68, 72
records, boxing
Armstrong double title 1938, **7**:64-65
Armstrong triple title 1938, **7**:66-67
Griffith 1963, **7**:151
knockdown, **7**:48, 132
Louis 1935, **7**:54; 1939, **7**:68
purse 1910, **7**:14
receipts 1927, **7**:39; 1974, **7**:183-84
records, bullfighting, **10**:144
records, college basketball
Arizin 1949, **3**:34
Boykoff 1947, **3**:27-28
Furman University 1955, **3**:50
Jaworski, 1939, **3**:15
Lavelli 1949, **3**:34
Maravich 1968, **3**:77; 1970, **3**:80
O'Brien 1953, **3**:47
Robertson 1960, **3**:59
San Francisco 1956, **3**:51
Selvy 1954, **3**:49
Seton Hall 1953, **3**:47
UCLA 1973, **3**:86-87
records, dog show victories, **11**:176
records, fencing, **11**:121
records, figure skating 1951, **9**:61-62
records, fishing, **10**:162
records, fly casting **10**:157-58, 163
records, football
Bradshaw, **1**:171
Brown, **1**:57, 62, 63, 126, 128

field goal, **1**:149-50
pass-catching, **1**:148
rushing, **1**:126, 128, 155
Simpson, **1**:156-57
Super Bowl 1977, **1**:167-68
records, golf
Blancas 1962, **5**:121
Hagen 1926, **5**:32; 1927, **5**:36-37
Hogan 1953, **5**:87-88
Jones 1927, **5**:35-36; 1930, **5**:44-46
Locke 1950, **5**:81
Masters purse 1963, **5**:122
Nicklaus 1965, **5**:130-31; 1967, **5**:144-45
Palmer 1962, **5**:119-20
Sarazen 1932, **5**:50-51
Suggs 1952, **5**:86
records, gymnastics, **11**:128-29
records, hockey
Esposito 1971, **8**:183-84
game length 1933, **8**:121
Geoffrion 1960, **8**:160; 1961, **8**:161
Howe, G. 1953, **8**:148; 1956, **8**:154; 1960, **8**:160; 1963, **8**:164-66
Howe, S. 1944, **8**:136
Hull, **8**:161-62; 1966, **8**:171-72; 1971, **8**:183
Moore 1954, **8**:149
penalties 1960, **8**:160
Richard 1945, **8**:137; 1952, **8**:147-48; 1953, **8**:148
Sawchuk 1952, **8**:147
records, horse racing
Adams 1956, **13**:62-63
Adios, Harry 1957, **13**:105
Arcaro 1952, **13**:56
Citation 1950, **13**:55-56
Count Fleet 1943, **13**:43-45
Cresceus, **13**:94
Directum I 1916, **13**:96
Emily's Pride 1958, **13**:106-07
Filion 1972, **13**:117
Fire Glow 1927, **13**:77
Gallant Fox 1930, **13**:22-23
Green Speed 1977, **13**:118
Greyhound 1938-39, **13**:102
harness racing 1914, **13**:96
Kelso 1964, **13**:69-70
Lee Axworthy 1916, **13**:97
Mahmoud 1936, **13**:53
Man o' War 1920, **13**:9-10
Moyers 1967, **13**:70
Nella Dillon 1917, **13**:97
Pincay 1974, **13**:77
Richards 1950, **13**:55
Seabiscuit 1938, **13**:34-35
Secretariat 1973, **13**:73-74
Shoemaker, **13**:57
Sir Barton 1919, **13**:8-9
Twenty Grand 1931, **13**:24
Volga 1916, **13**:96

War Admiral 1937, **13**:33-34
Whirlaway 1941, **13**:38-39
Whisk Broom II 1913, **13**:7
records, motorboating
    1920, **12**:118-20
    1921, **12**:121
    1930, **12**:129, 133-34
    1939, **12**:149
    1955, **12**:158-59
records, motorcycle, **10**:88-90
records, pistol shooting, **10**:50
records, plug accuracy, **10**:161
records, riflery, **10**:40, 44-45, 51
records, rowing
    Ward brothers, **12**:175-76
    Washington University crew 1925, **12**:124-25
    Yale University crew 1949, **12**:154-55; 1956, **12**:159
records, shooting, **10**:45, 52
records, skeet shooting, **10**:47-48
records, skiing 1940, **9**:43; 1964, **9**:104-05
records, ski jumping 1941, **9**:43-44
records, sled dog racing 1928, **9**:13
records, showshoe marathon 1938, **9**:42
records, soccer
    Aston villa 1957, **8**:38
    Bethlehem Steel Co. 1916, **8**:8
    English Football Association Cup 1952, **8**:33
    game length 1925, **8**:13
    Pélé 1969, **8**:65
    Tottenham Hotspurs 1962, **8**:47-48
records, speed-skating
    Anderson 1952, **9**:67
    Ballangrud 1936, **9**:37
    Ericsson 1956, **9**:79-80
    Grishin 1956, **9**:76-79
    Helgesen 1948, **9**:48-49
    Henning 1972, **9**:147-48
    Johannesen 1960, **9**:97-98
    Kulikov 1976, **9**:160
    Mathisen 1936, **9**:36
    Mikhailov 1956, **9**:78-79
    Mustonen 1968, **9**:127-28
    Nilsson 1963, **9**:103
    Shilkov 1956, **9**:77
    Skoblikova 1960, **9**:91; 1964, **9**:108-10
    Thunberg 1925, **9**:10
    Verkerk 1968, **9**:133-34
records, swimming
    at AAU championship 1915, **12**:5
    Abertondo 1962, **12**:67
    Australian relay team 1956, **12**:56
    Bleibtrey 1919, **12**:8; 1920, **12**:9
    Borg 1928, **12**:20
    Bottom 1977, **12**:103
    Breen 1956, **12**:59
    Chadwick 1950, **12**:49-50
    Curtis 1944, **12**:43
    Daniels 1907, **12**:2

Ederle 1922, **12**:10-11; 1923, **12**:11; 1926, **12**:15
Ender 1976, **12**:96-97
Ford 1943, **12**:43
Fraser 1962, **12**:67
Holm 1930, **12**:22; 1934, **12**:31
and interval training, **12**:71-75
Japanese 1932, **12**:24-25; 1936, **12**:35; 1949, **12**:49
Kahanamoku 1913, **12**:5
Kiefer 1936, **12**:40-41; 1940, **12**:42
Kight 1932, **12**:28
Kojac 1929, **12**:22
Langer 1915, **12**:5-6
Madison 1931, **12**:22
Mastenbroek 1936, **12**:41-42
Medica 1934, **12**:31
Montgomery 1976, **12**:98-99
Naber 1976, **12**:98-99
NCAA meet 1977, **12**:104-05
1917, **12**:8
1920 Olympic, **12**:9
1923 Olympic, **12**:11-12
1936 Olympic, **12**:34-42
1956 Olympic, **12**:59
1960 Olympic, **12**:66
1964 Olympic, **12**:69
1968 Olympic, **12**:78-79
Norelius 1928, **12**:20; 1932, **12**:28
Ris 1948, **12**:43-44
at Santa Clara meet 1967, **12**:75
Senff 1936, **12**:36, 38
Smith 1942, **12**:42-43; 1948, **12**:46
speed up in, **12**:74
Spence 1926, **12**:15
Spitz 1972, **12**:84, 88-90
Thumer 1976, **12**:99
and training, **12**:97-98
United States Olympic 1924, **12**:13-14; 1948, **12**:45-46; 1961, **12**:76, 81-82; 1976, **12**:93-94, 96-97
Weismuller 1921, **12**:9, 1922, **12**:9-10; 1926, **12**:14
Wenden 1968, **12**:77
women 1915, **12**:6
records, tennis
    Bridge 1938, **6**:73
    Laver 1969, **6**:164-66
    Perry 1936, **6**:65-69
records, track and field
    broad jump, 1904, **4**:8; 1924, **4**:35; 1925, **4**:43; 1928, **4**:47; 1936, **4**:79; 1960, **4**:132
    change in, by IAAF, **4**:198
    Coliseum Relays, 1962, **4**:148-49
    decathlon, 1928, **4**:52-53; 1936, **4**:84-85; 1956, **4**:128; 1972, **4**:181-82; 1976, **4**:194-95
    Dillard consecutive triumphs, **4**:89
    discus, 1902, **4**:8; 1928, **4**:48; 1929, **4**:55; 1932, **4**:62-63; 1936, **4**:79-80; 1962, **4**:148-50; 1968, **4**:164
    880-yard run, 1925, **4**:43
    800-meter run, 1912, **4**:18-19; 1928, **4**:46-47, 50; 1932, **4**:62-63; 1948, **4**:92-94; 1956, **4**:121

80-meter hurdles, 1929, **4**:56; 1931, **4**:56-57; 1932, **4**:66-67
1500-meter run, 1924, **4**:37; 1928, **4**:50; 1932, **4**:66-67; 1935, **4**:74-75; 1936, **4**:81-82; 1968, **4**:172
400-meter hurdles, 1920, **4**:27; 1948, **4**:92; 1976, **4**:189-90
400-meter relay races, 1924, **4**:41-42; 1956, **4**:127
400-meter run, 1924, **4**:39-40; 1932, **4**:67-69
½-mile run, 1928, **4**:43
hammerthrow, 1908, **4**:12-13; 1952, **4**:105; 1954, **4**:114; 1956, **4**:118-19
high jump, 1920, **4**:28; 1922, **4**:33; 1956, **4**:116-17; 1956, **4**:116-17; 1960, **4**:130-31; 1962, **4**:149-50; 1976, **4**:198-99
hurdles. *See* 80-meter hurdles, 400-meter hurdles, 110-meter hurdles
javelin throw, 1928, **4**:50; 1932, **4**:59; 1956, **4**:122; 1968, **4**:165-66; 1973, **4**:184
marathon race, 1932, **4**:58, 70-72; 1936, **4**:86-87; 1952, **4**:108-09; 1960, **4**:144-45
mile run. *See* 1-mile run
NAAU Meet, 1935, **4**:74-75; 1971, **4**:174
Olympic, 1920, **4**:32; 1932, **4**:64-65, 70-72; 1936, **4**:85; 1952, **4**:104-07; 1956, **4**:117-18; 1964, **4**:155-57; 1968, **4**:169-70; *see also* specific events
1½-mile run, 1922, **4**:33
110-meter hurdles, 1920, **4**:29; 1928, **4**:46-48; 1948, **4**:95-96; 1952, **4**:105; 1956, **4**:123-24
100-meter dash, 1928, **4**:46-47
100-yard dash, 1929, **4**:55; 1930, **4**:56; 1961, **4**:146-47; 1963, **4**:151; 1974, **4**:185-86; statistics, **4**:56
1-mile run, 1915, **4**:25; 1945, **4**:89; 1954, **4**:112-15; 1958, **4**:129-30; 1962, **4**:148-49; 1967, **4**:163; 1975, **4**:186; statistics, **4**:115, 186
by Owens, 1935, **4**:75-76; 1936; **4**:76-77
by Paddock, 1921, **4**:32; 1925, **4**:42
pole vault, 1906, **4**:9; 1920, **4**:29-30; 1926, **4**:43; 1928, **4**:43, 48; 1928, **4**:48, 1942, **4**:88; 1960, **4**:131; 1962, **4**:147, 148; 1963, **4**:152; 1966, **4**:161-62; 1970, **4**:173; 1973, **4**:183-84; 1978, **4**:201; statistics, **4**:173
by Ray, 1922, **4**:33
relay races. *See* 400-meter relay races
by Ritola, 1923, **4**:33-34
at Rose Festival Meet, 1970, **4**:173
running, 1907, **4**:12, 1921, **4**:32, 1922, **4**:33, 1923, **4**:33-34; 1925, **4**:42; *see also* specific runs
shot-put, 1928, **4**:44-45; 1932, **4**:59; 1954, **4**:112-13; 1960, **4**:133-34; 1962, **4**:148; 1964, **4**:158; 1965, **4**:160-61; 1973, **4**:184-85
steeplechase, 1924, **4**:37; 1928, **4**:52; 1936, **4**:85; 1952, **4**:106-07
10,000-meter run, 1924, **4**:34; 1948, **4**:89-90; 1952, **4**:102; 1964, **4**:153; 1972, **4**:178
2-mile run, 1925, **4**:42
women's events, 1928, **4**:46-47, 50, 54-55; 1929, **4**:55-56; 1931, **4**:56-57; 1932, **4**:62-63; 1964, **4**:158
records, trapshooting, **10**:42, 50-52
records, water skiing, **12**:106, 110
records, weight lifting
    AAU tournament 1929, **11**:105
    Alekseyev 1972, **11**:112
    Anderson 1955, **11**:108; 1956, **11**:108
    Bogdanovskii 1956, **11**:108
    Depthios 1972, **11**:112
    Galimberti 1924, **11**:105
    George 1953, **11**:107
    Golovanov 1964, **11**:111
    Jsmayr 1932, **11**:106
    Kangasniemi 1969, **11**:111
    Mesbah 1936, **11**:106
    Olympics 1924, **11**:105; 1948, **11**:106; 1952, **11**:107; 1960, **11**:110
    Soviet Union 1952, **11**:107; 1964, **11**:111
    Vlasov 1960, **11**:111
records, wrestling, **11**:92
records, yachting 1930, **12**:131-33; 1937, **12**:144-46
recruiting for
    basketball, **3**:96-97, 159-60, 170-71, 173, 180-81
    professional football, **1**:174-78
    track and field, **4**:199-200
Reddish, Jack, **9**:53-54
Redd, Lambert, **4**:62
Reed College basketball team, **3**:165-66, 168-69, 178
Rees, Dai, **5**:113-14
Reese, Peewee, **2**:88, 93
Reeves, Daniel, **1**:100
referees
    basketball, **3**:197-99
    boxing, **7**:20, 143-44
    hockey, **8**:120, 168-69, 194-95
    soccer, **8**:73-74
    tennis, **6**:12
Regas, Jack, **12**:159
Reichert, Ossi, **9**:75-76
Reid, James, **11**:6
Reiff, Gaston, **4**:92-94, 105-06
Reis, George, **12**:138-40
Remigino, Lindy, **4**:103
reporters, women, **8**:196
Resch, Glenn, **8**:197
Resolute, **12**:116-18
Resta, Dario, **13**:129-30
Revson, Peter, **13**:187-88, 191-92
Reynolds, Allie, **2**:92-93
Reynolds, Frank, **1**:52-53, 58
Reynoldstown, **13**:25
Rhodi, Abdeslam, **4**:144-45
Rhode Island University basketball team, **3**:26
Rhodes, James (Dusty), **2**:107-08
Rhome, Jerry, **1**:63
Rice, Jim, **2**:183-84
Rice University football team, **1**:50-51
Richard, Henri, **8**:184
Richard, Maurice, **8**:137, 145, 147-48, 151, 155-56
Richards, A.W., **4**:19
Richards, Golden, **1**:168
Richards, Gordon, **13**:55

Richards, Harry, **13**:30-31
Richards, Renée, **6**:198
Richards, Robert, **4**:104, 121, 123
Richards, Vincent, **6**:35-36, 43, 50-51, 82
Richey, Nancy, **6**:144
Richman, Sam, **4**:55
Richthoff, Johan, **11**:84
Rickard, Tex, and
    basketball, **3**:112
    bike races, **10**:97
    boxing, **7**:13-15, 17, 96, 114, 116
    hockey franchise, **8**:103
Ricker, Mrs. Edward P., Jr., **9**:13
Ricketts, Dick, **3**:50-51
Ridder, Eric, **12**:167-68
Riddle, Samuel D., **13**:10-12, 30-35
Ridlon, Jim, **1**:57
Riegel, Robert, **5**:82-83
Riegels, Roy, **1**:18
Riessen, Marty, **6**:190
riflery, **10**:40, 43-45, 51; *see also* hunting
Riggs, Robert, **6**:75-77, 86, 179-80, **10**:36
Righeimer, Francis E., **11**:121
Riley, Mickey. *See* Galitzen, Mickey Riley
Ring, Jimmy, **2**:38
Ring Magazine, **7**:168-69, 193-94
rinks. *See* skating rinks
Rio Grande basketball team, **3**:49
riots, baseball, **2**:54-56
riots, boxing, **7**:24-26
riots, football, **1**:28
riots, hockey, **8**:150-51, 155; *see also* hockey, melees,
    violence
riots, at 1932 Olympics, **12**:23
riots, soccer
    Argentina 1930, **8**:19-20; 1968, **8**:64
    England 1923, **8**:9
    Italy 1925, **8**:13
    Peru 1964, **8**:51
    Soviet Union 1955, **8**:37
    Turkey 1967, **8**:63
    World Soccer Tournament 1954, **8**:36
Ris, Wally, **12**:43-44
Risen, Arnold, **3**:23-24
Ritger, Dick, **11**:74
Ritola, Willie, **4**:33-34, 36-37, 39-41, 51
Ritter, R. Max, **12**:62
ritual, football, **1**:185-86
Rivers, Mickey, **2**:189-90
Rizzuto, Phil, **2**:203-04, 111-12
Robbie, Joe, **1**:158-59
Robert, Morris, **13**:40
Roberts, Dave, **4**:190-92
Roberts, Floyd, **13**:144-45
Roberts, Glenn, **13**:154, 159, 168-69
Roberts, Ken, **10**:94
Roberts, Robin, **2**:93, 97
Robertson, Charley, **2**:32

Robertson, Earl, **8**:129
Robertson, Floyd, **7**:159
Robertson, Lawson, **4**:9, 26, 50
Robertson, Oscar
    in All Star game 1964, **3**:147; 1970, **3**:165-66
    in NBA championship game 1971, **3**:172
    in Olympic game 1960, **3**:62
    player of the year 1958, **3**:55-56
    record 1960, **3**:59; 1962, **3**:143
Robertson, Ronnie, **9**:80-82, 88-89
Robie, Carl, **12**:81
Robiner, Abraham, **7**:138
Robinson, Albert, **7**:173
Robinson, Brooks, **2**:145-46
Robinson, Elizabeth (Betty), **4**:46-47, 55-56
Robinson, Jackie
    Dodgers purchase of, **2**:80
    on Montreal Royals, **2**:161
    in 1950 pennant race, **2**:89
    in Phillies game 1951, **2**:93
    in World Series 1953, **2**:103-04
Robinson, Frank, **2**:156-57, 175
Robinson, Rey, **4**:175-76
Robinson, Sugar Ray
    vs Basilio 1957, **7**:129-30
    death of Doyle, **7**:78
    vs Maxim 1952, **7**:109
    middleweight 1950, **7**:100-01; 1951, **7**:101, 105-06; 1955,
        7:122; 1957, **7**:127-28; 1958, **7**:130-31
    portrait of, **7**:128
    vs Turpin 1951, **7**:103
    welterweight 1949, **7**:95-96
Robledo, George, **8**:33
Robson, Fred, **5**:33-36
Roby, Douglas F., **4**:168-69, 181
Rocca, Antonino, **11**:104
Rocca, Peter, **12**:98-99
Roche, Tony, **6**:171-72
Rochester Lancers, **8**:70
Rochester Royals, **3**:113, 119-20
Rockne, Knut, **1**:7-8, 15-16, 22, 24
Rock Ridge Night Rocket, **11**:172
rodeo, **10**:130-36
Rodgers, Bill, **4**:200-01
Rodgers, Phil, **5**:119-20, 142-43
Rodnina, Irina, **9**:147, 156
Rodriguez, Luis, **7**:151
Rogallo, Francis, **10**:128
Rogers, Alfred (Doug), **11**:97
Roldau, Antonio, **7**:173
Rollow, Cooper, **1**:79
Rom, Dagmar, **9**:61
Roman, Ed, **3**:38
Roman Brother, **13**:69-70
Romanenko, Vitalii, **10**:49
Romanov, Nikolai, **9**:78
Roman Soldier, **13**:26-27
Romeo Hanover, **13**:115

Romig, John, **3**:37
Romnes, Doc, **8**:124-25
Ronnmark, Bertel Belhelm, **10**:46
Ronzoni, Gene, **1**:89-92
Roth, Al, **3**:38
Roosevelt, Franklin, **2**:56
Roosevelt, Theodore, **1**:2, **10**:151
Root, Elbert, **12**:41-42
Rose, Mauri, **13**:147-50
Rose, Mervyn, **6**:105
Rose, Murray, **12**:57, 61, 65
Rosemeyer, Bernd, **13**:143-44
Rosemont, **13**:28-29
Rosenberg, Butch, **12**:106
Rosenbloom, Maxie, **7**:41
Rose, Pete, **2**:180, 182
Rose, Ralph, **4**:8, 20
Rosewall, Ken
   in Davis Cup matches 1954, **6**:106-07; 1956, **6**:114
   earnings 1970, **6**:171-72
   French matches winner 1953, **6**:97-98
   in U.S. matches 1955, **6**:110-11; 1968; **6**:160; 1970,
      6:171-72; 1974, **6**:184-85
   U.S. matches winner 1956, **6**:113
   in Wimbledon matches 1954, **6**:104; 1956, **6**:112; 1968,
      6:158; 1970, **6**:169-70; 1974, **6**:183-84
Rosham Khan, **11**:20-21
Ross, Barney
   vs Armstrong 1938, **7**:64-65
   double title of, **7**:47-48
   lightweight champion 1933, **7**:45
   vs McLarnin 1934, **7**:49-50
   welterweight 1934, **7**:46-47; 1935, **7**:50
Ross, J.K.L., **13**:8, 11-12
Roth, Dick, **12**:69-70
Roth, George, **11**:128
Roth, Mark, **11**:75
Round, Dorothy, **6**:58-59
Rowan, Carl and Mrs., **6**:159
Rowan, Rip, **1**:36, 39, 40-41
rowing
   Ward Brothers and, **12**:175-76
   women in, **12**:114, 179
   see also crew races, intercollegiate; Olympic rowing,
      records, rowing
Royal Bay Gem, **13**:56-57
Royal, Darrell, **1**:68, 70-72
Rozelle, Alvin (Pete) and
   football strike, **1**:149
   merger with AFL, **1**:129
   NFL head, **1**:117-18
   player-reserve system, **1**:160-61
   rules change, **1**:159-60
   Super Bowl 1975, **1**:161
   suspension of players, **1**:124
   TV blackouts, **1**:154-55
   WFL, **1**:165
Rozsnyoi, Sandor, **4**:124-27

Rubenstein, Willie, **3**:11
Rudd, B.G.D., **4**:28
Rudenkov, Vasily, **4**:137-38
Rudi, Joe, **2**:176, 187-88
Rudolph, Edwin, **11**:58
Rudolph, Mason, **5**:131, 176-77
Rudolph, Wilma, **4**:135-36, 138, 142-44
Ruffa, Tony, **1**:30-31
Ruffian, **13**:78-79
rugby, **10**:72-79
rules, baseball, **2**:4, 154, 169, 171, 179
rules, boxing
   double titles, **7**:47-48
   fouls barred, **7**:41-42
   return bouts, **7**:119
   safety code, **7**:83, 149-50
   shotgun champs, **7**:74
   3-knockdown, **7**:149-50
rules, college basketball
   coaching, **3**:3-4, 33
   dribble, **3**:4, 7
   foul, **3**:7, 22, 33
   free throw, **3**:8
   girls', **3**:5
   goalie penalty, **3**:22
   halt, **3**:7
   Intercollegiate League, **3**:5
   Joint Rules Committee, **3**:8
   jump ball, **3**:13, 33
   pivot play, **3**:8, 10
   stalling, **3**:8
   stuff shot, **3**:52
   substitute, **3**:33
   tap off, **3**:8, 15
   violation of, **3**:46
rules, college football
   change in, **1**:2-9, 16-17, 25
   goal posts widened, **1**:60
   side line coaching, **1**:9-10
   speedier offense, **1**:33-34
   two-platoon system, **1**:49-50, 63
   2-point conversion, **1**:58
rules, golf, **5**:4, 7, 14, 139-40, 157
rules, hockey
   curbing fights, **8**:134
   defense restriction, **8**:113
   free penalty shot, **8**:125
   overtime, **8**:109, 135
   penalties, **8**:114, 155
   referees, **8**:120
   zoning, **8**:113
rules, horse-racing, **13**:94-96
rules, professional basketball
   eligibility, **3**:173
   personal foul, **3**:116
   stalling, **3**:123
   zone defense, **3**:199-200
rules, professional football, **1**:89, 159-60

rules, soccer, **8**:76, 90
rules, tennis,
  amateur tennis, **6**:5, 103
  champions, **6**:4-5
  conduct, **6**:194
  8-week, **6**:64
  expense money, **6**:134
  frowning ban, **6**:44
  tie breakers, **6**:170
rules, Olympic diving, **12**:62
rules, Olympic speed-skating, **9**:18
rules, swimming, **12**:6, 14
Rumania, gymnasts of, **11**:132
Run Dusty Run, **13**:80-84
running
  and heart trouble, **4**:26
  middle-distance, **4**:26
  sprint, **4**:16-17, 26
  starting blocks, **4**:73
  see also marathons; records, track and field, specific
    races, running
Runyan, Paul, **5**:54-56, 113-14
Rupp, Adolph, **3**:26, 42-45, 47, 104
Ruppert, Jacob, **2**:23, 67
Russell, Bill, **3**:51, 52, 127-30, 131
  as Boston Celtic coach, **3**:154-55
  vs Cincinnati Royals 1965, **3**:150
  in Hall of Fame, **3**:183
  in NBA championship game 1960, **3**:140-41; 1962, **3**:144;
    1965, **3**:151-52; 1966, **3**:155; 1968, **3**:162; 1969, **3**:162-63
  in NBA Eastern Division playoff 1968, **3**:160
  vs New York Knicks 1958, **3**:132-33
  records, **3**:131, 137
  salary, **3**:152
Russell, Cazzie, **3**:70
Russell, Doug, **12**:78
Russia. *See* Soviet Union
Russi, Bernhard, **9**:139, 145
Rutgers University basketball team, **3**:73-74, 102
Rutgers University football team, **1**:9, 60
Ruth, George (Babe), **8**:21
  in All Star game 1933, **2**:48-49; 1934, **2**:50-51
  bought by Yankees, **2**:23
  at Gehrig tribute, **2**:66-67
  home run records, **2**:40-41, 51-52, 129-30
  leader in League, **2**:21
  umpire-hitting, **2**:21
  in World Series 1926, **2**:36-38; 1932, **2**:45-46
Rutherford, S., **8**:20
Ruttledge, Jeff, **1**:82-83
Ruud, Birger, **9**:22-23, 29, 39
Ruuska, Weikko (Finn), **12**:72-74
Ryan, Elizabeth, **6**:14, 18, 34-35, 48-49
Ryan, Michael, **4**:21
Ryan, Nolan, **2**:170, 172, 174
Ryan, Pat, **4**:29
Ryan, Sylvester, **7**:128-29
Ryun, Jim, **4**:163, 170-72

Saarinen, Veli, **9**:24
Sabourin, Gary, **8**:182
Sachs, Eddie, **13**:166, 173-74
Sadat, Anwar el-, **1**:77
Saddler, Sandy
  featherweight champion 1948, **7**:91; 1950, **7**:97-99;
    1951, **7**:106-07
  vs Pep 1949, **7**:92-93
  suspension of, **7**:107
sailboats
  monotypes, **12**:135
  and ocean racing, **12**:166
  see also Olympic sailing; Olympic yachting; yachting
Sailer, Anton, **9**:77-89, 83-84, 115
sailplanes, **10**:122-24
St. Andrews Golf Club, **5**:11, 13
St. Cyr, Henri, **11**:155-56
St. Francis College basketball team, **3**:27-28
St. Godard, Emile, **9**:13
St. John, Jim, **11**:73
St. John's University basketball team
  vs Bradley 1959, **3**:57-58
  vs Cincinnati 1964, **3**:70-71
  vs Connecticut 1951, **3**:40-41
  Dayton 1962, **3**:66-67
  vs DePaul 1944, **3**:20
  vs St. Francis 1947, **3**:27-28
St. Joseph's College basketball team, **3**:63-64
St. Louis Blues
  vs Boston Bruins 1969, **8**:180-82; 1970, **8**:182-83
  vs Montreal Canadiens 1968, **8**:174; 1969, **8**:180
  vs New York Rangers 1974, **8**:195
St. Louis Browns
  and black spectators, **2**:75
  vs Cleveland Indians 1936, **2**:60; 1952, **2**:95-97
  vs Detroit Tigers 1925, **2**:34; 1938, **2**:63; 1942, **2**:76-77
  Gray's fielding, **2**:75
  move to Baltimore, **2**:101-02
  vs New York Giants 1933, **2**:46-48
St. Louis Cardinals baseball team
  and black spectators, **2**:75
  vs Brooklyn Dodgers 1934, **2**:52-53; 1946, **2**:77-78
  vs Brooklyn Robins 1924, **2**:33
  vs Chicago Cubs 1942, **2**:74; 1955, **2**:111
  vs Cincinatti Reds 1930, **2**:24; 1934, **2**:53-54
  vs Cleveland Indians 1918, **2**:12
  vs Detroit Tigers 1934, **2**:54-56; 1968, **2**:152-54
  farm clubs of, **2**:75
Hornsby trade, **2**:38-40
  vs Los Angeles Dodgers 1962, **2**:133
  vs New York Giants 1933, **2**:46-48; 1954, **2**:104-05
  vs New York Mets 1964, **2**:140-41; 1969, **2**:155-56; 1974,
    2:173-74
  vs New York Yankees 1926, **2**:36-38
  vs Philadelphia Phillies 1974, **2**:172-73
  and Robinson, **2**:80
St. Louis Cardinals football team, **1**:99, 103-04, 119, 182
St. Louis Eagles, **8**:126-27

St. Louis Hawks, **3**:124
   vs Boston Celtics 1957, **3**:130-31; 1960, **3**:140-41
   vs Cincinnati Royals 1964, **3**:150
   NBA championship 1958, **3**:133-35
   vs Philadelphia Warriors 1960, **3**:137
   record 1957, **3**:132
   vs San Francisco Warriors 1964, **3**:148
   vs Syracuse Nationals 1957, **3**:132
St. Louis Stars, **8**:76
St. Louis University basketball team, **3**:31
St. Louis University soccer team
   National Collegiate Soccer champions 1962, **8**:50
   NCAA champions 1959, **8**:43; 1960, **8**:46-47; 1970, **8**:70;
     1974, **8**:79
salaries. *See also* earnings
salaries, baseball, **2**:17, 188
salaries, basketball
   Barry, **3**:159
   Malone, **3**:182-83
   minimum, **3**:178
   NBA stars, **3**:186-88
   Russell, **3**:152
   Thompson, **3**:201
salaries, English athletes', **8**:21
salaries, football, **1**:115, 126-27
salaries, hockey, **8**:102, 188-89, 191-92, 200
salaries, soccer, **8**:68
Saling, George, **4**:64-65
Salo, Johnny, **4**:55
Sampson, Julie, **6**:97
Samuels, Dale, **1**:43-44
Samurai swordplay, **11**:96
San Antonio Spurs, **3**:200-201
Sande, Earl, **13**:11-13, 19-23
Sanders, Doug, **5**:142-43, 146, 161-62
Sanderson, Derek, **8**:193-94
San Diego basketball team, **3**:156
San Diego Padres, **2**:159
San Diego Toros, **8**:64
Sandler, Steve, **11**:24
Sanfield, Andy, **4**:104
San Francisco 49ers, **1**:128
San Francisco Giants
   vs Los Angeles Dodgers 1962, **2**:134
   vs Milwaukee Braves 1961, **2**:129
   move from New York, **2**:119-20
   vs New York Mets 1964, **2**:135-36
San Francisco State basketball team, **3**:51-52
San Francisco State soccer team, **8**:58, 85
San Francisco Warriors, **3**:146, 148-49, 158
Santa Clara international swim meet, **12**:75
Santana, Manuel, **6**:142-43
Santee, Wes, **4**:116
Santelli, Salle, **11**:124-25
Santo, Ron, **2**:171
Santos of Brazil, **8**:56-57
Santos, Valter, **8**:45
Saperstein, Abe, **3**:144

Sarazen, Gene
   British Open Golf Tournament 1928, second place,
     5:38-39; 1932, winner, **5**:50-51
   Professional Golfers' Association Tournament 1923,
     winner **5**:25-26; 1934, winner, **5**:54-55
   in Ryder Cup competition, **5**:54
   United States Open Golf Tournament 1922, winner,
     5:22-23; 1932, winner, **5**:51-52; 1934, second place,
     5:56-57
   World's Golf Classic 1922, winner, **5**:23
Sarron, Petey, **7**:63
Saubert, Jean, **9**:107-08, 111-12, 115
Sauer, George, Jr., **1**:140
Saunders, Willie, **13**:27-28
Savage, David (Swede), **13**:190
Savage, Joseph K., **9**:18
Saveliev, Sergei, **9**:153
Sawchuk, Terry, **8**:145, 147, 174
Saxton, Johnny, **7**:124-25
Sayers, Gale, **1**:128
Sceneshifter, **13**:33-34
Sceptre, **12**:160-61
Schaefer, Jacob, **11**:47, 53-58, 60
Schafer, Karl, **9**:15-16, 20-21, 37
Schaller, H.G. (Bus), **10**:89
Schayes, Adolph, **3**:23-24, 30, 132, 137, 142, 146
Schenk, Ard, **9**:142-45, 150
Schlee, John, **5**:174-75
Schlembeckler, Bo, **1**:78
Schlundt, Don, **3**:48
Schmautz, Bobby, **8**:203-04
Schmeling, Max
   heavyweight champion 1930, **7**:40-41
   as guest of Hitler, **7**:59
   Jewish manager of, **7**:50
   vs Louis 1936, **7**:56-59; 1938, **7**:65-66
   one-man fight, **7**:59-60
   vs Sharkey 1932, **7**:43-44
Schmertz, Robert, **1**:155
Schmid, Manfred, **9**:133
Schmidt, Fred, **11**:13
Schmidt, Mike, **2**:186-87
Schnabl, Karl, **9**:168
Schnelldorfer, Manfred, **9**:115-16
Schoendienst, Red, **2**:110-11
Schoenith, Joseph, **12**:157-58
Scholes, Clarke, **12**:50-51
Schollander, Don, **4**:157, **12**:69, 71-73, 80
Scholz, Jackson, **4**:34-37, 48
Schoonmaker, Mrs. Leon M., **11**:121-22
Schopf, Egon, **9**:61
Schramm, Tex, **1**:129
Schramme, Rudolf, **12**:100-01
Schranz, Karl, **9**:134-35, 137-39, 141-42, 146
Schroeder, Fred R. (Ted), Jr., **6**:78-79, 85-86, 90-92
Schuba, Beatrix, **9**:144-46
Schul, Bob, **4**:161
Schuler, Carolyn, **12**:64

Schultz, Dave, **8**:194-95
Schut, Johanna, **9**:129
Schwarcz, Erno, **8**:43
Schwartz, Morton, **13**:29-30
Schwartz, Walter, **11**:10
Schwartzwalder, Ben, **1**:180
Schwarz, Elisabeth, **9**:84
Schwarz, Jim, **10**:171
Schwarz, Wolfgang, **9**:133
Schwarzmann, Alfred, **11**:129
Sciarra, John, **1**:75
scoring
    Olympic diving, **12**:62
    in figure skating competition, **9**:96
Scotland, curlers of, **9**:5-6
Scotland, soccer team of, **8**:15, 20, 22
Scotland, tennis in, **5**:7
Scott, Barbara Ann, **9**:44-45, 52, 56-57, 60
Scott, Charlie, **3**:190
Scott, Clyde, **4**:95
Scott, Everett, **2**:66
Scott, Jack, **1**:182
Scott, Norman, **9**:2
Scott, Peter, **12**:167-68
Scott, Wendell, **13**:196
Scott Frost, **13**:105
Scotti, Alfred J., **7**:133-34
Scott-Paine, Hubert, **12**:137
Scriven, Margaret, **6**:58-59
sculls, **12**:149-51
Seabiscuit, **13**:34-35
Seagren, Bob, **4**:161-62, 165, 174, 176-77
Seaman, John, **11**:10
Seaman, Richard, **13**:143-44
Seamon, Manny, **7**:87
Sears, Ken, **3**:132-33
Sears, Mary Jane, **12**:59
Seaton, Pippin, **11**:144-45
Seattle Pilots, **2**:158, 185
Seattle Slew, **13**:80-84
Seattle Sounders, **8**:89-90
Seattle Supersonics, **3**:156, 172, 176, 202-03
Seattle University basketball team, **3**:56
Seaver, Tom, **2**:145-46, 159
Secretariat, **13**:73-77
Sedgman, Frank, **6**:90-92, 94-97
Segal, Abe, **6**:135
Segura, Francisco (Pancho), **6**:79
Seibt, Hellmut, **9**:69
Seitz, Peter, **2**:184-85
Seixas, Vic
    in Davis Cup matches 1954, **6**:106-07; 1955, **6**:108-10
        1956, **6**:114
    in French matches 1953, **6**:97-98
    in U.S. matches 1953, **6**:102-03
    in Wimbledon matches 1954, **6**:105
    Wimbledon matches winner 1953, **6**:98
Sellers, Johnny, **13**:67-68

Selvetti, Humberto, **11**:108
Selvy, Franklin Delano, **3**:49, 51
Senff, Dina **12**:36, 38
Seppala, Leonhard, **9**:13
Seton Hall University basketball team, **3**:47-48, 66
Setzler, Norbert, **11**:17-18
Sewgolum, Sewsunker, **5**:134
Sexton, Leo, **4**:59
Seyffarth, Ake, **9**:52
Shakespeare, Bill, **1**:28
Sham, **13**:73-76
Shamrock IV, **12**:116-18
Shamrock V, **12**:131-33
Sharif Khan, **11**:24, 26, 33
Sharkey, Jack
    vs Carnera 1933, **7**:45-46
    vs Dempsey 1927, **7**:34-36
    heavyweight champion 1932, **7**:43-44
    vs Schmeling 1930, **7**:40-41
shark fishing, **10**:181-84
Sharman, Bill, **3**:135-36, 176-77
Sharp, Paul, **1**:184-85
Shaughnessy, Clark, **1**:32-34, 51
Shaver, Gaius, **1**:23-24
Shavlakadze, Robert, **4**:134-35
Shaw, Quincy, **11**:2-3
Shaw, Tim, **12**:96
Shaw, Wilbur, **13**:142-47
Shea, Jack, **9**:16-18
Shea, William A., **2**:124, **8**:186
Sheffield United soccer team, **8**:14, 25, 53
Shelley, Ken, **9**:149
Shendan, Martin, **4**:8, 15-16
Shepard, Alan E., **5**:162
Sheppard, Melvin, **4**:9, 12-13, 17-19, 26
Sheppell, William, **8**:35
Shero, Fred, **8**:201
Shibe, Thomas, **2**:24
Shibicky, Alex, **8**:128
Shields, Frank, **6**:63
Shiley, Jean, **4**:57
Shoemaker, Willie, **13**:57-61, 63-64, 79
Shofner, Del, **1**:120-23
shooting, **10**:38-52
    King's rifle championship, **10**:46
    pistol, **10**:43-44, 46, 49-50
    records. *See* records, specific shooting events
    rifle, **10**:40, 43-45, 51
    running deer competition, **10**:43, 45, 49
    silhouette, **10**:194-95
    skeet, **10**:46-48
    trapshooting, **10**:40-43, 45, 48, 50-52
    world championship, **10**:52
Shore, Eddie, **8**:122, 124, 131
Shore, Ernest, **2**:21
Short, Robert, **2**:166
Shorter, Frank, **4**:182-83, 196-97
Shotton, Burt, **2**:81-85

Shoup, Herbert, **13**:132
Shula, Don, **1**:151-54, 157, 165
Shute, Densmore, **5**:54
Sidorova, Valentina, **11**:127
Siebert, Babe, **8**:106
Siemiontkowski, Hank, **3**:81-82
Seyfert, Gabriele, **9**:138
Shilkov, Boris, **9**:77-78
Sietas, Erwin, **12**:41-42
Sifford, Charles, **5**:113, 155-57
Silky Sullivan, **13**:65-67
siluetas metalicas, **10**:194-95
Silvester, Jay, **4**:164
Sime, Dave, **4**:134-35
Simes, Jackie, **10**:106
Simmons, Don, **8**:158
Simons, Monk, **1**:27-28
Simonsson, Ague, **8**:44
Simpson, George, **4**:55, 64
Simpson, O.J., **1**:71, 155-57
Simpson, Tom, **10**:106
Sinclair, Harry F., **13**:12-15
Singer, Al, **7**:42
Sir Barton, **13**:8-9, 11-12
Sisler, Dick, Jr., **2**:88-89
Sisler, George H., **2**:33
skating
    races 1920, **9**:6; 1926, **9**:10
    rinks, **9**:4-5
    rules, Olympic, **9**:18
    see also figure skating; Olympic figure-skating champions; Olympic speed-skating champions
skeet shooting, **10**:46-48
Skelton, Robert, **12**:12
skiing
    acrobatics, **9**:150-51
    artificial snow for, **9**:101-02
    Berkeley jump contest 1934, **9**:27
    cross-country, **9**:43
    injuries, **9**:140-41
    Lake Placid Sno-Birds jump, **9**:43-44
    safety at Olympics, **9**:103-04
    see also North American ski contest; Olympic ski jump champions; Olympic ski race champions; Olympic ski race champions; Olympic ski race champions, cross-country; Olympic ski race champions, marathon; Olympic ski race champions, military patrol; Olympic ski race champions, relay
ski-planing, **9**:7
Skoblikova, Lidiya, **9**:91-92, 104-11, 128-29
Skoglund, Bob, **1**:35-36
Skowron, Bill, **2**:132-33
Skrzypeski, Kazimierz, **9**:103
Skutnabb, Julius, **9**:7-8
skydiving, **10**:124-26
Slattery, Ann, **11**:73
Slattery, Jimmy, **7**:41
Slaughter, Enos, **2**:77-78

Sled dog race 1928, **9**:13
Slide Rule, **13**:41
Sloane, W.M., **4**:2
Slosson, George, **11**:57
Slusarski, Tadeus, **4**:190-92
Smith, Al, **2**:71, 113-14
Smith, Bill, **11**:92
Smith, Bill, **12**:42-46
Smith, Bud, **7**:124
Smith, Elmer, **2**:28-29
Smith, Graham, **12**:103-05
Smith, Harold, **12**:23-30
Smith, Hooley, **8**:109-10
Smith, Horton, **5**:42, 54-56
Smith, Janice, **9**:105
Smith, John Nelson, **5**:40-41
Smith LeRoy, **3**:38
Smith, Lester, **2**:185
Smith, MacDonald, **5**:26-27, 41-44
Smith, Margaret. *See* Court, Margaret Smith
Smith, Normie, **8**:127
Smith, Reynolds, **5**:61-63
Smith, Stan, **6**:173-77, 182
Smith, Steve, **4**:183-84
Smith, Tommie, **4**:165-69
Snead, J.C., **5**:194-95
Snead, Norm, **1**:120-23
Snead, Sam
    Los Angeles Open Golf Tournament 1950, winner 5:75-76
    Masters Golf Tournament 1939, second place 5:64; 1949, winner, 5:71-72; 1952, winner, 5:85-86; 1954, winner 5:93-94; 1955, third place, 5:97-98; 1957, second place, 5:101; 1963, third place, 5:122
    Professional Golfers' Association Tournament
    second place, 5:64-65; 1951, winner, 5:84
    United States Open Golf Tournament 1949, second place, 5:71-73; 1953, second place, 5:90-92
Snell, Matt, **1**:139-41
Snell, Peter, **4**:148-49, 159
Sneva, Tom, **13**:195-98
Snider, Duke, **2**:112-14
Snite, Betsy, **9**:97
snow, artificial, **9**:13, 101-02
snowmobiles, **9**:122-23
snowshoe marathon, **9**:42
Snyder, Jimmy (The Greek), **1**:133, **13**:143-44
soccer, **8**:2-98
    American Challenge Cup, **8**:8
    American Soccer League, **8**:8-9, 15-16, 18
    in Argentina, **8**:19-20, 64, 74; *see also* Argentina, soccer team of
    in Austria, **8**:16; *see also* Austria, soccer team of
    betting in, **8**:21-25, 38, 44-45
    in Britain, **8**:23-25, 47, 91-92; *see also* England and soccer; England, soccer team of
Challenge Trophy, **8**:8, 16-17
college, **8**:5-8, 74-75; *see also* National Collegiate Athletic

Asociation, Soccer champions; soccer champions, intercollegiate
vs cricket, **8**:9
Eastern League, **8**:17-18
in England. *See* England, soccer in; England, soccer team of
English Football Association Cup champions; English Soccer Cup champions
in Europe, **8**:43-44
European Soccer Cup, **8**:44, 50, 63
fans, **8**:32, 43-44; *see also* riots, soccer
vs football, **8**:5, 7-8
goaltending, **8**:75-76
heating of field, **8**:39
International Football Federation, **8**:78, 94, 96
International Soccer League, **8**:43, 45-46
law and order in, **8**:73-74
league mergers in, **8**:58, 63
listings, **8**:22
moat, **8**:31
National Challenge Cup, **8**:8
National Collegiate Athletic Association. *See* National Collegiate Athletic Association soccer champions
nationalism and, **8**:92-96
National Professional Soccer League match 1967, **8**:57-58, 62-63
night game, **8**:15
North American Soccer League. *See* North American Soccer League, North American Soccer League champions
Olympic. *See* Olympic soccer
at Polo Grounds, **8**:9-10
popularity of, **8**:5, 7-10, 15, 43-44
priests in, **8**:41
records. *See* records, soccer
referees, **8**:73-74
reserve clause, **8**:65-66
Rio de Janeiro field, **8**:31
riots. *See* riots, soccer
rules, **8**:76, 90
salaries, **8**:21, 68
Scottish Football Association Cup, **8**:20
and Scotland, 15; *see also* Scotland, soccer team of
selling of, **8**:86-89
techniques, **8**:59-61
terms, **8**:61
in Soviet Union, **8**:37; *see also* Soviet Union, soccer team of
in Spain, **8**:13
in Sweden, **8**:44-45; *see also* Sweden, soccer team of
on television, **8**:27
Toronto franchise, **8**:71
in Turkey, **8**:63
United Soccer Association championship, **8**:62-63
in United States. *See* United States, soccer in; United States, soccer team of
women in, **8**:67, 70

World Soccer Cup champions. *See* World Soccer Cup champions
world women's soccer championship, **8**:70
soccer champions, intercollegiate
Haverford 1915, **8**:8
Pennsylvania 1920, **8**:8
Princeton 1922, **8**:9
Yale 1912, **8**:7
softball, **10**:63-69
Somers, Alan, **12**:64-65
Son, Kitei, **4**:86-87
Sopwith, T.O.M., **12**:139, 144-45
Sorio, Sixto, **7**:191
Sorrell, Johnny, **8**:128
Soutar, Jack, **11**:5, 10-11
South Africa, golf in, **5**:134
South Africa, rugby team of, **10**:76
South Africa, tennis in, **6**:135, 185, 201
Southampton soccer team, **8**:85
Southern Cross, **12**:179-80
Southern Illinois University basketball team, **3**:73-74
Southern Methodist University football team, **1**:183
Souza, Ed, **8**:32
Sovereign, **12**:166-68
Soviet Union, aquatic team of, **12**:54-55, 60-61
Soviet Union, archery in, **10**:6
Soviet Union, basketball team of, **3**:52-53, 56-57, 69, 85-86
Soviet Union, boating and
Olympic canoe team, **12**:161, 174
Olympic crew team, **12**:156
Olympic kayak team, **12**:178
yachting, **12**:178
Soviet Union, equestrian team of, **11**:160
Soviet Union, fencers of, **11**:126
Soviet Union, gymnasts of, **4**:107, **11**:129, 131-32
Soviet Union, hockey team of
vs Canada 1973, **8**:189-90
in Olympics 1956, **9**:84-86; 1964, **9**:119; 1968, **9**:135; 1972, **9**:150
Soviet Union, mountain climbers of, **10**:120-21
Soviet Union, running deer shoot team, **10**:43, 45, 49
Soviet Union, shooting team of, **10**:49-50, 52
Soviet Union, ski team of, **9**:84-85, 116-17, 150
Soviet Union, soccer riots in, **8**:37
Soviet Union, soccer team of
barred from World Cup, **8**:78
vs Germany 1956, **8**:38
vs Indonesia 1956, **8**:38
Olympic victory 1956, **8**:38
vs West Germany 1955, **8**:57
vs Yugoslavia 1952, **8**:34
Soviet Union, tennis and, **6**:135
Soviet Union, track and field team of, **4**:109, 149-50
Soviet Union, volleyball team of, **11**:46
Soviet Union, water polo team of, **12**:57
Soviet Union, weight lifters of, **11**:107-08, 110-12
Soviet Union, Winter Olympics champions 1956, **9**:84-85;

1972, **9**:150
Soviet Union, wrestlers of, **11**:98
Spahn, Warren, **2**:120, 135
Spain, bullfighters in, **10**:140-43
Spain, soccer in, **8**:13
spearfishing, **10**:164, 166-67
speedboats. *See* motorboats
Speedie Mac, **1**:123
Speedy Scot, **13**:112
Spencer, Arthur, **10**:95
Spencer, Freddy, **10**:99
Spencer, Willie, **10**:97-98
Spence, Walt, **12**:15
Spero, Don, **12**:170
Sperry, Lawrence, **9**:7
Speyrer, Charles, **1**:70-71
Spiegelhoff, Johnny, **10**:89
Spinks, Mike, **7**:191, 196
Spinks, Leon
    heavyweight champion 1978, **7**:195-96
    at 1976 Olympics, **7**:191
    and WBC, **7**:196
Spitz, Mark, **12**:75, 81, 84-90
Spivey, Bill, **3**:41, 122
Sports Car Club of America, **13**:181-82
Spotts, Ralph, **10**:40
Spruance, Mrs. Halsey, **11**:25
Spy Song, **13**:45-46
squash racquets
    description of, **11**:25
    doubles championship 1974, **11**:25
    men's championships, **11**:4, 15, 21, 24, 26, 33
    Pakistani players, **11**:20
    popularity of, **11**:2, 12
    scoring, **11**:8
    vs squash tennis team 1926, **11**:11
    women's championship 1930, **11**:13
squash tennis
    championships, **11**:3, 6-7, 9-10, 15, 18, 24
    popularity of, **11**:11-13
    vs squash racquets team, **11**:11
Stable, José, **7**:160-61
Stabler, Ken, **1**:168
Stack, Allen, **12**:47
Stack, Tommy, **13**:80
Stagg, Alonzo, **1**:8, 48, 86, **8**:8
Stallard, H.B., **4**:36
Stallard, Tracy, **2**:129-30
Stallworth, John, **1**:170-71
Stammers, Kay, **6**:74-75
Stampf, Franz, **4**:115
Stanczyk, Stan, **11**:106-07
Stanfield, Andy, **4**:121
Stanford University basketball team, **3**:12, 19
Stanford University football team
    vs Alabama 1934, **1**:26-27
    vs Columbia 1933, **1**:25-26
    vs Michigan 1972, **1**:74-75

vs Nebraska 1940, **1**:33
vs Notre Dame 1925, **1**:15-16
vs Pittsburgh 1927, **1**:17; 1928, **1**:18
slush funds, **1**:177
T formation, **1**:34
vs UCLA 1924, **1**:15
Stanich, George, **4**:89
Stanley Cup champions
    Boston Bruins 1929, **8**:112-13; 1939, **8**:133; 1941, **8**:134; 1970, **8**:182-83; 1972, **8**:187-88
    Chicago Black Hawks 1934, **8**:125; 1938, **8**:129-30; 1961, **8**:161
    Detroit Red Wings 1936, **8**:127; 1937, **8**:128; 1943, **8**:135; 1950, **8**:144-45; 1952, **8**:147; 1954, **8**:149; 1955, **8**:152
    Montreal Canadiens 1924, **8**:103; 1930, **8**:113-14; 1931, **8**:118; 1944, **8**:137; 1946, **8**:137-38; 1953, **8**:149; 1956, **8**:155; 1957, **8**:156-57; 1958, **8**:158; 1959, **8**:159; 1960, **8**:160; 1965, **8**:169-70; 1966, **8**:172-73; 1968, **8**:174; 1969, **8**:180; 1971, **8**:184-85; 1973, **8**:191; 1975, **8**:201-02; 1977, **8**:203-04; 1978, **8**:205-06
    Montreal Maroons 1926, **8**:106-07; 1935, **8**:126
    New York Rangers 1928, **8**:110-12; 1933, **8**:121-22; 1940, **8**:133-34
    Ottawa Senators 1927, **8**:109
    Philadelphia Flyers 1974, **8**:193; 1975, **8**:199-200
    Toronto Maple Leafs 1932, **8**:119-20; 1942, **8**:134-35; 1945, **8**:137; 1947, **8**:141; 1948, **8**:143; 1949, **8**:143; 1951, **8**:145-47; 1963, **8**:163; 1964, **8**:167; 1967, **8**:173-74
    Victoria Cougars 1925, **8**:103
Stanley, Mickey, **2**:153
Staretor, **13**:38-39
Starks, Nathaniel, **5**:156
Starr, Bart, **1**:51, 130-32, 135-38
Stassen, Harold, **1**:48
Stassforth, Bown, **12**:55
Staub, Roger, **9**:91-92
Staubach, Roger, **1**:75, 151-53, 165, 168, 171
Stearns, Chuck, **12**:110
Stecher, Joe, **11**:81-82
Steele, Willie, **4**:91
Steenhoven, Graham, **11**:40
Steinkraus, Bill, **11**:158-61
Steinbrenner, George, **2**:192
Steiner, Bobby, **10**:134-35
Steinfeldt, Carl, **10**:10
Stenerson, Sverre, **9**:79-80
Stengel, Casey, **2**:102-03
Stengl, Manfred, **9**:113
Stennett, Rennie, **2**:178
Stenroos, Albin Oscar, **4**:41
Stepanskaya, Galina, **9**:153-54
Stephens, Helen, **4**:78, 79
Stephens, Olin, **12**:167, 172, 180
Sterkel, Jill, **12**:99
Sternaman, Joe, **1**:88
Sternberg, Brian, **4**:151
Steve Lobell, **13**:118
Stevens, Curtis, **9**:21-22

Stevens, J. Hubert, 9:21-22, 34
Stevens, Mal, 1:20
Stevens, Tom, 8:71-72
Stevenson, Chuck, 13:152
Stevenson, Teofilo, 7:179-81
Stewart, Jackie, 13:190
Stickles, Monty, 1:52-53, 58
Stiegler, Josef (Pepi), 9:118-19
Stiegman, John, 1:60
Stiles, Bob, 1:63-64
Stillman, Alfred, 11:3
Stingray, 11:177-78
Stirling, Alexa, 5:17
Stockton, Dave, 5:178-79, 188-89, 194-95
Stokes, Maurice, 3:156
Stolle, Fred, 6:132-33, 135, 144, 158
Stoneham, Horace, 2:119-20, 127
Stones, Dwight, 4:196-99
Storholt, Jan Erik, 9:166
Storm, 11:175-76
Stouder, Sharon, 4:156, 12:70
Stout, Elmer, 1:42, 45
Stout, J.A., 5:40-41
Stout, Jimmy, 13:35-36
Stove, Betty, 6:196-97
Stowe, Charles, 5:61-63
Stoyanov, Dimitro, 11:95
Stracey, John, 7:188
Strachan, Rod, 12:99-100, 103
Stranahan, Frank, 5:81, 92-93
Street, James, 1:68, 70
Streicher, Julius, 11:86
Streit, Saul, 3:44-45
Stribling, Young, 7:168
Strickler, George, 1:99-100
Stricklett, Elmer, 2:22
    baseball, 2:13, 166-67
    football, 1:149, 160, 163-64
    umpires, 2:159-60
Strobino, G., 4:21-23
Strong, Ken, 1:91-92
Stuart, Hugh, 5:162-63
Stubbendorf, Ludwig, 11:149
Stunyo, Jeanne, 12:57
Sturgess, Eric, 6:83-84
Sturrock, Alexander (Jock), 12:163-66, 172-73
Stutz, Harry, 13:130
Stydahar, Joe, 1:105-06, 108
Stymie, 13:48-49
Suburban Handicap, 13:7
Suggs, Louise, 5:74, 81, 86, 106
Sulaiman, Jose, 7:196
Sullivan, James E., 4:8-9, 19, 24
Sullivan, John, 7:2-4
Sullivan, Neil, 11:15
Su Mac Lad, 13:111-12
Summers, Jack, 11:15
Summer Tan, 13:58-59

sumo wrestling, 11:93-94, 98
Sunderland, 8:26, 76-77
Sun Meadow, 13:74
Supreme Court rulings on
    baseball, 2:167-68
    boxing, 7:139, 178
    football, 1:112-13
    Santee suspension, 4:116
surfing, 12:106, 11
Suton, May, 6:94
Sutton, George, 11:47
Sutton, Len, 13:169-70
Suyderhound, Mike, 12:110-11
Suzuki, Hiroshi, 12:50-51
Swann, Lynn, 1:166, 170-71
Swaps, 13:58-61
Swartz, Don, 12:91
Swearingen, Fred, 1:171
Sweden, equestrian team of, 11:140, 154-56
Sweden, Olympic hockey team of, 9:7
Sweden, Olympic ski marathon, 9:39
Sweden, soccer in, 8:40-41, 44-45
Sweden, tennis team of, 6:190-91
Sweden, Winter Olympics victory of, 1948, 9:52, 58-59
Sweden, wrestlers in, 11:83-84
Sweigert, William, 1:160-61
Sweikert, Bob, 13:154-57, 159
Swiacki, Bill, 1:40-41
swimming
    strokes, 12:2-4, 10
    style, 12:6-8
    training for, 12:71-75
    U.S. Olympic victory 1964, 4:157
Switzer, K., 4:162
Switzerland, equestrian team of, 11:158
Switzerland, Olympic military ski patrol, 9:59
Switzerland, Olympic bobsled team, 9:34, 84-85, 149
Switzerland, second place in Winter Olympics 1948, 9:58-59
Switzerland, soccer team of, 8:13
Swoboda, Ron, 2:155-56
Sylvester, John, 2:38
Symank, John, 1:119-20
Syracuse Nationals
    vs Boston Celtics 1953, 3:120; 1960, 3:137
    vs Detroit Pistons 1958, 3:133
    vs Los Angeles Lakers 1961, 3:142
    vs Minneapolis Lakers 1950, 3:119; 1954, 3:123
    NBA champions 1955, 3:124
    vs Saint Louis Hawks 1957, 3:132
Syracuse University football team, 1:57, 180
Syracuse University women's crew team, 12:114
Sysonby, 13:2-5
Szabo, Jaross, 9:10
Szekely, Eva, 12:52
Szordykowski, Henryk, 4:183

Taberski, Ralph, 11:59

table tennis, **11**:38-43
Tabori, Laszlo, **4**:115
tackle, football, **1**:7
Taiho, **11**:98
Takacs, Karoly, **10**:49
Takalo, Helena, **9**:156-57
Talbert, William, **6**:79-81
Talbot-Ponsonby, J.A., **11**:150
Tampa Bay Rowdies, **8**:85
Tanner, Elaine, **12**:79-81
Tannery, **13**:20-21
Tar Heel, **13**:103
Tarkenton, Fran, **1**:144, 157-58, 161-63, 167-68
Taruffi, Piero, **13**:158-59, 161
Taylor, Billy, **8**:142
Taylor, Chris, **11**:100
Taylor, F. Morgan, **4**:35
Taylor, Harry, **2**:82
Taylor, J.H., **5**:6-7, 9, 11
Taylor, Karen, **13**:80-81
Taylor, "Major", **10**:95
Taylor, Maxwell D., **1**:35, 38, 178-79
Taylor, Megan, **9**:28
Taylor, Otis, **1**:148
Taylor, Robert, **4**:175
Teague, Marshall, **13**:150
Tegart, Judy, **6**:157-58
television
    baseball on, **2**:67
    basketball on, **3**:192
    and black golf tournament, **5**:156
    bowling on, **11**:70-71, 75
    boxing on, **7**:63, 100, 114-17, 119, 128, 193-94, 198-99
    college football on, **1**:31-32, 47, 70, 77-78
    and hunting, **10**:185-90
    professional football on, **1**:108, 125, 139, 154-55
    soccer on, **8**:27
    tennis on, **6**:199-201
Temple University basketball team, **3**:13-14, 56
Temple University football team, **1**:27-28
Tendler, Lew, **7**:22-23
Ten Eyck, James, **12**:114
tennis, **6**:2-202
    All Comers' Tournament, **6**:8
    amateur, **6**:156
    and apartheid, **6**:135, 185, 201
    in Australia. *See* Australia, tennis in
    balls, **6**:30, 110
    and blacks, **6**:47, 87, 124-25, 135, 159, 185, 201
    Britain and. *See* Britain, tennis and
    Cannes matches 1926, **6**:32-33
    college, **6**:172
    courts, **6**:14, 125-26
    Davis Cup. *See* Davis Cup (matches)
    earnings in. *See* earnings, tennis
    Federation Cup, **6**:201
    Forest Hills matches. *See* United States tennis matches winners

French hard court tournament, **6**:48
French tennis matches champions. *See* French tennis matches champions
in India, **6**:185
International Lawn Tennis Federation, **6**:24
International Tennis Tournament, **6**:2
Lawn Tennis Club, **6**:2
'love', **6**:12-14
Madison Square Garden pro tennis tournament, **6**:145
misconduct, **6**:194
mixed doubles, **6**:12
national pro court championship, **11**:10-11
open, **6**:50, 154-202
outfits, **6**:53, 92
popularity of, **6**:20
prize money, **6**:163, 173; *see also* earnings, tennis
professional, **6**:145, 156
racquets, **6**:7-8, 150
records. *See* records, tennis
referees, **6**:12
rules. *See* rules, tennis
scoring, **6**:12-14, 170
Scottish Open Tournament, **5**:7
service, **6**:20
in South Africa, **6**:135, 185, 201
in Soviet Union, **6**:135
strokes, **6**:7-8
and television, **6**:199-201
tie-breakers, **6**:170
titles, world, **6**:24
training, **6**:16-17
and United States. *See* United States, tennis in
United States Lawn Tennis Association, **6**:103, 154-56, 172
United States tennis matches winners. *See* United States tennis matches winners
Virginia Slims-Thunderbird tennis tournament, **6**:175
West Side Tennis Club, **6**:8, 124-25
Wightman Cup matches **6**:58-59, 118-19, 131-32, 134
Wimbledon matches. *See* Wimbledon tennis matches champions
Wimbledon Stadium, **6**:21
women in. *See* women in, tennis
World Professional Tennis League, **6**:82
World Tennis Team, **6**:179
see also paddle tennis; platform tennis; squash tennis; table tennis
Terada, Norburu, **12**:41-42
Terrell, Ernie, **7**:168-69
Terry Bill, **2**:43
Testa, Tuesday, **13**:72
Texas Christian University football team, **1**:29-30
Texas University football team, **1**:68, 70-72
Texas Western basketball team, **3**:71-72
Tharp, Corky, **1**:51
Theismann, Joe, **1**:70-72
Thevenet, Bernard, **10**:107-08
Thoma, Georg, **9**:92, 110

Thomas, Clendon, **1**:58
Thomas, Dave, **5**:105, 142-43
Thomas, John, **4**:130-31, 134-35, 146-47, 150, 159
Thomas, Kurt, **11**:136-37
Thomas, Rene, **13**:127-29, 131
Thomond II, **13**:25
Thompson, Alexis, **6**:77
Thompson, David, **3**:200-01
Thompson, Earl J., **4**:26, 28-29
Thompson, Fred, **4**:185
Thompson, Paul, **8**:124-25
Thompson, R.M., **4**:17
Thompson, Tommy, **1**:102
Thoeni, Gustavo, **9**:152-53, 158-59, 167
Thompson, Wilbur, **4**:94
Thomson, Bobby, **2**:94-95
Thomson, E.F., **11**:142-45, 149
Thomson, Hector, **5**:61-63
Thomson, Peter, **5**:99, 105, 132-34
Thor, Hanover, **13**:110-11
Thorpe, Jim
    in baseball, **2**:21
    disqualification from Olympics, **12**:90-91
    in football, **1**:7, 43
    in track and field, **4**:17-18, 22-24, 101
Thumer, Petra, **12**:94-95, 99
Thunberg, Clas, **9**:10-11
Thurman, Arthur, **13**:130
Tibbott, Dave, **1**:9
Ticket, **13**:7
Tidwell, Charlie, **4**:130
Tiger, Dick
    vs Foster 1968, **7**:172-73
    vs Griffith 1966, **7**:166-67
    middleweight champion 1962, **7**:148
Tilden, William
    in Davis Cup matches 1923, **6**:25-26; 1927, **6**:40-42
    in French hard court tournament 1930, **6**:48
    in French matches 1927, **6**:37-38
    glare of **6**:44
    as greatest tennis player, **6**:87
    service of, **6**:20
    training of, **6**:16-17
    in U.S. matches 1926, **6**:35-37; 1927, **6**:42-43
    U.S. matches winner 1918, **6**:12; 1920, **6**:15; 1921,
        6:20-21; 1922, **6**:23-24; 1923, **6**:26-27; 1924, **6**:29;
        1925, **6**:31-32; 1929, **6**:47; 1931, **6**:50-51
    Wimbledon winner 1920, **6**:14; 1921, **6**:18; 1930, **6**:49-50
Tim Tam, **13**:65-66
Tipton, Eric, **1**:30-31
Tisdall, Bob, **4**:60-61
Titan Hanover, **13**:102-03
Titova, Ludmilla, **9**:125-26, 128
Tittle, Y.A., **1**:120-23
tobogganing
    electric block signals for, **9**:10
    International Luge Federation contest, **9**:133
    See also Olympic toboggan race champions

Tobian, Gary, **12**:60-61
Todd, Dick, **1**:97
Tokle, Torger, **9**:43-44
Tolan, Eddie, **4**:60-61, 64-65
Tolley, Cyril, **5**:40-41
Toomey, Bill, **4**:170-71
Tootell, Fred, **4**:37
Toronto basketball club, **2**:186
Toronto Maple Leafs
    vs All Stars 1947, **8**:141
    vs Boston Bruins 1933, **8**:121, 122; 1939, **8**:133
    vs Chicago Black Hawks 1938, **8**:129-30
    vs Detroit Falcons 1930, **8**:114-15
    vs Detroit Red Wings 1936, **8**:127
    vs Montreal Canadiens 1945, **8**:137; 1959, **8**:159; 1960,
        8:160; 1961, **8**:161
    vs Montreal Maroons 1932, **8**:118-19; 1935, **8**:126
    vs New York Rangers 1933, **8**:121-22; 1940, **8**:133-34
    Stanley Cup victors 1932, **8**:119-20; 1942, **8**:134-35;
        1945, **8**:137; 1947, **8**:141; 1948, **8**:143; 1949, **8**:143;
        1951, **8**:145-47; 1963, **8**:163; 1964, **8**:167; 1967,
        8:173-74
Toronto Northmen, **1**:158-59
Toronto soccer franchise, **8**:71
Torrance, T.A., **5**:40-41
Torres, Carlos Alberto, **8**:69
Torres, José, **7**:126, 160-61
Toth, Steve, **1**:28-29
Tottenham Hotspurs, **8**:47-48
Tour de France, **10**:100, 104-08
Tourischeva, Ludmila, **11**:132-34
Towns, Forrest, **4**:81-82
Toye, Clive, **8**:84-87
Trabert, Tony
    in Davis Cup matches 1954, **6**:106-07; 1955, **6**:108-10
    U.S. matches winner 1953, **6**:102-03; 1955, **6**:110-11
    in Wimbledon 1954, **6**:105
    Wimbledon winner 1955, **6**:107
track and field
    and Amateur Athletic Union. See Amateur Athletic
        Union, and track and field
    and blacks, **4**:76, 87, 166-69
    Bicentennial Meet of Champions, **4**:198-99
    Boston AA meet, **4**:88
    British Empire Games, **4**:113-14
    Coliseum Relays, **4**:148-49
    college. See college, track and field; Natinal Collegiate
        Athletic Union, and track and field
    cross-country run, **4**:16, 26
    decathlon. See decathlon winners, Olympic; records,
        track and field, decathlon
    disqualifications, **4**:8-9, 24, 72-73, 116
    drugs in, **4**:162
    fiber glass vaulting pole, **4**:148, 152, 174-75
    Gold Coast AAU meet, **4**:152
    foreign athletes and, **4**:199-200
    4-minute mile, **4**:87, 112-15; see also records, track and
        field, 1-mile run

Irish American Club meet, **4**:9-10

Knights of Columbus games, **4**:33-34

long jump, **4**:4; *see also* records, track and field, broad jump

marathons. *See* marathons

Millrose Games, **4**:33, 147, 183-84

and National Collegiate Athletic Association, **4**:55, 150-51, 161-62, 199-200

Olympic events. *See* decathlon winners, Olympic; marathon winners, Olympic; Olympic Games; records track and field, Olympic

records. *See* records, track and field

Rose Festival meet, **4**:173

runnings, **4**:16-17, 26, 73; *see also* specific marathons; records, track and field, specific races

San José meet, **4**:184-85

and Soviet Union, **4**:109, 149-50

spike shoes, **4**:163

starting blocks, **4**:73

Sunday sports competition, **4**:5-6

Supreme Court decision, **4**:116

Tom Black Classic track meet, **4**:185-86

Twenty-second Regiment Games, **4**:12

and United States, **4**:50, 149-50, 184

women in. *See* women, in track and field

training

baseball, **2**:75, 188-89

hockey, **8**:103

tennis, **6**:16-17

swimming, **12**:71-75, 97-98

trapshooting, **10**:40-43, 45, 48, 50-52

Trautmann, Bert, **8**:37-38, 40

Travers, Jerome, **5**:8

Travis, Walter J., **5**:7

Travis, Warren Lincoln, **11**:105

Trebilcock, Mike, **8**:53

Tremblay, J.C., **8**:174

Trenton State College basketball team, **3**:112

Trevino, Lee

British Open Golf Tournament 1971, winner, **5**:164-65; 1972, winner **5**:172-73

earnings, **5**:146, 147, 163, 165

portrait of, **5**:147-48

United States Open Golf Tournament 1968, winner, **5**:146-47; 1971, winner, **5**:163; 1972, fourth place **5**:166-67

trigonometry, **5**:99

Trinkle, Herbert, **10**:7

triple crown winners

Affirmed 1978, **13**:85-91

Assault 1946, **13**:45-48

Citation 1948, **13**:49-52

Count Fleet 1943, **13**:41-45

Gallant Fox 1930, **13**:19-23

Omaha 1935, **13**:26-29

Seattle Slew 1977, **13**:80-85

Secretariat 1973, **13**:73-77

War Admiral 1937, **13**:30-34

Whirlaway 1941, **13**:38-40

Triplett, Mel, **1**:113-15

Troeh, Frank, **10**:45

Trosky, Hall, **2**:60

Trowbridge, Theo, **11**:67

Troy, Mike, **12**:66

Truman, Bess, **1**:38

Truman, Christine, **6**:118-19, 134

Truman, Harry, **1**:36, 38, 44-45, **2**:109

Tse-Tung, Chuang, **11**:40

Tsuruta, Yoshiyuki, **12**:29-30

Tucker, Arnold, **1**:35-36, 38-40

Tulane University football, **1**:27-28

Tully, Mike, **4**:201

Tulsa University football team, **1**:63

tuna tournament, **10**:167-74

Tunney, Gene

heavyweight champion 1926, **7**:29-32; 1927, **7**:36-39

light heavyweight champion 1922, **7**:20

Turcotte, Ron, **13**:73-77

Turkey, soccer riots in, **8**:63

Turkey, wrestling team of, **11**:87

Turnbull, Loretta, **12**:134-35

Turner, Billy, **13**:81

Turner, Roger, **9**:14-16, 20, 27

Turner, Ted, **12**:185

Turnesa, Joe, **5**:30-34, 36-37

Turpin, Randy, **7**:105-06

Tuxedo Gold Racquet championship, **11**:11, 13, 15

Tweedy, Mrs. John, **13**:74-77

Twenty Grand, **13**:24

Twice a Prince, **13**:77

Twyman, Jack, **3**:156

Tyler, Francis W., **9**:31, 34, 56-58

Tyuus, Wyomia, **4**:156, 162, 164

Udvari, Frank, **8**:155

Uelses, John, **4**:147-48

Ulanov, Alexei, **9**:147

Unitas, Johnny, **1**:113-16, 121-23, 129-30, 139-41, 143-45, 149

United States, aquatic team of

dropping of Holm, **12**:32-33

in Olympics 1920, **12**:9; 1924, **12**:12-14; 1928, **12**:21; 1936, **12**:34-40; 1948, **12**:48; 1952, **12**:51-52, 54-55; 1960, **12**:66; 1964, **12**:71; 1968, **12**:76, 78, 81-82; 1976, **12**:93-94, 96-97, 99-100

United States, Army equestrian team, **11**:152

United States, auto racing in, **13**:134, 180-84

United States, basketball team of, **3**:52-53, 56-57, 69

United States, bicyclists of, **10**:97-98, 106-07

United States, boating and

Olympic rowing team, 1936, **12**:141; 1964, **12**:168; 1968, **12**:173; 1972, **12**:177-78; 1976, **12**:181

Olympic sailing team 1952, **12**:156

Olympic yacht race 1948, **12**:153-54; 1956, **12**:159; 1960,

12:163; 1964, **12**:168-69
United States, bobsled team of, **9**:21-22, 37-38
United States, boxing and
  Boxing Championships, **7**:193-94
  Olympics 1932, **7**:44, 193-94; 1952, **7**:110; 1956, **7**:126;
    1960, **7**:139; 1968, **7**:173; 1976, **7**:191-92
United States, clay-pigeon shooting team, **10**:52
United States, cricket in, **10**:60
United States, curling club of, **9**:27
United States, equestrian team of, **11**:151-52, 159-61
United States, field hockey team of, **10**:33-34
United States, golf in, **5**:8, 33-34, 40-41, 54, 61-63
  Amateur Golf Final, **5**:9, 106-07, 114-16
  barring of Didrikson from Open, **5**:70-71
  United States Golf Association, **5**:26, 50
  see also United States Open Golf Tournament winners
United States, hockey and
  National Hockey League, **8**:103
  in Olympics 1924, **9**:8-9; 1936, **9**:39; 1948, **9**:50; 1952,
    9:69; 1960, **9**:95-96, 98-99; 1972, **9**:150; 1976, **9**:160-61,
    164, 167
United States, lacrosse team of, **10**:81
United States, matador in, **10**:146
United States, pistol team, **10**:43, 49
United States, polo team of, **10**:15-20, 24-28, 32
United States, rifle team of, **10**:43-44
United States, rugby team of, **10**:72-74
United States, running deer shooting team of, **10**:43, 45
United States, skaters of
  crash of team 1961, **9**:100-01
  in Olympics 1924, **9**:7-8; 1928, **9**:10-12
United States, soccer in, **8**:16, 71-72
  disinterest in, **8**:64
  professional teams, **8**:58, 63, 74-75
  selling of, **8**:86-89
  United States Open Soccer Championship, **8**:17
  United States Soccer Football Association, **8**:7, 17-18,
    53, 64; *see also* soccer, Challenge Trophy
United States, soccer team of,
  vs Argentina 1930, **8**:19
  vs Chile 1950, **8**:32
  vs England 1950, **8**:32
  vs Italy 1934, **8**:21; 1952, **8**:33
  vs Mexican All-Stars 1954, **8**:35
  vs Mexico 1934, **8**:20
  in 1924 Olympics, **8**:12
  vs Paraguay 1930, **8**:19
  in World Open Soccer Tournament 1930, **8**:19
United States, table tennis team of, **11**:38-41
United States, tennis and
  Davis Cup winner 1923, **6**:25-26; 1954, **6**:106-07; 1958,
    6:121-22; 1963, **6**:131
  eligibility of Renée Richards, **6**:198
  Lawn Tennis Association, **6**:103, 154-56, 172
  Olympic tennis winners 1924, **6**:27
  televised Open, **6**:199-200
  tennis method of, **6**:6-7
  Wightman Cup winner 1933, **6**:58-59; 1963, **6**:134

see also United States tennis matches champions
United States, track and field team, **4**:149-50, 184
United States, trapshooting team of, **10**:42-43, 45
United States, weight lifters of, **11**:106-08
United States, Winter Olympics standing
  second in 1928, **9**:12-13; 1952, **9**:71-72; 1972, **9**:150
  third in 1948, **9**:58-59
United States, wrestlers of, **11**:83-84, 86-87, 92-93, 95, 103
United States Atlantic Tuna Tournament, **10**:167-74
United States Automobile Club, **13**:183
United States diet, **4**:50
United States Open Golf Tournament winners
  Armour 1927, **5**:34-35
  Boros 1963, **5**:123-24
  Burke 1931, **5**:49-50
  Casper 1966, **5**:140-42
  Dutra 1934, **5**:56-57
  Furgol 1954, **5**:94-96
  Hogan 1950, **5**:78-80; 1951, **5**:83-84; 1953, **5**:90-92
  Jacklin 1970, **5**:160-61
  Jones 1926, **5**:30-32; 1930, **5**:42-44
  Manero 1936, **5**:59-60
  Mangrum 1946, **5**:68-70
  Middlecoff 1949, **5**:72-74
  Miller 1973, **5**:174-75
  Nicklaus 1962, **5**:117-19; 1967, **5**:144-45; 1972, **5**:166-67
  North 1978, **5**:194-95
  Oimet 1913, **5**:9-11
  Palmer 1960, **5**:109-11
  Player 1965, **5**:131-32
  Sarazen 1922, **5**:22-23; 1932, **5**:51-52
  Trevino 1968, **5**:146-47; 1971, **5**:163
  Vardon 1900, **5**:6-7
  Venturi 1964, **5**:126-28
  Weiskopf 1973, **5**:175-76
United States Senate, **1**:154-55
United States tennis matches winners
  Anderson 1957, **6**:117-18
  Ashe 1968, **6**:160-62
  Betz 1942, **6**:77-78; 1946, **6**:81-82
  Budge 1938, **6**:73-74
  Bueno 1966, **6**:144
  Cochet 1926, **6**:35-37
  Connolly 1951, **6**:93-94; 1952, **6**:96-97; 1953, **6**:102-03
  Connors 1974, **6**:184-85; 1976, **6**:193
  Cooper 1958, **6**:120-21
  Court 1962, **6**:130; 1970, 171-72; 1973, **6**:182
  Doherty 1903, **6**:3
  duPont 1948, **6**:83-84; 1949, **6**:85-86
  Evert 1975, **6**:188-89
  Fraser 1960, **6**:126-27
  Gibson 1957, **6**:117-18; 1958, **6**:120-21
  Gonzales 1948, **6**:83-84; 1949, **6**:85-86
  Hard 1960, **6**:126-27
  Jacobs 1932, **6**:55-56; 1933, **6**:59-61
  King 1967, **6**:150-51; 1971, **6**:174-75; 1974, **6**:184-85
  Kramer 1946, **6**:81-82
  Lacoste 1927, **6**:42-43

Laver 1962, 6:130; 1969, 6:166
Mallory 1921, 6:19; 1922, 6:22-23; 1926, 6:34-35
Marble 1936, 6:66-69; 1938, 6:73-74
Moody 1923, 6:24-25; 1924, 6:28; 1925, 6:30-31; 1927, 6:39-40; 1928, 6:44-45; 1929, 6:45-46; 1931, 6:52-53
Nastase 1972, 6:177
Newcombe 1967, 6:150-51
Orantes 1975, 6:189-90
Palfrey 1945, 6:79
Parker 1945, 6:81
Perry 1933, 6:61-62
Rosewall 1956, 6:113
Sedgman 1952, 6:96-97
Smith 1971, 6:174-75
Stolle 1966, 6:144
Tilden 1920, 6:15; 1921, 6:20-21; 1922, 6:23-24; 1923, 6:26-27; 1924, 6:29; 1925, 6:31-32; 1929, 6:47; 1931, 6:50-51
Trabert 1953, 6:102-03; 1955, 6:110-11
Vilas 1977, 6:200-01
Vines 1931, 6:54-55; 1932, 6:56-57
Wade 1968, 6:160
University of California crew, 12:127-28, 152-53
University of California (Los Angeles) football team, 1:12-13, 15, 55, 63-64
University of California (Los Angeles) basketball team
vs Houston 1968, 3:75-76
vs Michigan 1965, 3:71
NCAA champions 1964, 3:68-69; 1967, 3:74-75; 1968, 3:77; 1969, 3:79; 1970, 3:80; 1971, 3:81-82; 1972, 3:83-84; 1973, 3:88-89; 1975, 3:99-100
vs Notre Dame 1973, 3:86-87; 1974, 3:95-96
record wins 1968, 3:75-76; 1973, 3:86-87
vs Rutgers 1976, 3:102
vs Wake Forest 1962, 3:68
Wooden as coach, 3:89-94
University of California (Los Angeles) soccer team, 8:70-79
University of California (Los Angeles) Southern California Pacific Coast Conference, 4:112-13
University of Southern California football team
vs Duke 1939, 1:30-31
vs Georgia Tech 1928, 1:18
Jones as coach, 1:24-25
vs Notre Dame 1931, 1:23-24; 1978, 1:79-80
vs Ohio 1975, 1:74
vs Purdue 1967, 1:66
vs Washington and Jefferson 1922, 1:10
vs Wisconsin 1953, 1:49; 1963, 1:62
Unruh, Paul, 3:37
Unseld, Westley, 3:160
Unser, Al, 13:87-89, 197-98
Unser, Bobby, 13:159
Unser, Jerry, Jr., 13:159
Unser, Louis, 13:146
Upset, 13:9
Urso, Frank, 10:87
Uruguay, soccer team of, 8:13, 16, 19, 32

Usery, W.J., Jr., 1:160, 163-64
Ussery, Bobby, 13:70-72
Utah Stars, 3:182-83
Utah University basketball team, 3:21, 28-29, 63-64, 72
Uto, Shumpei, 12:37, 40, 42
Utterstrom, Sven, 9:21
Utzshneider, Peter, 9:142-43

Vail Trophy, 9:123
Valdes, Eva, 11:153
Valdez, Rodrigo, 7:184-85, 190-91
Valentine, Lewis J., 3:22
Valentine, Police Commissioner, 13:30
Valenzuela, Ismael, 13:65-66, 69-70
Van Bebber, Jack, 11:84
Van Brocklin, Norm, 1:119-20, 122-23
Van Dellen, Buck, 1:25-27
Vanderbilt, Harold, 12:132, 139, 144-45
Vanderbilt University football team, 1:12
VanderMeer, Johnny, 2:62-63
Van Donck, Flory, 5:99
Van Egmund, Jacobus, 10:99-100
Van Horn, Doug, 1:164
Van Wie, Virginia, 5:46-47
Vardon, Harry, 5:4-7, 9-11
Vare, Mrs. Edwin H., Jr. See Collett, Glenna
Varipapa, Andrew, 11:67
Varia, Ilmari, 11:125
Vasquez, Jacinto, 13:78-79
Vedenine, Vyacheslav, 9:142
Veeck, Bill, 2:101-02
Velasquez, Jorge, 13:87-88
Velasquez, Ramon, 7:167-68
Venturi, Ken, 5:98-99, 107, 126-28
Verdeur, Joe, 12:48
Verker, Cornelis (Kees), 9:133-34
Vesper, Rudolf, 11:99
Vesper Boat Club crew team, 12:168, 170
Vexilar, Inc., 10:185
Vianelli, Peire Franco, 10:107
Victoria Cougars, 8:103, 106-07
Victoria Mary, Queen, 13:21
Vidali, Lynn, 12:84-85
Videman, Lydia, 9:71
Vigil, 13:12-13
Vignaux, Maurice, 11:47, 57-58
Vilas, Guillermo, 6:200-01
Villa, Leo, 12:171-72
Villanova University basketball team, 3:82-83
Villanova University football team, 1:59
Vines, H. Ellsworth, Jr., 6:53-57
Vinson, Maribel
death of, 9:100
national figure skating champion 1929, 9:14; 1933, 9:27; 1935, 9:28; 1937, 9:41-42
in Olympics 1936, 9:35, 38-39
in world figure skating contest 1930, 9:15, 16

Virdon, Bill, **2**:123
Viren, Lasse, **4**:178, 190-91, 194-95
Virginia Tech basketball team, **3**:87-88
Virginia University lacrosse team, **10**:85
Vlasov, Yuri, **11**:111
Vogel, Bob, **1**:145-46
Vogel, Matt, **12**:95-96
Voight, Angela, **4**:187
Voight, George, **5**:40-41
Voight, Stu, **1**:157-58
Volga, **13**:96
Volina, Sidney, **2**:158
volleyball, **11**:44-46
von Cramm, Gottfried, **6**:65-66, 69-72
Von Elm, George, **5**:29-30, 40-41, 49-50
von Saltza, Chris, **12**:66
Von Trips, Wolfgang, **13**:167-68
Voss, Carl, **8**:129
Vosters, Mrs. Francis, **11**:25
Vuarnet, Jean, **9**:92-93
Vukovich, Bill, **13**:153-55
Vulcan Forge, **13**:51-52

Wade, Virginia, **6**:160, 169, 196-97
Wadkins, Lenny, **5**:162-63, 176
Wagner, Barbara, **9**:89-90
Wagner, Mike, **1**:166
Wagner, Robert, Jr., **2**:119, 121, 124, 127-28
Wainwright, Helen, **12**:10, 12, 14
Wake Forest University basketball team, **3**:68
Walcott, Jersey Joe
   vs Charles 1949, **7**:94-95
   heavyweight champion 1951, **7**:103-04
   vs Louis 1947, **7**:82-83; 1948, **7**:85-87
   vs Marciano 1952, **7**:110-11
Walden, Bobby, **1**:161-63
Walker, Daphne, **9**:45
Walker, Dixie, **2**:78
Walker, Doak, **1**:75, 109
Walker, James, Jr., **5**:155-56
Walker, Jimmy, **1**:23
Walker, John, **4**:186-87, 196-98
Walker, Mickey, **7**:23-24, 32
Walker, Wade, **1**:184-85
Walkowiak, Roger, **10**:100
Wallard, Lee, **13**:150-51
Walling, Dow, **12**:121-22
Walsh, Stella, **4**:60, 62-63
Walter, Hanna, **9**:89
Walters, Phil, **13**:153
Walton, Bill, **3**:83-84, 88-89, 95-96
Walton, Joe, **1**:120
Walton, John, **10**:167-68, 172-74
Wambagans, Bill, **2**:28-29
Wanderers, **8**:102-03
War Admiral, **13**:30-35
Ward, Arch, **1**:99-100

Ward, Frank, **11**:15
Ward, Holcombe, **6**:2
Ward, Marvin, **5**:61-63
Ward, Norman, **1**:178
Ward, Pat, **6**:110-11
Ward, Roger, **13**:169-70
Ward brothers, **12**:175-76
Warfield, Paul, **1**:158-59, 164-65
Warmerdam, Cornelius, **4**:88
Warner, Ed, **3**:38
Warner, Glenn, **1**:24, 43
Warren, Helen, **4**:55-56
Warren Remedy, **11**:163
Washbond, Alan, **9**:36-38
Washburn, Mary, **4**:46
Washington and Jefferson University football team, **1**:10
Washington Bullets, **3**:185, 202-03
Washington Capitols, **3**:118
Washington Darts, **8**:67, 70
Washington, Kermit, **3**:196-97
Washington Redskins
   vs Chicago Bears 1937, **1**:93-94; 1940, **1**:95-96; 1942, **1**:96-97, 1943, **1**:97-99
   vs Cleveland Browns 1958, **1**:113
   and drugs, **1**:183
   vs Miami Dolphins 1973, **1**:153-54
   vs New York Giants 1962, **1**:120
   vs Philadelphia Eagles 1947, **1**:102
   transfer from Boston, **1**:92
Washington Senators
   vs Baltimore Orioles 1962, **2**:133
   vs Boston Red Sox 1917, **2**:21
   move to Arlington, **2**:166
   vs New York Yankees 1908, **2**:8-9; 1953, **2**:100-01; 1956, **2**:115-16
Washington State football team, **1**:89
Washington University crew, **12**:121-22, 124-25, 142-43, 152-53, 186
Washington Whips, **8**:62-63
Wasnie, Nick, **8**:114
Waterfield, Bob, **1**:105-06, 123
waterfowl hunting, **10**:157-58, 190-91
water polo
   international, **12**:4-5
   at Olympics 1932, **12**:23, 31; 1948, **12**:48; 1952, **12**:55; 1956, **12**:57, 60-61; 1960, **12**:67; 1964, **12**:71; 1972, **12**:87
water skiing, **12**:106-11
Watrous, Al, **5**:33-34
Watson, Harry, **8**:143
Watson, Phil, **8**:133
Watson, Phoebe, **6**:45-46
Watson, Pokey, **12**:81
Watson, Tom, **5**:190-93
Wayne Hoosiers, **3**:113
Wayne, Marshall, **12**:34-36, 41-42
Waynesburg University football team, **1**:31-32
Wear, Joseph, **11**:4

Weatherly, **12**:163-66
Weaver, George, **2**:25-28, 32
Weber, Dick, **11**:73
Weber, Wolfgang, **8**:55-56
Webster, Bob, **12**:70-71
Wehselau, Marichen, **12**:13-14
Weeghman, Charles, **2**:19
Weese, Norris, **1**:168
Wegeman, Keith, **9**:71-72
Wehling, Ulrich, **9**:142-43, 158-59
Weidemann, Carl, **13**:14-15
weight lifting, **11**:105-13, 117
  AAU championships, **11**:105-06, 108
  Olympic, **11**:105-08, 110-12
  records. *See* records, weight lifting
  world championships, **11**:106, 111-12
Weightman-Smith, G.C., **4**:47-48
Weir, Christy Lynn, **12**:111
Weiskopf, Tom
  earnings of, **5**:183
  Masters Golf Tournament 1972, second place, **5**:165-66;
    1974, second place, **5**:178-79; 1975, second place,
    5:182-83
  Professional Golfers' Association Tournament 1975,
    third place, **5**:184-85
  United States Open Golf Tournament 1973, third place,
    5:174-76; 1978, fourth place, **5**:194-95
Weismuller, Johnny, **12**:9, 11, 13, 14, 21, 49, 74
Welch, W.A., **9**:13
Weld, Therese, **9**:2, 6-7, 14-15
Welsh, Freddie, **7**:15
welterweight champions
  Armstrong 1938, **7**:64-65
  Basilio 1955, **7**:119-20; 1956, **7**:124-25
  Britton 1919, **7**:15; 1922, **7**:20-21
  Gavilan 1951, **7**:102, 104-05; 1953, **7**:114
  Griffith 1961, **7**:140; 1962, **7**:142-44; 1963, **7**:151
  McLarnin 1934, **7**:49-50
  Paret 1961, **7**:141-42
  Robinson 1947, **7**:78; 1949, **7**:95-96
  Ross 1934, **7**:46-47; 1935, **7**:50
  Stracey 1975, **7**:188
  Walker 1922, **7**:23-24
  Zivic 1940, **7**:70
Welu, Billy, **11**:72
Wenden, Michael, **12**:77, 80, 88
Wene, Sylvia, **11**:69
Wentworth, Mervin, **8**:117
Werner, Wallace (Buddy), **9**:74
West, Jerry, **3**:162-63, 173, 176-77
West Bromwich soccer team, **8**:19, 35
Westchester Field Hockey Club, **10**:34
Western Kentucky University basketball team, **3**:18-19
Western Maryland College football team, **1**:178
Westfall, Ed, **8**:196-97
West Germany. *See* Germany
West Ham United, **8**:27, 84
West Indies, cricket in, **10**:60

Westminster Kennel Club show. *See* dog shows
Westphal, Paul, **3**:191
West Virginia basketball team, **3**:18-19
Wethered, Roger, **5**:19, 40-41
Whichone, **13**:22-23
Whirlaway, **13**:38-40
Whisk Broom II, **13**:7
Whiskolo Home, **13**:26-27
Whitcombe, E.R., **5**:26-27, 54
White, Albert, **12**:12
White, Charles, **1**:79-80
White, Duncan, **4**:92
White, Jo Jo, **3**:189-91
White, Ruth, **11**:126
White, Sherman, **3**:38
White, Willye B., **12**:100
White Sulphur Springs Golf Course, **5**:11-13
Whitfield, Mal, **4**:90, 92-94, 96-97, 104
Whitney, George, **11**:3
Whitney, Harry Payne, **10**:15, 27, **13**:7, 9, 22-23
Whitney, John Hay, **13**:25
Whitney, Mrs. Payne, **13**:24
Whitney, William, **13**:15
Whiton, Herman, **12**:153-54, 156
Whittemore, Mary, **11**:34-35
Whittingstall, Eileen Bennett, **6**:52-53
Whitwell, E.W., **8**:18
Wichita State University basketball team, **3**:59
Wichman, Sharon, **12**:79-80
Wicks, Sidney, **3**:80-82
Wide, Edvin, **4**:37, 39-40
Widseth, Ed, **1**:28-29
Wightman, Hazel Hotchkiss, **6**:24-25, 27-28
Wightman, Mrs. George, **11**:13
Wilcox, Howard, **13**:132-33, 138
wild boar hunting, **10**:165
Wilding, A.F., **6**:5-6
Wilfong, Will, **3**:54-55
Wilkerson, Bobby, **3**:101-02
Wilkins, Mac Maurice, **4**:190
Willard, Jess, **7**:12-14, 16-17
Willard, Patsy, **12**:67
Williams, Archie, **4**:82-83
Williams, Billy, **2**:171
Williams, Bob, **1**:58
Williams, Bobby, **11**:74-75
Williams, Charles, **11**:5
Williams, Claude, **2**:25-28, 32
Williams, Cleveland, **7**:168
Williams, Dave, **2**:68-69, 72, 87
Williams, Herbert, **12**:159
Williams, John, **10**:5-6
Williams, Kevin, **1**:79-80
Williams, Percy, **4**:49, 53
Williams, Pete, **1**:38-39
Williams, Ralph, **4**:42
Williams, Randy, **4**:182
Williams, Richard, **6**:14, 25-26

Williams, Stan, **2**:124-25
Williams, Ted, **2**:116
Willing, O.F., **5**:40-41
Wills, Helen. *See* Moody, Helen
Wills, Maury, **2**:133
Wilson, Alex, **4**:62-63
Wilson, Don, **12**:169-70
Wilson, Hack, **2**:43
Wilson, Jean, **9**:10-22
Wilson, Jimmy, **2**:49
Wimbledon tennis matches winners
  Ashe 1975, **6**:187-88
  Borg 1976, **6**:192; **6**:197; 1978, **6**:202
  Brough 1948, **6**:83; 1950, **6**:87; 1955, **6**:108
  Budge 1937, **6**:69-70; 1938, **6**:72-73
  Bueno 1959, **6**:124; 1964, **6**:135
  Connolly 1952, **6**:95-96; 1953, **6**:100; 1954, **6**:105
  Connors 1974, **6**:183-84
  Cooper 1958, **6**:119-20
  Court 1963, **6**:133; 1965, **6**:142; 1970, **6**:167-69
  Drobny 1954, **6**:104
  Emerson 1964, **6**:135
  Evert 1974, **6**:182-83; 1976, **6**:191
  Gibson 1957, **6**:117
  Goolagong 1971, **6**:172-73
  Hoad 1956, **6**:112
  Jones 1969, **6**:163-64
  King 1962, **6**:128; 1966, **6**:143; 1967, **6**:146-47; 1968,
    6:57-58; 1972, **6**:176; 1973, **6**:180-81; 1975, **6**:186-87
  Kodes 1973, **6**:180-81
  Laver 1961, **6**:127; 1968, **6**:157; 1969, **6**:164-65
  Lenglen 1921, **6**:18; 1922, **6**:21-22; 1923, **6**:24; 1925, **6**:30
  McKinley 1963, **6**:132-33
  Marble 1939, **6**:74-75
  Moody 1927, **6**:34-39; 1929, **6**:45; 1930, **6**:48-49; 1935,
    6:64-65
  Navratilova 1978, **6**:201-02
  Newcombe 1967, **6**:146; 1970, **6**:169-70; 1971, **6**:173-74
  Olmedo 1959, **6**:122-24
  Perry 1936, **6**:65-66
  Santana 1966, **6**:142-43
  Seixas 1953, **6**:98
  Sedgman 1952, **6**:94-95
  Smith 1972, **6**:176-77
  Tilden 1920, **6**:14; 1921, **6**:18; 1930, **6**:49-50
  Trabert 1955, **6**:107
  Wade 1977, **6**:196-97
  Wilding 1913, **6**:5-6
Wingard, Lenore. *See* Kight, Lenore
Winnipeg Jets, **8**:190
Wing, Franklin F., Jr., **11**:151
Winkler, Hans Gunther, **11**:156, 158
Wint, Arthur, **4**:92, 96-100, 104
Winter, John, **4**:89
Winter Olympic Games
  1924, **9**:7-9
  1928, **9**:10-13
  1932, **9**:16-25

  1936, **9**:29-39
  1948, **9**:48-59
  1952, **9**:63-71
  1956, **9**:76-87
  1960, **9**:89-99
  1964, **9**:103-20
  1968, **9**:124-37
  1972, **9**:141-50
  1976, **9**:153-65
Winters, Fred, **4**:8
Wirtz, Arthur, **7**:128-29
Wisconsin University football team, **1**:12-13, 49, 62
Wisconsin University basketball team, **3**:18
Wisconsin University track and field team, **4**:26
Wise, Dorothy, **11**:64
Wittenberg, Henry, **11**:92
Woellke, Hans, **4**:76
Wohlhuter, Rich, **4**:188-90
Wolde, Mamo, **4**:171-72
Wolfermann, Klaus, **4**:184
Wolff, Bob, **8**:58
Wolverhampton Wanderers, **8**:27, 31
women in
  basketball, **3**:2, 5, 98-101,105-06
  billiards, **11**:48-49
  Boston Marathon, **4**:162
  boxing, **7**:179
  bullfighting, **10**:140
  crew, **12**:114, 179
  cricket, **10**:61
  curling, **9**:62
  fencing, **11**:121
  golf, 5-6, 15-17, 24, 70-71, 189-94; *see also* Ladies'
    Professional Golf Association
  gymnastics, **11**:129
  horse training, **13**:25
  horse racing, **13**:72-73
  karate, **11**:102
  motorboating, **12**:134-35
  mountain climbing, **10**:120-21
  Olympic equestrian contest, **11**:154
  polo, **10**:28-29
  racing, **13**:127
  skeet shooting, **10**:47
  soccer, **8**:67-70
  softball, **10**:67-69
  sports reporting, **8**:196
  swimming, **12**:6, 11, 75
  table tennis, **11**:41-43
  tennis, **6**:3, 6, 12, 135, 171-72
  track and field, **4**:33, 46-47, 54-57, 62, 63, 73, 106-07,
    158, 185
  trapshooting, **10**:50-51
  volleyball, **11**:46
  weight lifting, **11**:117
Wood, Craig, **5**:54-56
Wooden, John, **3**:89-94
wood, field and stream activities, **10**:150-95

Wood, Gar, **12**:118-20, 123-24, 129, 133-34, 137
Wood, Sidney, **6**:63
Wood, Tim, **9**:130-31, 133, 138
Woodruff, John, **4**:78-80
Woodward, William, **13**:19-23, 26-29, 35-36
Woolf, George, **13**:29-30, 34-35
Woolwich Arsenal, **8**:15
Woosnam, Max, **6**:18
Woosnam, Phil, **8**:57-58, 64, 71, 79, 90
world bobsled championship, **9**:100
World Boxing Championship, **7**:119
World Boxing Council, **7**:167-68, 184, 196
world figure skating champions
    Albright 1953, **9**:73
    Altwegg 1951, **9**:61-62
    Boeckl 1928, **9**:13
    Button 1948, **9**:59-60; 1951, **9**:61-62
    Fleming 1966, **9**:121; 1967, **9**:122; 1968, **9**:137-38
    Gerschwiler 1947, **9**:45
    Heiss 1956, **9**:87-88; 1959, **9**:89
    Henie 1930, **9**:15-16; 1931, **9**:16; 1934, **9**:27
    Jackson 1962, **9**:103
    Nepela 1973, **9**:151-52
    Scott 1947, **9**:45; 1948, **9**:60
world figure skating champions, pairs
    Belousova-Protopopov 1966, **9**:121
    Gorshkov-Pakhomova 1973, **9**:151
World Hockey Association, **8**:185-86, 188-90, 204-05
world ski race champions
    Allais 1937, **9**:42
    Killy 1966, **9**:122
    Pravda 1961, **9**:99
    Proell 1975, **9**:153
    Russi 1970, **9**:139
    Schranz 1969, **9**:138-39
    Thoeni 1974, **9**:152-53
World Soccer Champions
    Argentina 1978, **8**:96-97
    Brazil 1958, **8**:40-41; 1962, **8**:50; 1966, **8**:53-54; 1976, **8**:69-70
    England 1966, **8**:55-56
    Italy 1934, **8**:21; 1938, **8**:27
    nationalism ar.d, **8**:92-96
    rough tactics among, **8**:55
    Soviet Union banned as, **8**:78
    Uruguay 1950, **8**:32
    West Germany 1954, **8**:36; 1974, **8**:82-83
World War I, **2**:22
World War II, **7**:74
World Water Ski Union, **12**:110
Worsley, Gump, **8**:169-70
Worster, Steve, **1**:70-72
Wortmann, Siegfried, **8**:16-17
Wot No Sun, **13**:54-55
Wottle, Dave, **4**:175-77, 182
Wrede, Ludwig, **9**:15
wrestling, **11**:78-104
    AAU championship, **11**:92

Greco-Roman, **11**:84, 94, 98-99
popularity of, **11**:87-92
racism in, **11**:100-02
sumo, **11**:93-94, 98
unconscious hold, **11**:103
world championships, **11**:79-83, 85
Wright, Lorenzo, **4**:101
Wright, Mickey, **5**:111, 128
Wright, Warren, **13**:38-40
Wrightson, Bernie, **12**:77-78
Wykoff, Frank, **4**:45, 78
Wynn, Early, **2**:107
Wynne, Nancye, **6**:73-74
Wyoming University basketball team, **3**:19
Wysong, Dudley, **5**:114-16

Yablonski, Ventan, **1**:40-41
yachting, **12**:133, 178; *see also* America's Cup yachting competition; Olympic yacht race
Yale University basketball team, **3**:2-3, 34
Yale University crew
    vs Harvard University crew 1921, **12**:120-21; 1927, **12**:125-26; 1937, **12**:143-44; 1938, **12**:146; 1948, **12**:151-52; 1949, **12**:154-55
    in Olympics 1924, **12**:123; 1956, **12**:159
Yale University football team, **1**:18-20, 67
Yale University polo players, **10**:32
Yale University rugby team, **10**:75-76
Yale University soccer team, **8**:5, 7
Yale University swim team, **12**:43, 62
Yale University trapshooters, **10**:44
Yamanaka, Tsuyoski, **12**:65-67
Yancey, Bert, **5**:146-47
Yancey, Bill, **2**:163-64
Yang, C.K., **4**:138, 140-41, 159
Yankee Chance, **13**:40
Yarborough, Cale, **13**:190, 194-95
Yarbrough, Lee Roy, **13**:187
Yardley, George, **3**:133, 137
Yashin, Lev, **8**:67
Yastrzemski, Carl, **2**:145-47, 180-83
Yates, Charles, **5**:61-63
Yawkey, Tom, **2**:56
Yepremian, Garo, **1**:152-53, 157-58
Yerman, Jack, **4**:147
Yilmaz, Giyasettin, **11**:100
Yoder, Jim, **1**:70-72
Yomiuri Giants, **2**:191
Yonkers Futurity, **13**:105
York, Ruby, **2**:61
Young, Denton (Cy), **2**:8, 139
Young, George, **4**:165-66
Young, George, **12**:18-20
Young, Jimmy, **7**:188-90, 199

Young, Len, **1**:177
Young, Nat, **12**:110
Young, Sheila, **9**:153-56
Yost, Fielding, **1**:177
Yowarsky, Walt, **1**:46
Yrjola, Paavo, **4**:52-53
Yugoslavia, soccer team of, **8**:34, 38, 46

Zabala, Juan Carlos, **4**:70-72, 87
Zaharias, Babe, *See* Didrikson, Babe
Zahn, Wayne, **11**:73
Zaitsev, Alexandr, **9**:156
Zale, Tony
    vs Cerdan 1948, **7**:90-91
    vs Graziano 1947, **7**:80-81
    middleweight champion 1946, **7**:77-78; 1948, **7**:84-85
Zamora, Alfonso, **7**:188
Zaranka, Ven, **1**:46

Zarate, Carlos, **7**:199
Zaslofsky, Max, **3**:157
Zastrow, Bob, **1**:45
Zatopek, Dana, **4**:105-06
Zatopek, Emil, **4**:89-90, 102, 104-06, 108-09, **12**:73
Zbyszko, Wladek, **11**:80-82
Zdrazila, Hans, **11**:111
Zeppelin, Graf, **8**:18
Zev, **13**:12-15
Zhabotinsky, Leonid, **11**:111
Zimmere, Wolfgang, **9**:142-43
Zimmerman, Edith, **9**:115
Zimmermann, Egon, **9**:104-05
Zink, John, **13**:156
Zivic, Fritzie, **7**:70
Zollner, Fred, **3**:122
Zsivotsky, Gyula, **4**:167-68
Zunker-Benkovic bowling team, **11**:67
Zuppke, Bob, **1**:16, 22, 87